WRITING ACROSS LANGUAGES: ANALYSIS OF L$_2$ TEXT

ULLA CONNOR
ROBERT B. KAPLAN
Editors

SANDRA SAVIGNON
Consulting Editor

ADDISON-WESLEY PUBLISHING COMPANY

Reading, Massachusetts • Menlo Park, California
Don Mills, Ontario • Wokingham, England • Amsterdam • Sydney
Singapore • Tokyo • Madrid • Bogota • Santiago • San Juan

THE ADDISON-WESLEY SECOND LANGUAGE PROFESSIONAL LIBRARY SERIES

Sandra J. Savignon
Consulting Editor

DUBIN, Fraida, ESKEY, David
and GRABE, William
*Teaching Second Language
Reading for Academic Purposes*

HIGGINS, John and JOHNS, Tim
Computers in Language Learning

MOHAN, Bernard A.
Language and Content

SAVIGNON, Sandra J.
*Communicative Competence: Theory
and Classroom Practice*

SAVIGNON, Sandra J. and
BERNS, Margie S.
*Initiatives in Communicative
Language Teaching*

SMITH, Stephen M.
*The Theater Arts and the Teaching
of Second Languages*

VENTRIGLIA, Linda
Conversations of Miguel and Maria

WALLERSTEIN, Nina
Language and Culture in Conflict

Library of Congress Cataloging-in-Publication Data
Main entry under title:

Writing across languages.

Bibliography: p.
1. Discourse analysis—Addresses, essays, lectures.
2. Rhetoric—Study and teaching—Addresses, essays, lectures. 3. English
language—Rhetoric—Study and teaching—Addresses, essays, lectures.
4. English language—Study and teaching—Foreign speakers—Addresses,
essays, lectures. I. Connor, Ulla, 1948– II. Kaplan, Robert B.
P302.W74 1986   808′.00141   85-30611
ISBN 0-201-11184-5

ISBN 0-201-11184-5
3 4 5 6 7 8 9 10–MU–96 95 94 93 92 91

Foreword

This book makes an important contribution to two related aspects of language study which are currently of much concern both in the theoretical and descriptive domains of discourse analysis and in the practical pedagogy of language teachers.

The first aspect has to do with the nature of written language as a discourse process, as a mode of communicative behavior. Early developments in discourse analysis tended to focus attention on spoken language, on the management of talk and the speech acts of conversational utterances. This preference may in part be attributed to the orthodox linguistic belief in the primacy of speech. Old thought habits die hard. Pedagogy too has tended to the same belief, even to the extent of sometimes supposing that communicative language teaching involved only the development of the ability to converse—as if written language was not *really* authentic communication.

There have been, over recent years, challenges to this belief in the primacy of speech. One, particularly bold and strident, comes from the proponents of deconstruction, who, perversely enough, assert the very opposite. For them it is *writing* which is primary, in that it reveals the essential and inescapable paradoxical working of language as a quest for the stabilization of meanings which are of their very nature unstable, and elusive of intention and interpretation. The self-defeating nature of the striving for significance is concealed in speaking, where the negotiated outcomes of talk, centering on some purpose, give the illusion of stability as agreement. The contributors to this collection adopt a less extreme, more constructive perspective, content to explore the characteristics of writing as a *mode* of language use (not just an alternative *medium*) different from speech and worthy of particular attention, without commitment to any notion of its primacy. The perspective is descriptive rather than philosophical, with an emphasis on analysis rather than on speculation. This is appropriate, given the purpose of the book: to present recent research in a manner which will enable teachers to relate it to their practical concerns.

We come to the second aspect of language study which is prominently treated in this collection, namely, that texts have schematic structures which are culturally variable. I refer to the cultural differences of language users (and learners) which dispose them to realize meaning in writing in different ways and which tend to impede the convergence of world which interaction seeks to achieve. The roles of writing in the business of daily life vary in different societies, and they may be quite remote from the conventional functions of speech. Writing, dissociated by nature from immediate connections with context, and free to generate its own self-sustaining conventions, easily becomes an activity of access to the elite, a powerful means of control. Although it may be influenced by traditional patterns of thought as orally transmitted, it may also adopt different patterns in reference to some external cultural norm.

All this provokes problems of cross-cultural interaction. Such problems have been quite well documented in respect to reciprocal discourse, but their existence in writing has been less widely recognized. And yet they are clearly of immense importance, and of particular relevance to pedagogy. It should be noted that for very large numbers of language learners, especially in less privileged sectors of the world community, learning another language (or another dialect of their own) is a means of access to a world otherwise closed off to them, circumscribed by the written word.

The comparative study of rhetorical conventions, and the extent to which they reflect cultural thought patterns, is then of very substantial pedagogic relevance. It is particularly fitting therefore that the starting point of this volume should be Robert Kaplan's classic (if notorious) article of 1966 revisited on just this topic.

In the domain of pedagogy itself, as I began this Preface by saying, the significance of writing is now becoming widely recognized, the focus of attention widening from too exclusive a concern with spoken communication. If programs for teaching the use of written language are to be effective, they need to be grounded in an understanding of its nature; its mode of operation as a discourse process realized as text, its cultural variability, its conceptual and communicative character as a mediation. This book, which speaks in its different voices with authority but with a concern for practical relevance, offers such a grounding. To be thus informed is to be provided with the basis for initiative.

H. G. Widdowson
October 1985

Contents

Introduction
Ulla Connor and Robert B. Kaplan   1

Part **I** **Theoretical Backgrounds**   7

1. Cultural Thought Patterns Revisited   9
   Robert B. Kaplan

2. Text Linguistics for the Applier: 23
   An Orientation
   Nils Erik Enkvist

Part **II** **Models: Exposition and Argument**   45

3. Text as Interaction: Some Implications of Text   47
   Analysis and Reading Research for ESL Composition
   Patricia L. Carrell

4. Argumentative Patterns in Student Essays: 57
   Cross-Cultural Differences
   Ulla Connor

5. A Contrastive Study of English Expository Prose   73
   Paraphrases
   Ulla Connor and Peter McCagg

6. Observations on the Development of the Topic of   87
   Simplified Discourse
   Liisa Lautamatti

v

7. Contrastive Rhetoric and Text-Type Research   115
   William Grabe

Part III Inter-language Studies   **139**

8. Reader versus Writer Responsibility: A New Typology   141
   John Hinds

9. Written Academic Discourse in Korean: 153
   Implications for Effective Communication
   William G. Eggington

10. English in Parallels: A Comparison of English and   169
    Arabic Prose
    Shirley E. Ostler

Bibliography   **186**

About the Authors   **201**

Introduction

Ulla Connor and Robert B. Kaplan

During the past decade, there has been substantial growth in interest in analysis of texts of various types. To a large extent, emphasis has been given to the analysis of spoken text (e.g., Chafe 1980; Labov 1972; Sachs, Schegloff, and Jefferson 1974; Schank and Abelson 1977; Tannen 1981). More recently, attention has turned to the analysis of written text (e.g., de Beaugrande 1980, 1984; de Beaugrande and Dressler 1981; van Dijk 1985; van Dijk and Kintsch 1978, 1983; Dressler 1978; Grimes 1975; Halliday and Hasan 1976; Meyer 1975). Much of the work undertaken has in fact been concerned with theory; but some effort has been made not only to permit access to teachers but also to translate theory into practice in the form of materials available to teachers of L1 and L2 writing (e.g., Bander 1980; Kaplan and Shaw 1983; Raimes 1977; Winterowd 1980, 1983). It remains true, however, that relatively little has appeared to help teachers to understand the models deriving from theoretical studies and the methods into which those models have been adapted (although a few efforts have been made at least in some more limited areas—e.g., Kaplan *et al.* 1983).

The purpose of this volume is to make available recent research in linguistics, psycholinguistics, and rhetoric. The studies presented here look at written text not only as a product but also as a process—a creative activity in which information is interpreted as well as presented. A number of different theoretical formulations are examined in the several sections of this volume; namely, *semantic content structure analysis, cohesion and coherence, topic and comment (given vs. new), speech act theory, argumentative structure analysis,* and various *syntactic level analyses.* The several papers in this volume demonstrate that:

1. an interdisciplinary approach, incorporating insights from linguistics, psychology, education, philosophy, and rhetoric is necessary in order to examine L2 writing and the ways in which readers interact with it;

2. a text is an extremely complex structure, and in order to peform

1

comprehensive analyses of any text it is necessary to examine the various levels of language which constitute that text.

Some of the levels of language which interact within a text are: the *intrasentential* structure, the *intersentential* structure, and the *discourse* structure.

This volume makes these theories and applications available to teachers, administrators, and second-language researchers in the hope that they will be able to consider carefully the applicability of these views to classroom teaching and to materials development. The contributors to this volume have attempted to evaluate critically both the theoretical views and the related empirical research so that practitioners can have access to the thought and can evaluate for themselves the pedagogical usefulness of the insights.

The contributors to this volume are all directly involved in ESL and/ or EFL teaching or in teacher training. Because they represent a broad spectrum of professional experience, they offer insights and perspectives from different cultural perspectives. It is important to observe, however, that their primary concern is to provide practical applications rather than theoretical positions. The contributions are arranged into three primary sections: the backgrounds, models and methods, and contrastive studies in particular languages (with English held constant).

In the first section, Kaplan provides a state-of-the-art discussion on his notion of contrastive rhetoric and thereby provides a useful framework for the studies which follow. He issues a strong call for continuing study of written text in the hope that a comprehensive model of the structure of text may emerge. The papers which follow are, in a sense, answers to his call and contributions to the development of such a comprehensive model. In the second paper, Enkvist provides a broad-ranging survey of the available research models that have evolved in the recent past. His survey suggests the enormous complexity of text structure and the large number of variables that must be examined in order to arrive at an understanding of text; it speaks to both the formal analysis of text and the difficulty inherent in the reading process.

The second section opens with Carrell's argument for an integrative model of reading and writing. She describes a semantically based hierarchical analysis of expository texts. The model she proposes has been found useful in both research in reading comprehension and the teaching of reading and writing. Based upon the uniformly positive results reported for an approach based on outlining the top-level rhetorical organization of a text, she suggests ways in which the teaching of writing to ESL students can profit from this insight. Connor and McCagg examine paraphrases based on recall of a text. The subjects are native speakers of English, Spanish, and Japanese, and the text is in English. The study suggests that non-native speakers recall fewer supporting details than native speakers but follow the order of the original punctiliously, while native speakers tend to vary the order and to editorialize. Connor and McCagg suggest that the tendency to be constrained by the sequence of the original can be expected in teaching ESL writing. While the previous two studies employed expository texts, Connor examines persuasive and argumentative texts. The study is based on empirical evidence gathered from subjects in four different countries. She argues that, in order to explain the quality of text in argumentative essays, it is necessary to combine insights from linguistics, psycholinguistics, and sociolinguistics in the analysis. The multilevel analysis used in this study focused on the processes that writers employ when producing such text and on the processes that readers employ when deciphering the texts. The analytic procedure utilized both discourse-level genre characteristics and speech acts and their sequencing in the text structure. Lautamatti examines the relationship between sentence subject and sentence topic and then connects sentence topic to discourse topic. Her article originally appeared some years ago in a technical report (*Publications de l'association finlandaise de linguistique appliquée*) in Finland; it is the only contribution not specifically written for this volume, but it is of such importance (and it is not readily available in this country) that the editors decided to include it. Several subsequent studies have demonstrated the importance and the value of her study (cf., Witte 1983; Connor and Farmer 1985). The final article in this section takes the position that the notion *expository prose* has never been defined in linguistic terms but instead depends on various impressionistic definitions. Grabe argues that the various interpretations of the meaning of *expository prose* have led different researchers to produce conflicting and contradictory evidence. Through an analysis of a large corpus of texts, he goes on to propose the existence of a category of prose which is expository but also to suggest that it is not a monolithic type; rather, that there are a number of different sub-types of expository prose. He argues that valid studies must be limited to text types which are really comparable.

In the final section of this volume, a number of language specific studies are provided. Hinds undertakes to explain the variability across cultures of the concept of responsibility as it is shared between reader and writer. Demonstrating the inadequacy of existing typologies to explain cross-cultural differences in discourse on the basis of word order, subject prominence, topic prominence, focus on situation, focus on person, and the like, Hinds suggests a new basis for a typology based on the distribution of responsibility (for clarity and comprehensibility) between writer and reader. Hinds demonstrates the validity of the suggested basis for typology through the linguistic analysis of a text in Japanese. Eggington, on the other hand, discovers still another problem in the interpretation of text across cultural parameters. Based on an empirical study, he shows the existence of several rhetorical styles in Korean—one deriving from traditional Korean rhetoric, the other significantly influenced by English rhetoric (at least to the extent that English rhetoric has become universalized as the rhetoric of scientific and technical writing). Having demonstrated the existence of conflicting expository types, he examines the implications of this problem for language planning in an essentially monolingual, monocultural environment. Ostler looks at the structure of writing in English by speakers of Arabic. She finds a tendency toward elaborate parallel structures, supporting Kaplan's (1966) contention. That structure, she argues, has some relationship to preferences derived from Koranic writing. While her intent is not essentially to trace the origins of the preference for parallelism, she does provide some brief survey of the history and development of written Classical Arabic. An obvious problem in dealing with Arabic speakers is the diglossic situation, even in writing—that is, the coexistence of written Classical Arabic (in Koranic literature but also in some contemporary literature including some modern Arabic poetry) and what has come to be known as Modern Newspaper Arabic as well as other possible written varieties. Ostler's paper does not deal with all these issues but offers useful insights for ESL teachers.

It is the view of the editors that the structure and sequence of this volume, moving as it does from broad theoretical issues to narrow, language-specific illustrations, will help to make the whole area of written discourse analysis more accessible to teachers, teacher trainers, and material developers. It is further the view of the editors that information from this area of research has important implications for both the teaching of writing and the teaching of reading both to students of ESL and EFL and to mother-tongue speakers of English. Specifically, this volume focuses on reading and writing in the second-language environment rather than in the mother-tongue environment, but the editors believe that the underlying principles have applications to the teaching of reading and writing in the broadest sense.

In order to help readers new to this field, the editors have furnished sets of discussion questions at the end of each contribution. It is the intent of these discussion questions to help readers focus on the central issues in each contribution as well as to see the interrelationship among the several contributions that make up the entire volume. In addition, to remove some of the mystique associated with the people who do research, the editors have provided brief biographical notes which should help to identify the contributors and to place them in academic space and time. The editors have determined that an index to the volume, useful as it might be, would be so time-consuming (because of the very nature of the research) that it would be inefficient to prepare one. It has seemed to the editors that the ability to look up a particular concept would not be useful since identical or similar terminology is used in quite different senses by various authors even within this volume. It has seemed more important that readers be able to trace the interweaving of important concepts, rather than to be able to untangle the confusion of terminology which complicates the field of discourse analysis.

The editors hope, obviously, that this volume will find an audience. To the extent that it does, the editors are indebted to the scholars whose work is represented here. To that end, the editors have compiled a single composite bibliography for the volume, subsuming not only the sources cited by each of the contributors but going beyond directly cited sources to try to provide an introductory reading list to be pursued by anyone interested in learning more about this area.

The editors, of course, accept full responsibility for any errors which may occur in this volume; they do not, however, assume responsibility for the views of the several contributors or for the accuracy of their analyses. Finally, the editors wish to express their gratitude to Audrey Kaplan who typed the manuscript of this text and to Patricia L. Carrell and William Grabe for their helpful comments during the organizational stages of this project.

Part I
Theoretical Backgrounds

Chapter 1

Cultural Thought Patterns Revisited

Robert B. Kaplan
University of Southern California

About twenty years ago, I did a bit of research that has achieved some notoriety; that research was published in an article formally titled "Cultural Thought Patterns in Intercultural Education" (1966), though it has come to be known popularly as the "doodles article." In that study, I tried to represent, in crude graphic form, the notion that the rhetorical structure of languages differs. It is probably true that, in the first blush of discovery, I overstated both the difference and my case. In the years since that article first appeared, I have been accused of reductionism— of trying to reduce the whole of linguistics to this single issue. It was not my intent then, and it is not my intent now, to claim more for the notion than it deserves. Nevertheless, I have become gradually more convinced that there is some validity to the notion.

The title under which the article appeared was intentional; that is, it was my intent to call attention to what seemed to me a pedagogical problem. It was my experience that students in ESL programs, who were brought to the level of proficiency necessary to the writing of text, wrote texts which were different in important ways from the texts written by native speakers of English. What that early article attempted to do was to define the differences. It was clear that one kind of difference occurred at the syntactic level; in the original study, I tried to minimize such differences, because it is not at the level of the discrete sentence that the important distinctions occur, though of course there *are* differences at the level of the discrete sentence and even at the level of the phrase and the word. The interesting distinctions occur, it seems to me, at what I have decided to call the rhetorical level; i.e., at the level of organization of the whole text. There are, it seems to me, important differences between languages in the way in which discourse topic is identified in a text and in the way in which discourse topic is developed in terms of exemplification, definition, and so on.

While my memory suggests that I was not fully aware of the distinction between emic and etic considerations at the time I wrote the original article, I understand that to a certain extent my observations were constrained by virtue of the fact that my focus was on the English language, while my conclusions implicated other languages. It is interesting to note that a number of researchers looking at written texts from the standpoint of a number of other languages have come to similar conclusions, though the graphic representation has been significantly different; i.e., my suggestion that there is a direct and uninterrupted flow of information in English has been taken as also implying that directness and specificity are highly valued, and, as a consequence, each researcher studying a language other than English has described that language as direct and uninterrupted in its flow of information. The disagreement is not significant; rather, the point is that scholars looking at other languages have perceived significant differences between languages in their rhetorical structure, even if, in all fairness, they have not agreed on the nature of the differences.

Since the mid-1960s, I have continued to study these differences. To my good fortune, the study of written text has expanded substantially over the time span. While I have written a good deal on the subject since 1966, apparently nothing I have written since has so captured the imagination of others in the field. The "doodles article" has been reprinted a number of times, and its wide dissemination has caused it to come home to haunt me. Let me say, then, that I admit having made the case too strong. I regret having done so, though I in no way regret having made the case.

In fact, it is now my opinion that all of the various rhetorical modes identified in the "doodles article" are possible in any language—i.e., in any language which has written text. The issue is that each language has certain clear preferences, so that while all forms are possible, all forms do not occur with equal frequency or in parallel distribution. My contention is that any native speaker of any particular language has at his disposal literally hundreds of different mechanisms to signify the same meaning. To illustrate—once, when I had some idle time, I made a list of all the ways I could think of to combine the structures "It was raining" and "We did (not) go swimming." In a relatively short time, I was able to list over 300 alternatives; to be sure, these alternatives spanned a wide range of sociolinguistic constraints. That is exactly the point; the variations are marked for sociolinguistic constraints, for written versus oral usage, and for a number of other features. The native speaker can choose among them, presumably recognizing the various pertinent constraints. Since all of the variants identified were grammatical, grammaticality is not one of the constraints (though ungrammaticality is). Not only does the native speaker recognize circumstances in which the various forms may be used, but the native speaker also recognizes that the choice constrains in important ways any text which may follow.

The non-native speaker does not possess as complete an inventory of possible alternatives, does not recognize the sociolinguistic constraints on those alternatives, and does not recognize what sorts of constraints a choice imposes on the text which follows. From a pedagogical point of view, these are important issues; if the contentions about non-native speakers are correct, then it is the responsibility of the second-language teacher to increase the size of the inventory, to stipulate the sociolinguistic constraints, and to illustrate the ways in which a choice limits the potentially following text.

The psycholinguistic evidence that thinking, reading, and writing seem somehow to operate in terms of schema is growing. It seems to me, though it remains to be demonstrated, that schema are not only reticulated sets of ideas but are also prefabricated sets of syntactic structures; i.e., the "restaurant schema," for example, does not only permit us to recognize the fit of a set of events—Harry sat down, scanned the menu, chose Chateaubriand, ate, paid his bill, and left—it also permits us to infer that there were other people involved (e.g., a maître d', a waiter), that the restaurant was not an ordinary one (i.e., McDonalds does not yet include Chateaubriand in its menu), that the bill was probably a pretty hefty one, and so on. But it seems to me, in addition, the schema permits us to infer that certain structures are *unlikely* to occur in the normative playing out of the schema (e.g., no one is *likely* to say "Your place or mine?"—certainly a possible part of a subsumed schema, but not necessarily inferred because we have no evidence that Harry was accompanied). The schema also permit us to infer that whole segments of text are *likely* to occur; e.g.,

Are you ready to order, sir?
Yes, I'd like the Chateaubriand, rare please. I'll have escargot to start, followed by the Caesar salad. And I'd like the rice pilaf. Can you suggest a good red wine? I'll order coffee later.

While there may be small variations (e.g., *house* salad for *Caesar* salad, etc.), there will not be huge variations. The text—

Can I help you, sir?
Yes, I'd like a book of 20s—the ones with flowers—and a sheet of overseas airmails, please.

—is not likely to occur in the restaurant schema even as a sub-schema. These example schema are rather obviously oral schema; written schema will be somewhat different. Space does not allow analysis of a developed written schema, but I refer you to the whole paper which I am delivering. An elaboration of the schema implied by the question "Your place or mine?" is not likely to occur in this paper, except perhaps as a self-conscious example. A point that I am trying to make is that written text *is* different from spoken text in nontrivial ways.

Elsewhere I have argued that, at least *historically*, written language is different from spoken language. In brief, while it is now widely held that all human children are born with a natural, biologically conditioned predisposition to acquire language, and that all it takes to trigger that predisposition is the presence of a language in the environment, the language that is acquired is *oral* language. It is also widely accepted that the predisposition to acquire is, at least initially, self-appetitive and self-rewarding; it is, at least initially, impervious to formal teaching, though it is probably enhanced by an accepting encouragement from caretakers in the environment. But what is so readily acquired is oral language. Indeed, it is relatively well-established that the ability to speak is one of the characteristics of the species and that all human beings within the normative ranges have that characteristic; conversely, the absence of that characteristic defines the normative range.

While all human populations have the ability to speak, not all human populations have the ability to write. It appears that spoken language has a very long history—almost as long a history as the species itself. From the earliest emergence of the species, the combination of group hunting, territoriality, nomadism, and the reality of a very slowly developing young have combined to create a selection pressure in favor of the emergence of spoken language. But writing is a much later and not universally distributed phenomenon. There is some archeological evidence that the evolution of the skull and of the buccal cavity reached a point at which "modern" speech became possible something on the order of 100,000 years ago. And this evolutionary pattern is built into the DNA, the genetic code of the species; thus, it is the property of all human beings.

However, about 10,000 years ago, a subset of the total human population underwent a post-biological evolutionary step; it invented writing. The step is *post-biological* because it was not built into the genetic code and it was not universally distributed in the species, though it had an enormous impact. About 1,000 years ago, a somewhat smaller subset of human beings invented movable print, a second post-biological evolutionary change, again not built into the genetic code and not universal for the species. Most recently, within our lifetimes, a third post-biological evolutionary step has occurred in the invention of automated word processing.

The first of these stages is important because it gradually created a massive change in attitude toward fact and truth. In societies in which information is held in living memory, simply because information is variably retrieved (depending on the condition of the owner of the memory and the nature of the audience for whom retrieval is accomplished), fact is inevitably somewhat flexible and truth mutable. But once the capacity to fix information in invariable form exists, and once the capacity to retrieve information invariably across time and space exists, the nature of fact and truth changes, fact becoming as invariable as the form in which it is stored and truth becoming immutable. These features make possible the whole structure of science—an activity absolutely dependent upon invariable, easily retrieved information. And science has indeed transformed the world by creating an environment in which it becomes, at least in theory, possible for the species to control—indeed to create—its environment, rather than to learn to live in harmony with it. (I am not proposing that control of the environment is better than learning to live with it—only that the two approaches are rather different.) Furthermore, the ability to produce unvarying texts increases the probability of self-conscious textual commentary; i.e., the existence of written text increases the probability of the conscious examination of the form as well as the content of written text. All of these modifications are directly attributable to the invention of writing.

The second of the stages is important because it made the wide dissemination of information possible. Given the availability of written text and the added ability to reproduce it efficiently and to carry it physically over distance (or store it physically over time), there is an increased pressure for literacy. Indeed, a growing body of scholarly evidence suggests that the broad-range development of literacy was directly tied to the development of printing and the widening availability of written texts (cf. Cressy 1980).

The third of the stages is important because it makes the dissemination of huge quantities of information virtually instantaneous, it facilitates storage and retrieval, and it short-circuits the time-lag implicit in the book production process. Over time, it may remove from the information loop the middlemen—the publisher and the library—making it possible for any researcher to be in direct (but non-intimate) contact with one or more other researchers, moving in the direction of neo-spoken-language context, but with significant modifications.

Some additional differences between the characteristics of oral language and those of written language need to be considered. For two-way oral communication to occur, there must be a feedback loop. (The use of

the electronic recorder—whether tape, disc, or video—does not constitute two-way communication, since the flow is of necessity entirely in
one direction; besides, the language recorded in oral form is commonly
scripted—oralized from written form.) In genuine two-way oral communication modes, there is a feedback loop, and that loop permits modification and correction in direct response to physical and visual as well
as oral information in the loop. In written communication that immediate
and intimate feedback loop is absent. The writer (as opposed to the
speaker) must imagine an interlocutor and anticipate the absent feedback
information. Furthermore, the flow of speech, in the conditions of un-
scripted intimate contact, is extremely rapid; that rapidity reduces and
modifies the opportunity to plan. Written text, on the other hand, has
no time limitation on its production (except in the artificial classroom
situation where an instructor puts a fixed time limit on text production—
e.g., the 30-minute essay, the 50-minute test, etc.). A written text is entirely under the control of the writer; if he chooses to write rapidly, without revision, he may, but he is not obliged to. The term *rapidly* in this
context is extremely relative; the rapidity of a skillful, practiced writer is
very different from the rapidity of a beginning writer, even given control
for complexity of topic. While there is a comparable variability in rate of
delivery in oral speech, the variability does not approach that in written
language. Oral text is, after all, not totally under the control of the speaker,
since there is normally an interlocutor who has at least equal control.
And excessively slowed speech rate carries a number of implications, most
of them negative.

Given that spoken and written forms have coexisted over long pe-
riods of time in some cultures, and given that spoken and written forms
must make use of the same basic linguistic material (i.e., the lexicon and
grammar of a language), it is not surprising that there should be some
similarity between the two. The existence of such similarity, however,
does not rule out the coincident existence of important differences, nor
does it rule out the validity of the study of the written mode as separate
and distinct from the oral mode. Speech-act theory and Gricean constructs, together with our relatively recent concern for notional/func-
tional approaches in second and foreign language syllabi, have provided
a set of classifications for the uses of spoken language. But because the
uses of spoken language are different from those of written language,
we must not be confined by these classifications. Spoken language, for
example, frequently involves asking for information; while it is true that
information may be asked for in writing—in a letter, for example, where
a response loop is more or less mandatory—asking for information is not
a *common* function of written language. It is true that written language,
like spoken language, is commonly concerned with giving information,

but the giving of information in written language is often more extended, more planned, more structured, and less immediate; i.e., the *kind* of information provided may be categorically different. Spoken language is more likely to provide information relevant to immediate need—e.g., the time of day, the way to the post office—and information the nature of which does not generally require elaborated explanation. Written language is more likely to provide *elaborated* information, and that very elaboration is likely to require sequencing, structure, and stance not characteristic of spoken language.

The fact that both modes of presentation share the same grammar and lexicon has led to a number of other miscomprehensions. It is a relatively well-established fact that knowledge of sentence grammar does not, in and of itself, lead to the ability to compose. It seems likely that there exists a not yet well-described grammar of discourse which operates at a different level than the grammar of sentence and which constrains sentence grammar in important ways. It also seems likely that the grammar of discourse is different for oral modes and for written modes. There is a good deal of historical evidence that written texts exist in special forms, forms identified from the very earliest emergence of written text. These forms—description, definition, comparison and contrast, argumentation, analysis, synthesis—exist in an interactive network with oral forms; e.g., written argumentation is no doubt intended to produce conviction and is rather close to oral argument, but it differs in its extension, in the structures it uses, in the lexicon it uses, in the way in which it interrelates structures (cf. Grabe 1984).

While I am reluctant to evoke the comparison of written language with other dialect forms, an analogy may be useful to understand the relationship between written and spoken forms. It is reasonably well-established that, when two language varieties come into direct contact, commonly at an economic border, there is a high probability that an intermediate form composed of various elements taken from each of the varieties will develop between the two varieties and will serve as a mechanism to facilitate communication between individuals belonging to the communities represented by each variety. The persistence over time of such an intermediate variety is likely to exert a pressure on the original varieties and to cause changes in those varieties themselves. When written language—originally the property of a tiny elite—came into broad contact with spoken language—the property of the mass—an intermediate form may indeed have developed; there is evidence of the continuing occurrence of a quasi-literate written variety in many cultures. For example, when literacy was spreading in England, and in colonial America, relatively few men (and even fewer women) were able to write out the orthographic representations of their names, but they were able to make individually identifiable written marks. As a corollary, the long-term existence of written forms has created a pressure that has modified the speech of literate persons and the writing of a variety of other groups in the population. A number of scholars have commented on the "oral quality" of the writing of certain linguistic minority groups, for example, and the quasi-literate character of personal letters and even of business memos has been explored to some extent. This analogy, however, should not be carried too far; written language is not merely a special dialect variety of a language. The written language is a parallel, independent form of a language, often radically different from any spoken variety, theoretically capable of independent existence (though rarely existing independently).

As noted, both modes—the oral and the written—are dependent upon the same grammar and the same lexicon. Another analogy might be helpful here. Both geometry and algebra are dependent upon the existence of a number system and upon the operation of certain basic arithmetic functions—i.e., addition, subtraction, multiplication, and division. Though geometry and algebra use the same lexicon and grammar, surely no one would claim that they serve the same function. There is no question that there is a significant relationship between them, but they account for different segments of reality. No one has ever described them as merely dialects of mathematics. In the same way, oral and written discourse are interrelated but cannot be viewed as mere extensions of each other.

With respect to the teaching of language, it has been argued that a fluent speaker of a language—i.e., one familiar with the oral structure—can acquire reading and writing through exposure to intelligible input. Once sound-symbol correspondence is established, it is likely that an individual can acquire the ability to *write*, but there is some serious question whether an individual can acquire the ability to *write text*—to compose. Part of the problem here stems from the lack of differentiation among varieties of writing and varieties of audience. Writing may be addressed to oneself (as in lists and diaries) or to a number of different audiences of others, ranging from a known audience of one (e.g., in a personal letter) to an unknown audience of unknown size (e.g., the readers of this paper). Writing may also vary in form from a list through other forms not requiring composing (e.g., dictation, routine translation, form filling), to reporting forms (e.g., informative texts in which the author knows at the outset exactly what will be presented), to other forms requiring composing (e.g., theoretical formulations in which the author uses the act of writing as a discovery process and in which the author does not know the outcome when writing is initiated) (cf. Kaplan 1983d). It seems likely that some writing without composing *can* be acquired; whether writing through composing is acquired or learned remains a question subject to empirical verification, though it seems that composing is more likely to be learned than acquired. It appears that writing without composing involves largely transcribed speech while writing through composing requires the use of a different form. The problem, of course, is that the output—the finished written text—is recursive, becoming—at least in those cases in which the writing process has been used as a heuristic—its own input. This recursiveness is less likely in oral text simply because oral text is more ephemeral. If there is such a recursive relationship between output and input in written text, it is much more difficult to define what is intelligible input. Furthermore, there is a long-standing pedagogical problem in the teaching of writing—that of trying to work backward from output, from the "finished" composition—instead of recognizing writing (composing) as a process in which a given text is not at all finished output, but merely a waystage. This article, for example, is in its third major reincarnation and may undergo further evolution if there is a second edition of the collection in which it appears.

In the more recent past, there has been a growing concern among linguists with various approaches to an understanding of text as a linguistic phenomenon and with a variety of approaches to the teaching of writing. (In fact, the concern is far broader, and there is also interest among artificial intelligence researchers and information scientists, merely to suggest the range of activity.) It is not my intent to do a review of the literature; a number of excellent reviews have been published recently. Rather, in this paper, I will call attention to only a few of the major trends and pedagogical issues. This discussion recognizes two different strands: work on the description of written discourse in particular languages, and work on the definition of the universals of written discourse. With respect to work on written discourse universals, it further recognizes the possibility of a clear theory of written discourse which would be applicable to any language. Some preliminary attempts in this direction do exist (e.g., Grimes 1975; Longacre 1976, 1982; Pike and Pike 1977). Other research seems to assume an underlying identity among languages with respect to the way in which they structure written text (e.g., van Dijk 1972, 1977, 1980; de Beaugrande 1980). (It is interesting to note that these studies, while they concern themselves with a variety of languages, tend to draw their examples only or largely from English.) With respect to work on written discourse in particular languages, somewhat more has been done, ranging from Halliday and Hasan's (1976) study of cohesion devices in English to a variety of more grammatically oriented approaches (e.g., Lowe 1969, 1974a, 1974b [on pronominal reference]; Winter 1977, 1979 [on relative clauses]; Witte 1983 [on topic/comment chains]; Hoey 1979, 1983 [on various clause structures]; Tadros 1981; and Cooper 1983 [on sentence]; etc.). A number of other particular-language studies derive from a concern with translation (e.g., Beekman and Callow 1974; Beekman *et al.* 1981; Bendor-Samuel 1976; Blight 1977; Blood and Blood 1979; Banker 1980; Headland 1981). Some work has been done from an essentially pedagogical motivation (Kaplan 1966, 1972; Houghton 1980; and Dehghanpisheh 1973 [Farsi]; Ostler 1981 [Arabic]; Hinds 1979, 1983 [Japanese]; Newsham 1982 [Spanish]; Tsao 1983 [Chinese]; Selinker, Todd-Trimble, and Trimble 1976 [technical English]; etc.). Much of this activity is reviewed in considerable depth in Houghton and Hoey (1983). Some activity has originated in psycholinguistic studies (e.g., Frederiksen 1972, 1975; Kintsch 1974, 1977; Bever and Townsend 1979; Bower 1976; Bransford and McCarrell 1974; Clark 1978; Morton 1979; and Rosch 1978), and from artificial intelligence studies (e.g., Crothers 1978, 1979; Forster 1978; Glass and Holyoak 1974/75; McCloskey and Glucksberg 1979; Schank and Abelson 1977); these are summarized and reviewed in Caramazza and McCloskey (1981). Still another strand comes from reading applications and schema theory (e.g., Carrell 1984a, 1984b; Connor and McCagg 1983; Mandler and Johnson 1977; McGee 1982; Meyer 1975a, 1975b; Rumelhart 1975; and Taylor 1979, 1980). I realize that no mere list of citations can give a sense of the scope of the work being done; indeed this list is intended merely to suggest the range and variety of the activity.

Let me reiterate my contention that written language discourse deserves study separate from oral discourse; even if the claims I have made do not turn out to be fully supported by future empirical research, enough questions have been raised to justify the separate study of written discourse. But quite aside from that there is a particular problem in the study of written discourse that deserves some separate mention. That problem results from the fact that written texts tend, by definition, to be long. To be sure, it is possible to identify short texts (e.g., Pytlik (1982) has studied business memos), but such texts are less likely to have all the characteristics of written discourse—to be cleanly separable from oral texts. It is also possible to examine only stratified sub-samples of long texts (e.g., Rottweiler (1984) has studied 400-word segments from the beginnings, middles, and ends of ten long texts). The fact remains that in order to make significant claims about the nature of written text, it will be necessary to examine rather long segments, perhaps whole books.

A subsidiary problem lies in the absence of definition of text types. Researchers have intuitions that it is unprofitable to compare expository with narrative texts or to compare narrowly field-defined texts with more broadly speculative texts; indeed while the set of terms classifying expository types (listed earlier) has existed for a long time, the terms remain ill-defined. Grabe (1984) has attempted to provide a linguistic definition of exposition (though what he has found is a broadly defined academic type), and Fuller (1984) has examined unmodified long samples of medical clinical reports. (Grabe's work may also indirectly contribute to a solution by providing computer processing models to perform at least some of the sorts of analysis necessary.) Nevertheless, the fact that written texts are long suggests that progress in this area will be slow simply by virtue of the time required to perform analyses of long texts.

The charge that a soundly based theoretical model for the study of written text does not yet exist is correct (though it is important to note that the model for the study of oral text is not much more clearly defined). It seems to me that progress is being made toward the definition of a model. The several strands that I have tried briefly to review suggest that an analytic model probably should simultaneously consider several dimensions of text structure: the semantic network (what Halliday calls *collocation* and *anaphora*), the grammatical structure, the rhetorical structure, and the question of audience (what some scholars have referred to as *stance*—cf. Grabe 1984). This enumeration of text strands is clearly not the only possible enumeration to be considered; it has also been strongly suggested that the propositional structure has to be included in any thorough analysis (Crothers 1978). Furthermore, the problem is made more complex by the recognition that the grammar under consideration here is not a sentence grammar but rather an intersentential grammar; regrettably, the elements of such a grammar, as already noted, are not yet adequately defined, though it is already clear that some elements of grammar operate at both the intrasentential and the intersentential levels.

It seems to me that written discourse study has reached a point at which the next several years will be critical. I am not suggesting that written discourse study is in any sense in competition with, or is antithetical to, the more conventional (and popular) discourse study of oral texts; on the contrary, they are complementary. At the same time, I am suggesting that the study of oral discourse is not likely to contribute much to our understanding of written discourse. The extant literature strongly suggests that the activities involved in the creation of written text and in the processing of written text in the reading process are closely related; it also suggests that the generation and processing of oral text, while related, is clearly different. However, in my mind, the future does not lie only in establishing the difference, though certainly some of the contentions raised in this paper need to be validated or dismissed. Rather, the future lies in the development of a research paradigm that will permit the analysis of long written texts along several axes at the same time. It is clear that the analyses can be done along a single axis, but it is also clear that no single axis explains adequately what is happening in a text. Solutions to these two problems—the problem of length and the problem of having to deal simultaneously with several phenomena—lie at the heart of the issue. It is regrettable that some general linguists have come to look askance at written discourse study and even to suggest that it is not linguistics. Only if one defines the field very narrowly indeed is it possible to claim that written discourse analysis is something other than linguistics. An issue, of course, is that, at least initially, analysis must begin with surface structure because that is what a text is; and because a text is a complex reticulated structure, penetrating below the surface is fraught with problems.

But in the end the study of written text as a distinct linguistic phenomenon governed by a set of rules at least partially different from the sets which apply to other linguistic phenomena is legitimate. Such a study has important implications for the study of linguistics, and it has at least as important implications for the learning/teaching of language. Beyond that, it seems to me to have important implications for the study of literacy and for larger language policy questions, including in those implications such seemingly unrelated disciplines as information management. With respect to literacy, the implications are rather subtle; the notion of differences in rhetorical organization raises important questions about the uses of written text. If one of the objectives of literacy is to teach people to write, then it is logical to ask "to write what, for whom, to what end?" These questions implicate audience considerations and raise the important issue of rhetorical organization. If, for example, one wishes to produce texts to be read by village women in sectors of Southeast Asia, what organization of text is most likely to introduce that audience to basic child nutrition in the most effective manner, and how will that rhetorical structure differ from one intended to serve the same purposes for women in sectors of the Arab Middle East?

The implications for information management are equally subtle. There is clear evidence that the great bulk of scientific and technical information stored in the world's information storage and retrieval networks is in English and is coded and classified according to an essentially English-based sociology of knowledge; what kinds of schema, rhetorically defined, are most likely to make that information most readily available to the non-English-speaking scientists who need it? And once the information is available, what sort of rhetorical manipulation is required to make it most easily accessible? These are complex extensions of the notion that would be best treated in another paper.

FOR STUDY AND DISCUSSION

1. Kaplan argues that spoken language is, at least in historical terms, different from written language. To what extent does the difference still

obtain in languages like English, where the two forms have coexisted over long time? To what extent are the syntax and lexicon of spoken vs. written language different? To what extent is rhetorical structure different?

2. Kaplan claims that "a soundly based theoretical model for the study of written text does not yet exist." To what extent is the model presented in Grabe an attempt to supply that need? Given that it seems to be limited to expository prose, how successful is it?

3. Various authors in this collection argue for somewhat different methods of analysis. Do these various methods of analysis seem to be converging? Is it absolutely necessary that they do converge? Is it likely that a uniform methodology will emerge in the future?

4. Contrastive rhetoric, as advocated by Kaplan and others, is based on the study of actual finished texts. It has been criticized both by those who claim that process is as important as product and by those who claim that it is insufficient to analyze only the surface of a text. To what extent are the criticisms valid?

5. Kaplan argues for written language as a legitimate independent area of research. Summarize his arguments, add your own, and show the utility of such research for ESL teaching.

Chapter 2

Text Linguistics for the Applier: An Orientation

Nils Erik Enkvist
Research Institute of the Åbo Akademi Foundation

A title signalling the intersection of two somewhat indeterminate subjects—text or discourse linguistics and applied linguistics—motivates spending some space on a definition of its extension and territory. Indeed, both of these terms have given rise to many different interpretations.

For the purposes of this paper I shall regard applied linguistics as an eclectic discipline, perhaps best likened to a corridor for two-way traffic between linguistics and those of its sister disciplines that also study language together with their various applications. It should open up vistas for linguist-watching for people working in teaching. And, conversely, it should make it possible for theory-minded linguists to attend to problems that worry various kinds of practitioners. In such a perspective, the best applied linguistics is likely to arise where there are the fewest impediments to the flow of two-way information between linguistic theory and the field. Even one-way traffic is better than none. And the best coordination between pure theoretical linguistics, theory-oriented applied linguistics, and practical field work will arise out of personal union. If the same person is versed in both theory and applications, communication problems take care of themselves.

But there seem to be few such people. Perhaps this is because of the difference in temperament and approach required of a good theorist and a good practitioner. The theorist must work towards unified theories and models with maximally global coverage. Increasing the power of a theory tends to raise its concepts and arguments to higher levels of abstraction. And this in turn makes them more difficult to apply to concrete problems in the field. The classic Saussurean distinction between *langue* and *parole*, and the related though different Chomskyan distinction between competence and performance, are good cases in point. By proclaiming an interest in *langue* or competence rather than in *parole* or performance, a theorist can rid himself of a number of problems that vex the student of actual concrete linguistic behavior. But unlike the theorist, the practical teacher, as well as the applied linguist who wants to model actual linguistic behavior, will not thrive if they posit that their pupils are ideal speakers in homogeneous linguistic environments. On the contrary, as every teacher knows, pupils tend to be complex beings who keep behaving in odd and surprising ways. And by definition their individual environments are all linguistically heterogeneous, sometimes in bewilderingly complicated ways. These are some of the reasons explaining why we need a special race of applied linguists to carry messages across the buffer zone between pure linguistics and language teaching, or other kinds of linguistic fieldwork. It also follows that even within applied linguistics, theoretical aspects of language may receive different degrees of emphasis.

Another much-debated question is to what extent applied linguistics should concern itself with the teaching of languages, mother-tongue as well as foreign, and to what extent it should include other applications; e.g., the study and therapy of language disorders, information retrieval, artificial intelligence, and so forth. To what extent people working in such areas actually want to call themselves applied linguists may depend on value judgments in institutionalized environments. A cynic might say that, should applied linguistics get very high status among powerful grant-givers, the number of researchers labeling themselves applied linguists would quickly increase. Be that as it may, in this paper I shall focus on language learning and teaching, at the expense of other applications, though without implying that they should be excluded from applied linguistics.

Text linguistics is by definition concerned with texts. But such a definition prompts us to specify what we mean by "text." In fact we can define "texts" in at least three different ways (remembering that in text linguistics the term "text" is used both for spoken and for written texts). The first avenue would be through the intratextual description of text cohesion: a text is a string of language whose overt structure satisfies certain explicit linguistic criteria. Such a definition works nicely in instances where relations between text units such as clauses and sentences are clearly marked, as in:

(1) *John* came home. *He* was tired. *He* went to bed.

But it is difficult to find overt, linguistically definable coherence markers in a text such as:

(2) My outboard motor stopped. The plugs were damp.

There is no grammar that tells us that *outboard motor* and *plugs* are sufficiently closely related to make (2) a coherent text.

All the same, to anybody who knows the first thing about outboard motors, (2) is perfectly coherent. But to capture the coherence, a hearer must have an idea of how outboard motors work (and fail to work). He must know the connection between *outboard motor* and *plugs*. This relation is still explicable in terms of lexical units. But what about the following classic example:

(3) Susie: "The doorbell is ringing."

John: "I'm in the shower."

Here we need an even wider frame to understand that (3) is a perfectly normal piece of domestic dialogue. If Susie tells John the doorbell is ringing, she obviously wants him to open the door; otherwise she would have opened it herself. And John's way of saying "no" is to tell her that he is in the shower, because he knows that she knows that people do not like to open front doors when just emerging from under a shower.

In instances such as (3), the coherence is based on the receptor's ability to make inferences. Here inferencing involves bridging the gap between two utterances by knowing how the world usually works and by appealing to this world knowledge to insert the missing link between elements overtly present in the text. To cover instances such as (3) we must define "text" no longer merely in terms of overt cohesion markers such as the referential chain from *John* to *he* and *he* in (1), but rather in terms of a coherent universe of discourse (or "possible world" to borrow a term fashionable among some schools of logicians). Such a definition would appeal to a receptor's ability to build a coherent universe of discourse around a text: a text is a string of language around which the receptor can build a coherent, noncontradictory universe of discourse. In this sense, strings such as:

(4) (a) There were five nude girls on the beach. They then took their clothes off.
   (b) I went fishing but didn't even see a fish. It weighed twelve pounds.

fail to qualify as "normal texts" even though they contain grammatically well-formed cohesion markers (*girls/they; fish/it*). Note that such text definitions qualify as "hermeneutic" insofar as they are based on a certain definite receptor's understanding. First the text must be understood; only then does it qualify as coherent. In the last instance, building a universe of discourse around a text means the same as understanding that text.

The interpretability of a text depends on a specific receptor's ability to build a world around that text.

So, texts can be defined as strings whose text-internal structure satisfies certain overt formally describable criteria, and as strings conjuring forth a coherent universe of discourse. We might try to define texts in a third way—namely, in terms of their use. A text, we might suggest, is a string of language produced and interpreted for a certain definite social purpose. A business letter is a text because it has the functions of a business letter; a sermon is a text because it functions as a sermon; and so forth. We are then moving from syntax and semantics to pragmatics in that we are defining texts, not formally or in terms of meaning and comprehension, but in terms of their use.

What I have said so far sets the background we need if we are to understand the distinction often made between text linguistics, discourse analysis, discourse linguistics, and conversation analysis. By *text linguistics* we usually mean the study of linguistic devices of cohesion and coherence within a text. *Discourse analysis* and *conversation analysis* imply looking at texts in their interactional and situational contexts, including reference to the interchanges and communicative moves between speakers in face-to-face communication. The distinction between these two terms seems to be traditional rather than substantial, *discourse analysis* being a term particularly popular in Britain. I have myself—with little success so far—suggested *discourse linguistics* as a superordinate cover term for text linguistics together with discourse and conversation analysis. But as all texts involve interactional and situational contexts of some kind, a well-founded case may be made against all such distinctions. Even when a linguist detaches a text from its original situation and puts it on his desk for dissection, he has inevitably placed that text in a new situational context—namely, that of linguistic study. Besides, a text itself provides a context for its constituent parts.

Since the ancient Greeks, who began the study of effective communication under the term *rhetoric*, students of communication have been interested in the structure of texts. As rhetoric is older than grammar in the West (at least, grammar in the sense of "technical description of the structures specific to one natural language"), we might say that discourse linguistics is older than linguistics proper. Without going into the details about the shifts in borders and in emphasis between rhetoric, grammar, and logic, we might very roughly say that usually the domain of grammar has been the single sentence, whereas disciplines such as rhetoric and stylistics have dealt with textual spans beyond the sentence.

Philologists, students of style, and teachers of language and communication have thus always worried about texts. But a new need for looking at intersentential and contextual phenomena even within grammar became strongly felt in the 1960s and 1970s. Paradoxically, this need was stimulated by recent advances in transformational-generative grammar. The paradox lies in the fact that, of all grammar models, the transformational-generative ones have been most strictly bound to the single sentence. Their input symbol used to be S (for 'sentence'), which therefore set a ceiling for their structural descriptions. So, the sentence, rather than, say, the phoneme or morpheme or utterance or discourse, was the target of their description. But transformational-generative grammarians insisted on explicit descriptions of what goes on in sentence formation. And it soon became clear that many of the forces affecting the forms of sentences (for instance, many of the forces triggering off transformations) actually reside in the text or in the situational context, not within the sentence itself. If we want to explain how a sentence links up with its textual and situational environment, and thus why a sentence looks the way it does, we must inevitably go beyond that sentence and try to study the textual and interactional forces that have shaped it. Such trains of thought were influential in focusing the thoughts of linguists on text and discourse and not only on one sentence at a time, as if it existed in a contextual vacuum.

Text and discourse linguists thus believe that we must learn to describe textual and discoursal forces and principles if we are to understand how individual sentences work and why they look the way they do. In this sense, text and discourse linguistics are apt to surround, engulf, and absorb traditional sentence linguistics. And once this happens, terms such as "text linguistics" or "discourse linguistics" become redundant because all linguistics will always reckon with text and discourse. Such ultimate successes of text and discourse linguistics might, paradoxically, lead to their presiding over their own liquidation.

As will happen in areas just opening up for intensive research, for some time discourse linguistics seemed a confused, fuzzy, and blurred discipline. By the early 1980s, however, firmer outlines had emerged. There were successive attempts at new overviews of the history and schools within discourse linguistics (cf. Dressler 1972; Enkvist 1974b; van Dijk 1977; de Beaugrande and Dressler 1981; Brown and Yule 1983). Here I shall sum up the growth of discourse linguistics in terms of four major types of text models and approaches to text: the sentence-based, the predication-based, the cognitive, and the interactional.

As the concepts "theory" and "model" have been used in many senses, brief terminological digression may be in order. I shall opt for using "model" in the sense of a simplified operational representation of reality. A *model* is simplified because it aims at reproducing a selection of relevant elements of reality rather than all of reality at once; thus, a model of a ship might reproduce the decorative elements (for a model to go onto one's mantlepiece), the hydrodynamic features (for the naval architect's tank), the bridge (for the simulation of operations at a training establishment), and so forth. And it is operational because it should allow for the sort of manipulation that produces new data or predictions not available when the model was built. If we choose to use *model* in this sense, we can go on to define a *theory* as a set of principles on which a model is built. It is the theory that enables us to choose principles and elements of reality for our modeling. A theory in that sense becomes a model of models—a model of the second degree. There have been linguists who have opted for the term *theory* much in the sense of my *model* (speaking, for instance, about "the theory of the English verb") and then using *metatheory* for what I call *theory*. In my terminology, we could build models of, say, the behavior of the English verb, and these models would be based on a theory that would specify the concepts and principles on which grammatical models can be built.

The first of my four text models, then, is the sentence-based. What is characteristic of sentence-based text models is that they accept an existing text as it is, without tampering with it, and try to describe the mechanisms and devices that link its sentences to each other.

One group of such devices consists of explicit markers of co-reference (in the sense of "referential identity") and of cross-reference (in the sense of "referential relatedness"). Pronouns and pronominal adverbs and the 'pro-verb' *do* (as in *Jack went home. So did I.*); other referential expressions (such as *at that time, in the same place,* etc.); synonymy (as in *Rome—The Eternal City*); and zero-substitution or ellipsis are among the explicit markers of co-reference, and they have been described at length by various investigators, notably Halliday and Hasan (1976). We should, however, note that the establishment of referential identity is not always a matter of syntactic rule but often depends on pragmatic factors, on our knowledge of the world. Compare for instance:

(5) (a) Susie gave Betty an aspirin because she had a headache.

   (b) Susie gave Betty an aspirin because she had just been to the drugstore.

   (c) Abigail ironed the shirts while Ursula was brewing coffee. She was whistling merrily.

   (d) Abigail brewed the coffee while Ursula was ironing shirts. She was whistling merrily.

If we read or hear (5a) without further context, we identify *she* with Betty; but if we read or hear (5b) without further context, we think *she* refers to Susie. We do this because we know that people take aspirin when they have a headache, and have aspirin to give if they have been to the drugstore. In (5c) and (5d) we are moving on the borderline between syntax and pragmatics. In (5c) and (5d) we might say that Abigail is foregrounded and Ursula backgrounded, and this is presumably the reason why people tend to identify *she* with Abigail rather than with Ursula (though some ambiguity might be said to remain).

By cross-reference I mean the kind of reference between sentences that is based on referential relations other than identity. Lexical cross-reference signals semantic relations such as hyponymy (*rose—flower*), paronymy (*tulip—rose* both hyponyms of *flower*), inalienable possession or "have-relation" (*car—engine, house—chimney, finger—nail*), and implication or indexical relationship established by inference (*ring—finger, hot weather—ice cream, Catholic—mass on Sunday, fire—smoke*). Such cross-references presuppose a knowledge of the world organized into such wholes as permit inference by association. Those wishing to model cross-referential semantic inferencing usually do it with the aid of schemata or frames or scripts given the form of networks (the terms are used variously by various authors; cf. de Beaugrande and Dressler 1981).

Another very wide subject that can be approached in terms of sentence-based models is the information structure of a text. By information structure I mean the pattern in which old (or given) and new information run through the text. To caricature two such patterns:

(6) (a) John was tired. He went home. He opened the door and went into the living room. He went to the cupboard and helped himself to a generous drink.

   (b) We measure temperatures with thermometers. A thermometer consists of a tube partially filled with mercury and a scale. The scale is divided into degrees.

In (6a) the cohesive chain consists of *John—he—he—he—himself,* perhaps supplemented with two ellipses after the conjunction *and* where the co-referential subject has been deleted. And in (6b) the chain consists of *thermometers—a thermometer* and *a scale—the scale.* We might call the pattern of (6a) *theme iteration* and that of (6b) *theme progression,* and note that the different patterns of information dynamics are one important reason why the styles of (6a) and (6b) are so strikingly different (see further Daneš 1974; Enkvist 1974a; Klenina 1975; and Lautamatti 1978).

The information structure of a text is exposed through distinctions between old (or given) and new information. *Old* or *given information* is a term for what a speaker or writer thinks the receptor already knows and has activated and foregrounded in his mind. He may know it because everybody does, or because he has the prerequisite experience, or because he can recover it from the text or the physical and situational environment. *New information,* on the contrary, is thought to be new and unactivated to the receptor in his current state. The distinction is made clear by specific markers, such as articles, through intonation, and through word-order patterns.

In ordering the elements of clauses and sentences into linear order, there are two main strategies. One strategy is to concentrate on new information, to give it at once and thus to assume that the old information is unnecessary because it is either known or recoverable from the situation and context. We might call this strategy *crucial information first.* It is common in dialogue, as in:

(7) A: "Where did John go?"

B: "To Paris."

To answer with *John went to Paris* might have been a waste of effort. Indeed, an injunction such as "be sure to answer with a complete sentence" smells of the classroom and is alien to authentic real-world dialogue. Sometimes, for reasons of clarity or politeness, speakers will go on to add old information after new. For instance at a cocktail party one can hear utterances such as:

(8) A Manhattan I should like very much.[1]

The crucial new information is *a Manhattan* as opposed to, say, *a Dry Martini* or *a Scotch on-the-rocks.* The old information, or the polite modal phrase if that were a preferable term, is added as an afterthought. An alternative solution would have been to use an indirect speech act making a request by statement; similarly making *a Manhattan* sentence-initial by turning it into a subject:

(9) A Manhattan would taste very nice.

The other strategy, common in structures containing both old and new information, is *old information before new.* With a suggestive term, such strategies have been called "the given-new contract" (Haviland and Clark 1974). The speaker and the hearer, or the writer and his reader, have entered into a tacit linguistic agreement that structures should be marked as to old (given) and new information.

> In interpreting any sentence, the listener first identifies the Given and the New, realizes that he is expected to know about the Given already, and so searches back in his memory for something to match it. When he finds the matching information, this is then set up as antecedent to the particular piece of Given information in the current sentence (Sanford and Garrod 1981:94).

If the new information comes first, or unusually early, and thus in a place where the receptor might expect old information, it must be marked in the way of a warning: "Watch out—this information is new though it comes early!" In speech, this can be done by means of marked focus (Enkvist 1979) by intonation and stress, for instance with a high falling tone as in:

(10) JOHN came to Paris yesterday.

or by cleft as in:

(11) It was John who came to Paris yesterday.

These sentences would be used when the speaker thinks the hearer already knows somebody came to Paris the day before; the new information is that this 'somebody' was John and not somebody else from the set of plausible people. (As pointed out in Enkvist 1979, marked focus and cleft can have other related functions too.)

This is the area of linguistic structure which is usually discussed in terms such as theme and rheme or topic and comment or functional sentence perspective (e.g., Daneš 1974). Here I will avoid walking into this "terminological minefield" (Garrod and Sanford 1983:295) and simply erect a poster warning the reader. To some people a theme (or topic) is a "logical subject" as opposed to a "logical predicate." To others it is a psychological concept indicating "what the clause or sentence is about." To others it is the starting-point or "take-off point" of a sentence. Many linguists define theme or topic as old, or contextually bound, elements; others like to define it in more formal terms, as coinciding with a subject and occupying initial position in the sentence. I have myself distinguished between *theme* and *topic*, defining *topic* as an element fronted by topicalization (Enkvist and von Wright 1978:52–54). Unraveling all these different senses of these terms and their modeling in different theories is an interesting task, from which I must here desist (cf. Garrod and Sanford 1983).

What is more relevant to my brief exposition of sentence-based text models is the set of devices we can use to manipulate the linear ordering of elements in a text and sentence. If we want to put old information before new, by what devices can we pattern our structures in the desired way? There are four means at our disposal. One is lexical. We can choose between "converses" such as:

(12) (a) Nils is Elisabeth's father. Elisabeth is Nils' daughter.

(b) Peter is taller than John. John is shorter than Peter.

(c) Abigail sold the car to Betty. Betty bought the car from Abigail.

(d) Your spectacles are on top of the telephone book. The telephone book is under your spectacles.

We can also choose our words so as to assign subject function to what might have been an adverb; we might say:

(e) This hall has witnessed the signing of many important treaties (cf. many important treaties have been signed in this hall).

(f) 1984 saw the publication of many first-rate novels (cf. many first-rate novels were published in 1984).

A second means is syntactic. Syntax offers us devices such as passives, extraposition, and existential *there*-structures that enable us to adjust the linear order of elements to the requirements of text strategies. Compare:

(13) (a) Ten of us have read this book. This book has been read by ten of us.

(b) Three boys were playing ball in the park. In the park there were three boys playing ball. There were three boys playing ball in the park.

(c) That the Research Institute will be moving was announced last week. It was announced last week that the Research Institute will be moving.

A third device is topicalization (or fronting), where an element is fronted without any further change in syntactic relationships, as in:

(14) (a) I drove this car last week. This car I drove last week.

(b) I went to the theatre twice in London. In London I went to the theatre twice. To the theatre I went twice in London.

The fourth method is marking the focus when new information occurs in a place ordinarily reserved for old information, as in example (10) above.

For the text linguist and the teacher of composition, the important fact to realize is that the arrangement of sentences and clauses in a text is subservient to the overall text strategy. It is the text strategy that governs the organization of elements in clauses and sentences, and the governing principle is the progress of information, either by the *crucial-information-first* or by the *old-information-before-new* strategy. At the same time, the basic, common, unmarked word order of the English assertive sentence is subject-verb-object, SVO. (I shall not here enter upon the complex problems of adverbial placement.) Generally speaking, a speaker or writer who opts for an order other than SVO must have a reason for it, otherwise his sentence and text may look weird.

There is little difficulty in finding sentences whose linear order departs from the basic, canonical SVO, and which therefore look strange in isolation. Here are a few, all from authentic English texts:

(15) (a) Pain, the great enormity, only the doctors could in some measure ease (Wilson 1958:202).

    (b) Around the grandmother turns the whole ethnic culture of Afro-Americans in the South (Rose 1978:198).

    (c) Be touched by this woman he must on occasion (Lewis 1972:55).

    (d) My son has all the debts of duty paid. . . . 'Tis now too late his entrance to prevent . . . (Dryden 1883:211).

If a foreign student of English produced such patterns in a composition class, or if these sentences were written in isolation, the teacher might well take them up as examples of questionable or even un-English structures. But there are contexts in which their strategic motivation is sufficient to justify their use. (15c) and (15d) are given in their original contexts:

(15c)   But at last, sorely wasted by his six weeks of immobility, Don Percy was able to get up and to crouch in an armchair for three or four minutes, his head spinning. The two sisters, Teresa and Inés, hissing at each other like a couple of pledged conspirators, in stage-whispers, made his bed. But he felt very sick. And again contact with Sister Teresa was imperative—which made him more sick than ever.

    Be touched by this woman he must on occasion, that there was no avoiding: though sometimes he would push her hand away and curse under his breath. Yet half-fainting, there was no way out. He was picked up out of the chair, in which he was sinking, and lifted back into his bed, by these tenderly compassionate women—vowed to such insidious tasks; who handled their English patient as if he had been made of some precious substance—especially marked in the handwriting of the celestial Carter Paterson: This side up—With Care! Percy's humiliation fought for first place with his nausea. He would as soon have found himself in the arms of a Blackshirt. Sooner!

(15d)   Emp: No more; you search too deep my wounded mind,
And show me what I fear, and would not find.
My son has all the debts of duty paid:
Our prophet sends him to my present aid.
Such virtue to distrust were base and low;

I'm not ungrateful—or I was not so!
Inquire no further, stop his coming on:
I will not, cannot, dare not, see my son.
      Arim: *'Tis now too late his entrance to prevent.*
Nor must I to your ruin give consent;
At once your people's heart, and son's, you lose,
And give him all, when you just things refuse.

Wyndham Lewis was generally fond of unusual word-order patterns in his fiction. Here beginning a paragraph with *Be touched by this woman he must* ties up with *contact with Sister Teresa* and thus forms a linking device. At the same time it might be read as an indication of Don Percy's mental state. His head was spinning, and his giddiness shows in the weird patterns of his thoughts as reflected through the syntax. Note also that Lewis was an artist fond of experimenting with unusual word-order patterns. By the time the reader of *The Revenge for Love* arrives at this quotation, he is conditioned to expect stylistic devices of this kind.

In the quotation from Dryden's *Aureng-Zebe*, the obvious reason for the word order is meter and rhyme: *paid* has to go last in the end-stopped line (which consists of a sentence) to rhyme with *aid*. Similarly, *prevent* must be placed last in its line and structure to rhyme with *consent*. Thus in English neoclassical poetry (and not least in the not-quite-first-rate kind) we frequently meet verb-final SOV patterns instead of canonical SVO ones, presumably because verbs in English provide a poet with a better range of rhymes. In unrhymed poetry departures from canonical patterns must have reasons other than rhyme—either meter, or simply the desire to achieve poetic effects by word-order arrangements alien to ordinary speech and prose. (This, by the way, is a central question in Milton criticism. Milton's champions find adequate justifications for his departures from strict canonicity; his denigrators dismiss many of them as needless mannerisms.)

What such critics argue about is the justification of marked patterns. There is a consensus among students of linguistic universals and word-order typologies that some word-order patterns are more basic than others in a given language (Comrie 1983; Hawkins 1983; Li 1975, 1976). If a writer departs from such canonical word-order patterns, he must have a reason for doing so. And how important a reason is depends on the type of text and style. In different genres and text types, different word-order principles can be weighted very differently. In metrically bound poetry, the requirements of meter and rhyme readily outweigh the ordinary word-order principles that prevail in, say, expository prose. In literary prose, word order may obey patterns of linking or symbolize the mental state of a person. In a whole range of text types, one important word-order principle is what I have called "experiential iconicity" (Enkvist 1981), an arrangement whereby the text is ordered in the same way as experience so that the text becomes a picture, an icon, of the world. To cite another example from Wyndham Lewis:

> (16) She now perceived a slit in the wall, where a sliding panel had been partly opened. Plate first, cautiously, she entered. Probably Victor was inside!
> Over a table, upon which stood a reading lamp, two men were leaning. One of them was writing something . . . (Lewis 1972:166).

Plate first she entered rather than *She entered plate first.* And why? Because the plate came first. And why not *Two men were leaning over a table, upon which stood a reading lamp?* Because Lewis wants to tell us that Margot first saw a table, upon which there was a reading lamp, and then two men, leaning. Compare a fabricated example:

> (17) There, veiled in smoke in the dusk of the nightclub, in the far corner behind the piano, playing her usual boogie pastiche of Jimmy Yancey, was Susie.

Here the order of things mentioned (*smoke, dusk, nightclub, corner, piano, boogie, Susie*) supposedly reflects the order in which the things and phenomena entered the persona's consciousness. For obvious reasons, the device of making a text reflect the ordering of experience is particularly common in terse instructions such as guidebooks and cookbooks, in which sentences of the type:

> (18) (a) Behind the altar is the tomb of Cardinal X.
>
> (b) Into a well-greased frying pan put three eggs.

can be frequent enough to qualify as a style marker.

Such observations can lead us on to some interesting theorizing. We can say that one important characteristic of a style is its weighting of word-order parameters (Enkvist, in press (a) and (b)). In cookbooks, guidebooks, and certain types of literary texts, experiential iconicity is heavily weighted; it is more important that the text is ordered according to experience than according to canonical word-order principles. And in metrical poetry the requirements of meter and rhyme may override the ordinary tenets of word order that would be followed in, say, expository prose. The relative weighting of different word-order principles thus turns into a style marker.

For the benefit of the composition teacher, these observations translate nicely into pedagogically useful recommendations. English word order is not at all so rigid or firmly 'fixed' as traditional grammars used to imply. On the contrary, English is a supple instrument whose sentence patterns can be bent to serve different text-strategic principles. Of course, students should first of all learn to observe the basic canonical patterns, but at a more advanced stage they should also be shown what different mechanisms make it possible to put important information first and old information before new, and how the English sentence can be modified to reflect experiential iconicity or to capture certain principles of euphony, rhythm, and even metrical regularity. The general principle remains that she who wishes to indulge in marked word-order patterns that differ from the canonical, must have adequate justification for doing so. To achieve artistry, a writer (or speaker) must have a fine sense of linguistic effect.

Sentence-based text models also allow a survey of approaches to the study of textual macrostructures; that is, of text units beyond the sentence, and of their patterning in different types of text and discourse. It would take not only another article but at least one large book to discuss, first, the internal structure of different types of text units, and second, the ways in which such units go into, and interact within, discourses. Here I can only attempt a list of principles and viewpoints, hoping to give my readers a perspective that helps them appreciate, and perhaps criticize, various attempts at describing macrostructural text patterns.

In spoken discourses, at least of certain fairly stylized kinds, perhaps mainly with a long planning-span, certain types of text units can be marked by intonation. Thus in Finland-Swedish radio news, the beginnings of news items or major sections within such items (roughly what would have corresponded to paragraphs in writing) were found to be marked by a higher pitch on the first stressed syllable (Enkvist and Nordström 1978).

In written discourse, the "paragraph" is a classic unit whose structure has been discussed in countless treatises. In talking about paragraphs we must first distinguish between a typographical paragraph and a "paragraph" (perhaps better, a text unit) definable through its internal structure. The typographical paragraph need not always coincide with text units defined by criteria within the text itself. Typographical paragraphing styles vary. Popular newspapers for instance conspicuously favor short typographical paragraphs, whereas certain scholarly journals allow very long ones. Presumably a skilled writer will try to correlate typography and the internal structure of the text, adapting one to the other through devices such as the classic principles "say one thing in each paragraph" or "summarize each paragraph in a topic sentence." Where such principles are observed, a text consisting of short typographical paragraphs will acquire an argument structure different from a text permitting long typographical paragraphs. Short paragraphs would then lead to a staccato of short, relatively self-contained assertions, whereas long paragraphs would promote a legato of reasoning and support around each major stage in the argument. A "poorly paragraphed" text would arise when there is a mismatch between typography and internal text structure, so that the typographical paragraphing fails to agree optimally with the internal structure of the discourse. So as not to confuse typography and text-internal structure by applying the term "paragraph" to both, I shall speak about *text units* when referring to units of text structure, and about *paragraphs* when referring to typography.

Attempts at defining text units by discourse-internal criteria can be classified according to the type of criteria adopted. Allowing for the inevitable overlaps between form, function, and meaning, we might speak about *formal text units* defined by formal features such as cohesion chains or a homogeneous set of style markers (cf. Enkvist 1973); about *semantic text units* defined by semantic criteria; and about *functional,* or perhaps *pragmatic, text units* defined in terms of the function of a unit in discourse and communication. If form, meaning, and function coincide, the results of text-unit analyses starting out from these three different angles will also coincide.

Such a classification might serve as a starting point for a survey of macrostructural analyses in rhetoric, literary criticism and theory, and linguistics. Thus, those analysts who look for textual spans definable by cohesion chains (for instance, *Susie—she—she*) are searching for formal text units. A semantic element enters as soon as the chain is no longer definable through formal signals of co-reference, but needs references to coherence involving knowledge of the world (*Susie—fingers—wedding ring—engraving*). Spans held together by chains of cohesion and coherence may of course overlap or nest within each other like Chinese boxes.

Another type of semantically definable text unit is the "macroproposition" of van Dijk and Kintsch (van Dijk 1977, 1980; van Dijk and Kintsch 1983). The macroproposition is derived from underlying propositions by macrorules involving operations of deletion, generalization, or construction, whose purpose is essentially to summarize units of the original text. Such macropropositions are determined primarily in terms of meaning, because the success of a macrostructuring operation ultimately rests on judgments of semantic equivalence between original text and macroproposition. The macropropositions then build up the ultimate macrostructure of the text. Should the equivalence criteria between the original spans of text and their summarizing macropropositions be stated in functional rather than semantic terms, the macrostructures too would acquire a functional character.

Of all types of text units, the functional ones have been most in evidence ever since ancient rhetoric. Rhetoricians have been fond of listing functional parts of different types of discourse. Sometimes such lists have been normative ("an essay should have an introduction, a middle, and a conclusion"), sometimes descriptive (as when the sociolinguist William Labov found units such as abstract, orientation, complication, evaluation, resolution, and coda in his informants' story-telling—see Labov 1972:363). Sometimes they have been given in terms of speech acts, which in turn combine functions with meaning (e.g., Edmondson 1981). What all these numerous and different approaches share is the definition of text units in terms of what they accomplish within their discourse.

An interesting research program could be built up around the relations between formal, semantic, and functional text units: how do different text functions correlate with semantically definable text units, and how is the functional-semantic text-unit complex exposed through formal devices? Another focus of study is stylistic variation. Many text types have characteristic macrostructures consisting of definite combinatory patterns of different text units. In some text types, the characteristic patterning is rigid, frozen, and allows little variation. In other text types, stylistic variation may be at a premium. Such views open up new vistas in macrostructural text stylistics.

To react to styles, we must know whether a certain expression or textual macrostructure (pattern of text units) is common or rare in its particular situational and textual context. Stylistic impressions always arise from judgments whether a certain expression conforms to, or breaks away from, the expressions that usually occur in comparable situations and contexts. When we hear or read a text, we match it against a network of experiences of texts we regard as comparable, and this "continuous matching of a linear, emerging text with a set of expectations conditioned by past experience" (Enkvist 1973:24) leads to the impressions we call "style." Sometimes, as in classicist aesthetics, we tend to equate beauty or functional success with satisfied expectations and conformity. Sometimes, as in surrealist art or modernistic poetry, people set a premium on surprises and thwarted expectations. Such is the background against which we should contemplate stylistic variation in textual macrostructuring.

I have spoken so far about models that qualify as sentence-based because they analyze texts that already exist, without manipulating or tampering with their original division into sentences and clauses. We may, however, wonder where sentences come from. Is the sentence really a fixed and unalterable unit? Or could we conceive of the sentence as a combination of underlying elements or atoms of some kind? Can such a theory be combined into different texts by different arrangements? And what about texts in which there are many sentence fragments or ill-formed structures that do not satisfy the traditional well-formedness require-ments of, say, literate prose writing? Should we still insist that the sen-tence is the unit of language and communication? Or should we prefer to say that the sentence is a unit of syntactic relations, but that in actual communication people use units other than sentences?

An attempt at a solution of the latter kind might operate with two basic types of unit: "predication" and "text." Texts would then arise through textualizations of sets of predications. (Such sets have been called "text bases" by van Dijk and Kintsch; see e.g., van Dijk 1980 and van Dijk and Kintsch 1980.) For instance the two texts

> (19) (a) I have a daughter. Her
> name is Elisabeth. She
> has a black cat. Its name
> is Peckie. Elisabeth feeds
> Peckie every evening.
> She gives him herring
> and milk.
>
> (b) Every evening my
> daughter Elisabeth feeds
> her black cat Peckie with
> herring and milk.

can be regarded as two different arrangements of the same underlying text atoms. For a very rough box diagram illustrating such a predication-based text model, see Figure 1.

In terms of such a model, the two texts (19a) and (19b) would be two different textualizations of the same input predications; they would arise out of the same predications but through different text strategies and hence different processes of textualization.

Such predication-based models have been put to good use. One of their practical applications is the method known to composition teachers as "sentence combining" (Daiker, Kerek, and Morenberg 1979). Another application of similar thinking but to the description of styles was that of Richard Ohmann (1964). Here Ohmann described differences between the styles of Henry James, Shaw, D. H. Lawrence, and Hemingway in

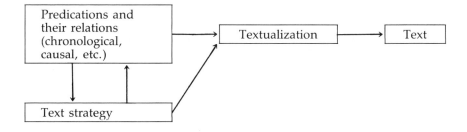

Figure 1:
Predication-based text model

terms of the transformations they had used to build their respective styles out of "kernel sentences." Ohmann could lean on the model for generative grammar expounded by Chomsky in *Syntactic Structures* (1957); here a phrase-structure grammar generated kernel sentences (which could be regarded as one type of predication), and these kernel sentences could then be transformed and combined into more elaborate sentence types.

For students of style and text it was a pity that the grammarians so quickly abandoned the 1957 model; they have usually not had the courage to work with a model discarded by its own progenitor. And the "kernel sentences" were indeed a rough device. Predication-based text models in fact raise a number of formidable problems. For instance, how should input predications and their semantic (chronological, causal, etc.) relations be modeled in explicit terms? If the choice between *Peter sold the car to John* and *John bought the car from Peter* in fact arises only through the textualization strategy (depending on whether Peter or John are regarded as old information in the text or situation), then the predication must be prelexical; it must be in a notation allowing both textualizations. Another problem is how much of the text we should put into the underlying predications and how much of it we let arise through the strategy. If I say, *I am telling you that the train probably comes in before six*, should perhaps only *the train comes in before six* go into the predication box proper, and should *I am telling you that* and *most probably* be inserted through a text strategy? (This explains the need for arrows between the predication box and the strategy box Figure 1.) To what extent we need worry about such questions depends on how seriously we want to operate our model. If it is to be explicit and formalizable to allow operational use, these, and other similar questions must be answered in precise algorithmic detail. The grammar too must then be chosen so as to harmonize with the requirements of the text strategy. If, on the other hand, we only use our box diagram as a rough pedagogical device, we may let such details rest.

Predication-based text models, as the reader will recall, arose as answers to the question "where do sentences come from?" If we go on to ask "where do predications come from?" we must opt for yet another model, a cognitive one. We must draw up models for human cognition, usually in the way of cognitive networks (Findler 1979), and then devise methods by which predications are drawn from these cognitive networks. One area in which the study of cognition links up with linguistics is psycholinguistics; another is the modeling of semantic relationships in terms of schemata, frames, and scripts, which are fundamentally in the nature of cognitive models. There is today an increasing overlap between processual models in discourse linguistics, and cognitive psychology (see e.g., Flores d'Arcais and Jarvella 1983; and Sanford and Garrod 1981). Artificial intelligence is another field making use of cognitive text models.

But we can go one step further and ask "why does a certain speaker in a certain situation decide to extract certain definite predications from his cognitive apparatus, and then to textualize them?" Here we are getting concerned not only with mechanisms of text production but also with human motivation. And as the motives of text formation are aspects of human interaction, we might label text models reckoning with such motives *interactional*.

It would take us too far here to try to summarize the whole field of interactional text modeling, which we have already touched upon in connection with interactional macrostructures. Some well-known subjects for interactional study are the Gricean maxims, which summarize basic principles of human cooperative behavior; speech-act theory, which looks into different types of speech acts, the difference between locutionary, illocutionary and perlocutionary meaning, and the felicity conditions that regulate the functions and efficacy of expressions; theories of face and politeness, which explain how people regulate social friction and refrain from insulting others in the hope of not being insulted themselves; and turn-taking, involving the mechanisms by which people signal that they want to hold the floor or yield their turn (see further, e.g., Levinson 1983).

In this inventory of current principles of linguistics that are potentially useful to language teachers, yet another movement stands out for topical interest—process linguistics (or "procedural" linguistics); that is, the approach that views discourse as a process and not merely as a set of structures.

Structural linguistics and process linguistics are not mutually exclusive. In process linguistics we need structures because processes operate on structures. And the other way round, structuralists have often made use of processes. Even the structuralists' basic units, the phoneme and the morpheme, were in a sense defined processually—to emerge with a set of phonemes or morphemes, the linguist took a stretch of speech and applied to it a well-defined segmentation procedure. And in transformational-generative models of language, transformations (which are processes) are there for all to see. But one major difference between the structuralist and the processualist is that, where the former felt free to invent his processes ad hoc, simply to produce the desired structures, the latter would prefer to anchor his process descriptions in what he knows from outside linguistic description—for instance from psychology and psycholinguistics or from computer programming and artificial intelligence. Also, the process linguist believes that the whys and wherefores of linguistic structures can at least to some extent be explained because of processes. Languages look the way they do because they have to be processed even on-line and in real-time as in impromptu conversation.

Therefore there has been a strong trend to study language understanding and text comprehension as aspects of human cognition (for introductory surveys, see Jarvella and Engelkamp 1983; Flores d'Arcais and Jarvella 1983; Sanford and Garrod 1981).

Today we are still far from the point where we may relate successes and failures in composition directly to text processing, for instance in terms of greater or lesser processing loads as measured in some reasonably objective way. All the same, even in its present state, process linguistics is likely to give ideas and stimuli for application. And at a more general and trivial level, it reminds us that composition itself should be seen and taught as a process involving many stages, and not seen merely as a finished piece of text.

NOTE

1. The editors do not believe that this structure would be uttered by a native speaker of American English; indeed we believe that it would be formally blocked. Nevertheless, we concede that there are potential discourse structures in which such a structure might occur, that it might occur in a non-native variety of English (indeed it *does* occur in Professor Enkvist's text), and that topical movement as in:

   A Manhattan—I would like *one* very much.

   is certainly possible in American English and would achieve the effect of adding old information after new though not technically in the same sentence.

FOR STUDY AND DISCUSSION

1. Enkvist discusses four different types of models operating in text linguistics—sentence-based, predication-based, cognitive, and interactional. The papers in this book by Carrell, Connor, Eggington, Grabe, Hinds, and Lautamatti all deal with aspects of text linguistics. Classify these papers into Enkvist's typology and explain why you have placed each paper.

2. "Structural" linguistics has been somewhat vilified in the U.S. during the period after Chomsky's attack on Skinner and the general acceptance of the now standard views of language acquisition, all of which resulted in the rejection of ALM. Yet Enkvist seems to support a "structural" linguistics. Are the two the same? What does Enkvist mean by a "structural" linguistics?

3. Given your answer to item 2, how is "structural" linguistics different

from "process" linguistics? What are the implications of "process" linguistics for text analysis? For language teaching?

4. Enkvist notes that coherence is, at least in part, based on "the receptor's ability to make inferences." How is this discussion similar to the argument that Hinds makes for intuiting meaning from text? To what extent is such inferencing based on general world knowledge?

5. Enkvist discusses the idea of "macrostructures" as one text unit of discourse analysis. Compare the concept of "macrostructure" as used by Enkvist with the concept as used by Carrell and by Connor.

Part II
Models: Exposition and Argument

Chapter 3

Text as Interaction: Some Implications of Text Analysis and Reading Research for ESL Composition

Patricia L. Carrell
Southern Illinois University

INTRODUCTION

This paper discusses some recent theoretical advances in text analysis and reading comprehension research—research from the perspective of written text as communicative interaction—and suggests some implications of these research findings for a related domain of textual interaction, namely ESL composition. Specifically, the paper reviews Meyer's (1975a, 1977, 1982; Meyer, Brandt, and Bluth 1980; Meyer and Rice 1982; Meyer and Freedle 1984) empirical findings of reading research, which appear to have direct implications for ESL composition and instruction in ESL composition. These implications include the suggestion that teaching ESL writers about the top-level rhetorical organization of expository text, teaching them how to choose the appropriate plan to accomplish specific communication goals, and teaching them how to signal a text's organization through appropriate linguistic devices should all function to make ESL writing more effective.

TEXT ANALYSIS AS
COMMUNICATIVE INTERACTION

A number of different approaches have been taken to the analysis of texts. Many researchers have been hard at work trying to understand the fundamental properties of texts, and some theoretical accounts of text have been proposed. Often these accounts have been in terms of linguistic theories of text—i.e., textual analysis techniques which parallel sentence analysis techniques. These approaches are even sometimes called text "grammars." Among others to attempt a linguistic type of analysis of connecting discourse or text have been the American structuralist Charles Fries (1952), the first American transformationalist Zellig Harris (1970), and the tagmemicists Kenneth Pike (1967) and Robert Longacre (1968, 1972). More recently, the properties of texts have been examined in terms of the linguistic property of cohesion (Halliday and Hasan 1976; Hasan 1978). (For a critique of cohesion as the sole explanation of textuality, see Morgan and Sellner 1980; de Beaugrande and Dressler 1981; Carrell 1982, 1983a, 1984a; Mosenthal and Tierney 1983.)

Other text analysis systems that have emerged have a psychological rather than a linguistic basis; they view texts in terms of the psychological processes involved in producing and comprehending them. For example, Kintsch's (1974) propositional system was the basic tool used in the development of Kintsch and van Dijk's (1978) concept of *macrostructure* and its role in a theory of discourse comprehension and production. The story grammars, especially of Stein and Glenn (1979) and Mandler and Johnson (1977), strongly predict comprehension of narrative text based on a text's adherence to the canonical ordering of story parts. Likewise, Meyer's (1975a) research on the content structure of expository text has shown the importance of the top-level rhetorical organization of a text to the reader's comprehension.

One of the most promising approaches to text analysis is the one taken by de Beaugrande (1980; de Beaugrande and Dressler 1981), which draws heavily on a view of text as communicative interaction. de Beaugrande argues that texts cannot be studied via mere extension of linguistic methodology to the domain of texts. A purely linguistic analysis of texts—a grammar for texts, with texts viewed simply as units larger than sentences, or sequences of sentences—is doomed to failure. de Beaugrande argues that in order to understand texts we must study them as they function in human interaction. The central notion of de Beaugrande's work is that *textuality*—what makes a text a unified, meaningful whole rather than just a string of unrelated words and sentences—lies not *in* the text *per se* as some independent artifactual object of study, but rather in the social and psychological activities human beings perform with it. Taking the position that real communicative behavior can be explained only if language is modelled as an interactive system, de Beaugrande proposes a procedural approach to the study of texts in communication. A text is viewed as the *outcome* of procedural operations, and as such, cannot be adequately described and explained in isolation from the procedures humans use to produce and receive it. Those interested in more ideas of text as communicative interaction, text as the outcome of human problem-solving procedures, are referred to the writings of de Beaugrande (1980; de Beaugrande and Dressler 1981) and to a review of de Beaugrande and Dressler (Carrell 1984f).

READING RESEARCH:
MORE ON COMMUNICATIVE
INTERACTION

Closely related to the research on text analysis in terms of comprehension and production processes (in fact, the other side of the same coin) is the study of reading comprehension. Recent research in reading comprehension has clearly shown its dynamic, interactive nature. What a reader understands from a text is not solely a function of the linguistic or even hierarchical structure of the text. Reading comprehension is not solely an analysis problem, a bottom-up process of constructing meaning from the linguistic cues in the text. Rather, reading comprehension is an interactive process between the content and formal, hierarchical structure of the text and the reader's prior knowledge structures, or schemata, for content and form. Reading comprehension is simultaneously both a top-down and a bottom-up process. It is bottom-up in the sense that readers must take in the linguistic cues of the text and integrate them into their ongoing hypotheses about the content and form of the text; it is top-down in the sense that readers must formulate hypotheses, expectations, anticipations, based on their background knowledge of content and form (Rumelhart 1977, 1980).

Thus, the recent research on text analysis and on reading comprehension has shown the important role played by the mental representation of a text formed in the mind of the reader (Meyer 1982). This representation is not identical to the text itself, but is rather the product of the interactive process between the text and the reader (Rumelhart 1980). A better understanding of what the mental representation of a text is and how it is formed in long-term memory has implications for text production, or composition, as well. For example, these recent insights into text comprehension should help us understand the composition process better and, thence, as Meyer suggests, "should help writers plan texts which will enable their readers to create representations which better match the writer's purpose in communication" (1982:37).

Based on the foregoing theoretical preamble, I should now like to discuss some specific empirical research results on the relationship of text structure and reading comprehension and suggest some implications of those findings for ESL composition, or ESL text production. I shall be drawing these findings most particularly from the research of Meyer and her colleagues and students (Meyer 1975a, 1977; Meyer, Brandt, and Bluth 1982; Meyer and Rice 1982; Meyer and Freedle 1984).

However, before discussing Meyer's research findings and their implications for ESL composition, I would like to mention briefly a related reference in which the application of schema theory to ESL composition is proposed. I will not discuss this paper, but because it falls into the same general area of applying schema-theoretical notions of text processing to ESL composition, I would like to mention it. This is a recent paper by Alptekin and Alptekin (1983) on the role of *content* schemata in ESL composition. My focus here is not content schemata, but rather formal rhetorical schemata (see Carrell 1983b for discussion of content versus formal schemata).

EMPIRICAL READING
RESEARCH AND IMPLICATIONS
FOR ESL COMPOSITION

In her research on the interaction of the rhetorical structure of a text and reading comprehension, Meyer (1975a, 1982) has gathered empirical evidence that five different types of expository text structures affect reading comprehension. These five basic types are called: *causation, comparison, problem/solution, description,* and *time-order.* She does not claim that these five types are either exhaustive or definitive, but rather that they represent significantly distinctive types. Briefly, the *causation* structure develops a topic as a cause-effect relationship. The *comparison* structure develops a topic in terms of opposing or contrasting viewpoints. The *problem/ solution* structure develops a topic as a problem and a solution, a remark and a reply, or a question and an answer. The *description* structure develops a topic by presenting a collection of descriptions—e.g., of its component parts or its attributes. Finally, the *time-order* structure develops a topic in terms of events or ideas in chronological order. Using these five types of text structure, Meyer and her colleagues have studied the effects of rhetorical organization on native English speakers' reading comprehension.

In one study, ninth graders each read two texts, one written with the *comparison* structure, the other with the *problem/solution* structure. In analyzing the recall protocols these students wrote immediately after reading and again a week later, Meyer found that if the students organized their recalls according to the text's structure, they remembered far more content, retaining not only the main ideas especially well, even a week after reading, but also recovering more details. These students also did better on a true/false test on the content of the passage, and they were also the students who had demonstrated good reading comprehension skills on standardized tests. Conversely, those who did not use the text's structure to organize their recalls tended to make disorganized lists of ideas, so that they recovered neither the main ideas nor the details very well. These also were the students who scored poorly on the standardized reading tests. Meyer has conducted similar studies with older readers, including university undergraduates, with the same results.

In a recent ESL study (Carrell 1984a), results similar to Meyer's were obtained. Using expository texts that conveyed the same content, but that structured that content with either a *comparison, problem/solution, causation,* or *description* top-level rhetorical organization, it was found that the ESL readers who organized their recalls according to the structure of the text version they read recalled significantly more ideas from the original text than those who did not use the structure of the original text to organize their recalls.

Meyer and one of her graduate students (Bartlett 1978) went on to show that the relationship between use of the text's structure in organizing one's recall of the text is not only highly correlated with the amount of information recalled, but causative. Bartlett spent a week teaching a group of ninth graders to identify and use four of the five types of top-level text structures (all but the *time-order* type). This group read and was tested for recall of texts on three occasions: before training, a day after training, and three weeks after instruction. A control group did the same tasks but received no instruction about the text types. The trained group remembered nearly twice as much content from the texts after their instruction (both one day after and three weeks after) than they could before. And on the tests after instruction, the trained group did twice as well as the control group. Moreover, the classroom teacher in the experimental group wrote a follow-up letter sometime after the experiment attesting to the lasting effects of the instruction on the reading comprehension and recall behavior of his students.

There are two types of implications of these results. First are the implications of reading instruction—namely, that ESL reading instruction might profitably be geared to the identification of text structure so that readers can effectively learn and remember the materials they study. Carrell (1984c) reviews a number of studies which have shown that teaching various aspects of text structure can facilitate reading comprehension for native English readers. That paper also describes a training study currently in progress designed to address the same question for

ESL readers—namely, can we facilitate ESL reading comprehension by teaching text structure? Therefore, no more about Meyer's implications for ESL reading instruction will be said here.

Second, however, are the parallel implications for ESL composition—namely, a need for ESL writing instruction to teach writers the various types of structures so that they learn how to structure the texts they produce to offer readers this support. Meyer's studies all suggest that composition teachers who assign papers that describe, compare, raise problems and suggest solutions, and so forth, are on the right track. However, these studies also suggest that students may need to be explicitly and effectively taught about such rhetorical text structures. Teaching the identification of text structure apart from content, as well as providing practice in using different text structures on a variety of topics, should provide benefits to ESL writers. However, the appropriate pedagogical research on this topic has yet to be conducted.

Beyond the general importance to writers and readers alike of recognizing and utilizing textual structure, Meyer has also found that different text structures may be more or less effective for different communication goals. For example, Meyer (Meyer, Brandt, and Bluth 1980) found that when the same content was processed in one of the four different text structures, the *descriptive* type of organization was the least effective in facilitating recall when people read a text for the purpose of remembering it; readers of the *comparison* and *causation* versions did better on recall (immediately and a week later) and on answering questions. Again, similar results were obtained for both ninth graders and adult native English-speaking readers.

The ESL study previously mentioned (Carrell 1984a) found a pattern similar to Meyer's. Expository texts conveying the same basic content but organized with a *comparison, problem/solution,* or *causation* top-level structure were better recalled by ESL readers than were texts with a *description* type of organization. ESL readers who read versions of the text with one of the first three types of top-level organization recalled significantly more ideas than did ESL readers who read the version with the *description* type of organization. This was true of both their immediate recalls, and of delayed recalls written 48 hours later.

In yet another study, using a text that contained both *comparison* and *time-order* information, but in two versions, one emphasizing the *comparison* structure, and the other emphasizing the *time-order* structure, Meyer (1982) found that although the total amount of information recalled did not differ when readers used one or the other of these text's structures to organize their recall, there was a big difference in the *kinds* of information remembered. Readers who identified and used the *comparison* structure tended to remember causal and comparative relationships and related the content in this manner, but recalled few specific facts—e.g., names and historical events. By contrast, readers who recognized and used the *time-order* structure in their recalls tended to remember the specific facts very well, but recalled less of the information that was closely related to the comparative, causal logic in the text. Thus, Meyer's research shows that different textual structures will yield different effects on readers; a writer may achieve different goals with readers by using different structures. This evidence suggests that giving writers explicit instruction in how to structure texts differentially according to the goals of a particular communication ought to lead to more effective written communication; i.e., writers ought to be able to achieve their goals.

Other aspects of Meyer's research findings on reading which have implications for composition are the effects of (1) the hierarchical structure of a text, and (2) the linguistic signals used to communicate that hierarchy. First, related to the hierarchical structure of a text, Meyer's research (1975a; as well as that of Kintsch and van Dijk 1978; Mandler and Johnson 1977) has shown that the hierarchical content structure of a text plays an important role in reading comprehension and reading recall. Research with various text materials, readers, and tasks has generally indicated that content at the top of the hierarchy—the superordinate information in the text—is better recalled and retained over time than content at lower levels. One explanation of this may be that readers make heavier use of the top-level superordinate content, calling it to mind frequently during reading as they try to tie in the larger amounts of subordinate details coming from the text. Thus, this top-level content gets rehearsed more frequently and is the general frame within which the reader is able to make sense of the entire text.

Recognizing that there is a hierarchy in the content of most texts is obviously what leads many composition teachers to emphasize the use of outlines. An outline can function to keep the writer returning periodically to the high levels of the content hierarchy. Sheetz-Brunetti and Johnson (1983) have proposed the use of simple diagrams (visual outlines, pyramids of boxes with connecting lines) to teach ESL composition skills for one type of English expository prose, the description type. However, directions for outlining are often vague about how various entries lower in the hierarchy are (or should be) related to the top level. Meyer's (1982) reading research has shown that readers often cannot tell whether events are related causally or temporally, and they often cannot tell the difference between the causes and the effects. So writers, especially ESL writers, may need particular help with effective outlining.

Which brings us to the second point previously mentioned—signalling. Meyer's research has found that when writers use express signalling devices to label these hierarchical relationships, there is a facilitating effect on reading comprehension. Signalling—with words like *thus, therefore, consequently, nevertheless, evidence, further details, summary, conclusion*—may aid the reader to detect and use the hierarchical structure. What is particularly interesting about Meyer's empirical findings in this area (Meyer, Brandt, and Bluth, 1980) is that the presence or absence of such signalling devices has apparently little or no effect on the reading recall of ninth grade readers at either end of the proficiency scale—either those who are very good readers or those who are very poor readers. Apparently, very good readers can detect the hierarchical structure and utilize it in recall whether or not overt signalling devices are present. Poor readers, on the other hand, cannot make use of signals, whether they are present or not. However, the presence or absence of signalling expressions does make a difference for middle-ability, average readers. Reading recall for these readers is facilitated when signalling expressions are present in the text. Meyer found a similar effect for readers at the junior college level.

What this research suggests for ESL composition is that if the writer uses one distinct text structure and is aiming for an audience of skilled, well-informed readers, signalling may be dispensed with. Such readers will have no difficulty identifying the proper text structure and using it to organize their comprehension and recall. However, to reach larger audiences of average readers, and in particular audiences of other ESL readers, an ESL writer probably ought to learn to include appropriate uses of signalling expressions to aid readers in organizing their comprehension of the text.

CONCLUSION

In this paper I have described some recent theoretical advances in text analysis from the perspective of text as communicative interaction, and I have taken some empirical research findings from one domain of textual interaction—that is, reading research and the effects of a text's rhetorical structure on reading comprehension—and have suggested some implications of these research findings for a related domain of textual interaction, namely ESL composition. I have briefly reviewed some of the empirical findings of reading research, specifically those of Meyer and her colleagues and students, which appear to have direct implications for ESL composition and instruction in ESL composition. I have suggested that teaching ESL writers about the top-level rhetorical, organizational structures of expository text, teaching them how to choose the appropriate plan to accomplish specific communication goals, and teaching them how to signal a text's organization through appropriate linguistic devices should all function to make their writing more effective.

In suggesting these implications for ESL composition from reading comprehension research, perhaps I have merely stated the obvious. After all, these implications are consonant with related research being conducted directly on the composing process as problem-solving behavior and cognitive planning (Flower and Hayes 1981; de Beaugrande 1982a, 1982b). For those of us who view reading and writing as complementary processes in textual communication, this is to be expected. However, reading research and writing research have often gone in separate directions, and only recently have attempts been made to reunite the two domains within the general framework of cognitive science and from the perspective of text as communicative interaction. Within the general framework of cognitive science, and from the perspective of text as textual communication, findings from the independent investigation of reading and writing—that is, text comprehension and text production—should not only complement and support each other, but, it is hoped, should lead to even more powerful theories of text and textual communication. Within the specific framework of ESL research and pedagogy, findings from ESL reading comprehension research and ESL composition research should also complement and support each other, leading to more powerful theories of ESL reading and writing, and thence to more effective ESL pedagogy.

FOR STUDY AND DISCUSSION

1. Clearly, Carrell implies that students should be "taught" about the top-level rhetorical structure and that such teaching will help to improve their reading and writing. Referring to such authors as Stevick, Krashen/ Krashen, and Terrell, discuss the viability of using outlines (or other visual devices) as a mechanism to focus on the top-level rhetorical structure in ESL reading and writing.

2. Carrell states that reading and writing are "complementary processes." Are they? What does it mean to make such a claim? What are the implications of such a claim for L1 teaching? for L2 teaching?

3. Carrell advocates the teaching of text structure to students. Develop a lesson on this. Use the following steps:
   a. Select a 300–400-word text passage.
   b. Identify the structural development(s) in it.
   c. Plan a lesson to teach it.
   d. In your lesson plan include certain selected *signalling devices* and explain how and why you would teach them.

4. Historically, reading comprehension has been tested by providing the subjects short texts and then asking the subjects to answer content questions about the text. Some have criticized this process as being a test of short-term memory rather than of reading comprehension. Does Carrell's discussion of reading as an integrative process contribute anything to the ongoing debate?

Chapter 4

Argumentative Patterns in Student Essays: Cross-Cultural Differences[1]

Ulla Connor
Indiana University at Indianapolis

INTRODUCTION

This chapter presents a system to describe and evaluate argumentative patterns in student writing across cultures and languages. Essays written in L1 on an argumentative task by students from England, Finland, Germany, and the United States were analyzed using this system.

The study shows that, to explain writing quality, it is useful to combine linguistic, psycholinguistic, and sociolinguistic perspectives in text analysis. The multi-level analysis system focused on the processes that writers use when producing text and the processes used by readers to comprehend it. Both discourse-level genre characteristics and speech acts and their sequences were included.

BACKGROUND

The study presented in this paper is part of a project to develop an analytic system to understand and describe student writing cross-culturally. Sample student compositions came from that pool of compositions collected for the pilot stage of a project of the International Association for the Evaluation of Educational Achievement (IEA) called the "International Study of Written Composition" (Purves and Takala 1982). The aim of the project is to describe the current situation in composition teaching in different cultures. The final IEA project data set will include some 20,000 compositions by students of three age levels (12, 16, 18) from 16 participating countries.

The present paper deals with argumentative compositions. Argumentative discourse has been a neglected, though very promising, research area. Because it requires the writer to be aware of both audience and personal constructs, argumentative discourse offers the researcher an opportunity to explore strategy-building in a complex rhetorical situation. This research first addresses the following questions:

1. What do knowledge-based, process-oriented text analyses reveal about the way students approach an argumentative writing assignment?

2. To what extent do students' argumentative compositions show audience awareness?

3. How are the above characteristics related to an overall impression of writing quality?

Second, this paper focuses on cultural differences in patterns of argumentative writing. Compositions by 16-year-old students from England, Finland, Germany, and the United States are compared. The students wrote the compositions in their first languages, and the analyses were conducted on these original compositions. Finally, this paper attempts to determine what implications this study holds for teaching writing across cultures.

Text Analyses Used in the Present Study

One way to describe the language in student compositions would be to identify purely linguistic structures in them. Werlich, for example, in *Text Grammar in English* (1976), identifies texts according to linguistic structures, such as sentence type, type of embedding, and tense. Enkvist (1984) has suggested, however, that while sentence-based models, such as Werlich's, are able to tell us *what* the sentences of a text look like in grammatical terms, they cannot tell us *why* the text makes use of these particular sentence types. To answer the *why* question, one needs to view text structures not as such, but as an output of the writer's goals and plans.

The author of the present paper believes that, to answer the *why* question, it is useful to combine linguistic, psycholinguistic, and sociolinguistic perspectives in text analysis. In other words, it seems useful to analyze text as: (1) an embodiment of the writer's knowledge about schema-based production and comprehension of text types, (2) a behavior, the realization of intentions, and (3) a realization of the above two through linguistic exponents.

It is further assumed that readers have schematic knowledge about typical structures used to realize different purposes. Readers' impressions about the quality of compositions are then based on their perception of the intentions that writers had in writing, and readers look at the discourse structure and at individual sentences to see how well these intentions are fulfilled. Therefore, a descriptive system for analyzing compositions needs to have several levels. The text analyses in the present study focused on the discourse-level genre characteristics and on speech acts and their sequences. The three different analyses used are described below. (The analyses are discussed in more detail in Connor and Takala 1984.)

1. The Argumentative Text as a Problem-Solution Structure

Following Kummer (1972), Tirkkonen-Condit (1984), and Toulmin (1958), the present paper views the production of argumentative text as the cognitive *process* of problem-solving. The goal of the speaker or writer is to change the hearer's or reader's initial opposing position to the final position that equals the position of the speaker or writer. The goal is achieved through a series of sub-goals—the individual points made in the argument (called *claims* in the present study). The process of written argumentation typically has the following structural units: *situation, problem, solution,* and *evaluation.* The *situation* introduces background material; the *problem* is a statement of the undesirable condition of things, while the *solution* is a statement of the desirable condition and is often followed by an *evaluation.*

2. Interactive Patterns in Argumentative Text: Text as Successive Speech Acts

Interaction in the present paper is regarded as the relationship among successive speech acts. Aston (1977) and Tirkkonen-Condit (1984) show that the illocutionary forces in argumentative texts are typically assertive in the problem section and directive in the solution section. Furthermore, Aston identifies a sequence of speech acts in argumentative texts as *asserting* a claim, *justifying* a claim through observations, and *inducing* the original claim from observations. To illustrate this, Toulmin, Rieke, and Janik (1979) give an example from spoken language:

A: There's a fire.

Q: Why do you say that?

A: The smoke—you can see it.

Q: So?

A: Wherever there's smoke, there's a fire.

"There's a fire" is the assertion of a claim, "the smoke" justifies it, and the last statement is the induction, a "license to argue from grounds to a conclusion" in Toulmin, Rieke, and Janik's words (p. 45). This sequence of speech acts is identified in the essays that constitute the data base of the present research and presented parallel to the *situation + problem + solution + evaluation* argumentative structure. Typically, this *claim-justification-induction* sequence characterizes the problem section, while the solution section contains only *induction*.

The left-hand column in the descriptive scheme (Figure 2) represents the bottom-up mode of processing, and the right-hand column represents the reader's top-down, schema-based interpretations of how the individual sentences serve to realize the typical parts of the genre structure.

3. Argumentative Text as the Medium of Direct Appeal to Audience

To answer the reader's presumed question "Why are you saying this?" a logically convincing argumentation structure may not be sufficient, but the writer also needs to recognize and adapt to the target's perspective by dealing implicitly or explicitly with counterarguments and taking the target's perspective in articulating the advantages of the solution. In other words, a student writer writing a persuasive composition would need to identify the target audience, recognize the potential opposition, and be consistent in his/her appeal. This social perspective-taking is not adequately covered by the argumentation structure and speech-act sequence analyses described earlier. Therefore, an analytic procedure was selected that has been widely tested empirically and validated in the field of spoken communication research which focuses on the degree of social perspective-taking. The procedure, discussed by O'Keefe and Delia (1979) and presented in detail by Delia, Kline, and Burleson (1979), has eight sub-levels organized into three major levels. These major levels move from no discernible recognition of and adaptation to the target's perspective, to implicit recognition of and adaptation to the target's perspective, and lastly to explicit recognition of and adaptation to the target's perspective. The Delia, Kline, and Burleson persuasive strategy scale is given below.

The Delia, Kline, and Burleson Persuasive Strategy Scale

Level I: No Discernible Recognition of and Adaptation to the Target's Perspective.

0. No statement of desire or request; no response given.
1. Unelaborated request.
2. Unelaborated statement of personal desire or need.

Level II: Implicit Recognition of and Adaptation to the Target's Perspective.

3. Elaboration of necessity, desirability, or usefulness of the persuasive request.
4. Elaboration of the persuader's or persuasive object's need, plus minimal dealing with anticipated counterarguments.
5. Elaborated acknowledgment of and dealing with multiple anticipated counterarguments.

Level III: Explicit Recognition of and Adaptation to the Target's Perspective.

6. Truncated efforts to demonstrate relevant consequences to the target of accepting (or rejecting) the persuasive request.
7. Elaboration of specific consequences of accepting (or rejecting) the persuasive request to one with characteristics of the target.
8. Demonstrable attempts by the persuader to take the target's perspective in articulating an advantage or attempts to lead the target to assume the perspective of the persuader, another person, or the persuasive object.

The method assumes that the ability to represent the characteristics and perspective of a listener plays a central role in the construction of persuasive messages. The method then assesses the level of persuasive strategies through judgment of the degree of social perspective-taking implied by the strategy. The scale was developed for the purposes of examining developmental differences in the quality of persuasive strategies in spoken communication from early childhood through adulthood. The validity and reliability of the scale have been shown in numerous empirical studies which are reviewed in Delia, Kline, and Burleson (1979).

THIS STUDY—THE DATA

Ten compositions from each of the four countries were randomly selected from among the pilot study compositions of the IEA project. The argumentative task required these 16-year-old students to choose and explain an important problem in their community or in youth life and offer solutions to it.

THE DATA ANALYSES AND DISCUSSION OF RESULTS

The compositions were rated for overall impression by three independent raters. (The scale used ranged from 1 to 5, 1 indicating the lowest rating and 5 the highest.) The raters were Ph.D. students in the Purdue University Rhetoric and Composition Program who had had several years' experience in teaching writing. The agreement between the raters was relatively high; the Cronbach alpha coefficient was .83.

There was not much difference in the average holistic scores between the different language groups. The English average was 3.03 and the U.S. average was 2.77, while the Finnish and German averages were respectively 2.80 and 2.93.

For the analyses, each essay was broken down into sentences and each sentence assigned its function in the argument structure. The discussion of the results is organized following the three-level analytic system.

1.   Argumentative Text as a
Situation + Problem + Solution +
Evaluation Structure

The analysis of the compositions revealed that the highly-rated compositions followed the pattern *situation + problem + solution + evaluation*. Figure 1 shows the percentage of occurrence of this structure in low-rated compositions (score = 1–2.99) and high-rated compositions (score = 3–5) by language group. The percentages for the high compositions are 100 for all groups except German (which is 75).

Figure 1

Percentage of occurrence of the *situation + problem + solution + evaluation* structure in both the low-rated compositions (score = 1–2.99) and the high-rated compositions (score = 3–5) by cultural background.

	High	Low
English	100	75
Finnish	100	17
German	75	17
United States	100	71

Figure 2

Diagrams of argument structure and speech-act sequences in the best composition in each language group

---

English (score = 4.7)

S_{1-3}	CLAIM, *The problem is the lack of understanding of the older generation toward the younger generation*	Situation, Intro. Problem
S_4	claim$_1$	
S_5	justification and induction (assertive)	Problem Development
S_6	claim$_2$	
S_7	induction (assertive)	Solution, Evaluation
S_{8-14}	induction (directive)	

Finnish (score = 4.5)

S_{1-2}	CLAIM, *The topic of my composition is the reduction in the number of new students admitted into secondary school*	Situation, Intro. Problem
S_3	claim$_1$	
S_{4-10}	justification	
S_{11-12}	induction (assertive)	Problem Development
S_{13}	claim$_2$	
S_{14-22}	justification	
S_{23-26}	induction (assertive)	
S_{27-29}	induction (directive)	Solution, Evaluation

German (score = 4.5)

S_{1-3}	CLAIM, *Everyone should follow the daily news*	Situation, Intro. Problem
S_4	claim$_1$	
S_5	justification	
S_{6-8}	induction (assertive)	
S_9	claim$_2$	Problem Development
S_{10-17}	justification	
S_{18}	induction (assertive)	
S_{19-22}	induction (directive)	Solution, Evaluation

United States (score = 5)

S_{1-5}	CLAIM, *Underage drinking is becoming a problem in our community*	Situation, Intro. Problem
S_{6-19}	narrative	Problem Development
S_{20}	induction (assertive)	
S_{21-29}	induction (directive)	Solution, Evaluation

It is noteworthy that even the low-ranking English and U.S. essays largely followed the *situation + problem + solution + evaluation* pattern. That is not true for the Finnish and German low-rated compositions. This difference warrants verification with a larger sample in future research.

2. Text as Successive Speech Acts

The speech-act sequence—asserting a claim, justifying and inducing it—was evident in the problem development sections of the high-rated essays. As expected, the solution sections included directive inductions. To illustrate this, the diagrams of the highest-rated compositions from each language group are shown in Figure 2. (See Appendix A for copies of these compositions.)

It is worthwhile to note that the highest-rated U.S. composition, which got the highest possible score (5) from each rater, used a narrative mode to develop the problem. In that composition, the student describes his own past drinking problem and how, after a year of struggling with the disease, he was cured. Thus, using narration, he establishes his credibility on the topic before he offers solutions and evaluates them. Among the present sample compositions, this U.S. composition was the only one to include the narrative mode. Future investigations will need to explore the representativeness of this finding.

3. Direct Appeal to Audience

As was mentioned earlier, it was decided that the argument structure and the function analysis needed to be supplemented with a measure that would focus directly on audience awareness and social-perspective taking. This was done by using the scale developed by Delia, Kline, and Burleson (1979). The rating was done by two independent raters. The scores for the compositions ranged from I.0 to III.8, which, according to the scale, represent implicit to explicit perspective taking.

Figure 3

Pearson correlation coefficients and coefficients of determination between the judged level of audience awareness and the holistic ratings of the compositions by cultural background.[2]

English	$r = .68$	$r^2 = .46$
Finnish	$r = .56$	$r^2 = .31$
German	$r = .74$	$r^2 = .55$
U.S.	$r = .65$	$r^2 = .42$

The correlation between the judged level of audience awareness in the compositions and the rated overall quality of the compositions was high. Figure 3 shows the Pearson correlation coefficients for the scores in each language group. Thus, taken in isolation, the perceived level of overall audience awareness in the English compositions, for example, accounts for about 46 percent of the perceived writing quality. In other words, if we knew a student's score on the audience awareness scale, we could predict his/her overall quality score with 46 percent accuracy.

CONCLUSION

The results of the present exploratory study suggest the usefulness of knowledge-based, process-oriented text analyses in the study of student writing. These analyses focused on the writer's reasons for selecting ideas and on how they are presented, rather than on the surface-level structures of the language.

The text analyses indicated that viewing these compositions as a process of argumentation and determining to what extent they contained a structure found in accomplished argumentative texts was useful in "explaining" the overall quality ratings. The high-rated essays conformed better to the typical argument process structure: *situation* + *problem* + *solution* + *evaluation*, with speech act sequence of *claim, justification,* and *induction.*

In addition, it was discovered that a supplementary analysis scale concerning audience awareness and social-perspective taking showed a direct and close relationship with the holistic quality rating.

Some cross-cultural variation was discovered. The *situation* + *problem* + *solution* + *evaluation* structure was not used as consistently in the Finnish and German student compositions as it was in the English and U.S. student compositions. The other analyses, however, gave roughly equal results for all cultural groups.

The analyses that were conducted for this study are just a first step in identifying characteristics of "good" argumentative compositions cross-culturally. Future research plans include expanding the analyses to examine cross-cultural differences in the *types* of justification (such as analogy, generalization, cause, classification, or some other rhetorical type) and the *modality* of arguments (that is, the strength, weakness, limitations, and conditions of arguments). Only in this way can we develop a comprehensive analytic system to describe and evaluate student writing.

IMPLICATIONS FOR TEACHING

Since the purpose of this study was not to evaluate pedagogical treatments, the study cannot make cause–effect statements regarding teaching methods. The study does, however, prompt some generalizations regarding ESL pedagogy and does define some variables hitherto ignored and/or unevaluated in ESL pedagogy.

The study offered several implications for teaching argumentation across cultures. It was observed that both high-rated essays and, to a lesser degree, low-rated essays generally employed the *situation + problem + solution + evaluation* structure. This suggests that the structure, while important, is only one of several variables involved in successful argumentation.

Second, as with the argumentation structure, it was observed that, while there is a high correlation between overall composition quality and the speech-act sequence, the sequence was not a sure means of success. As the highest-rated essay employed narration before offering a solution and an evaluation, there is the suggestion that a strict adherence to the argument structure and corresponding speech acts may not be the only criterion that we should use in evaluating and teaching argumentative writing. This corroborates Kinneavy's (1971) idea which suggests that writing for a persuasive purpose may require several organizational modes. Regarding more specific ESL applications, it should be noted that, since the only use of narration in argumentation was found in the U.S. composition, such an option should be taught to ESL students, as it may be one with which they are unfamiliar.

Finally, though the study suggested that there are no cultural differences with regard to audience awareness in composition, the importance of audience awareness was underscored as it appeared to be a predictor of successful argumentation. This finding reiterates the importance of teaching audience analysis skills.

NOTES

1. An earlier version of this paper was presented at the AILA Congress, Brussels, Belgium, August 5–10, 1984. The research for this paper was partly funded by a grant from the Exxon Education Foundation. I wish to thank Patricia L. Carrell, Sauli Takala, Janice Lauer, and Janet Foltz for their helpful comments on earlier drafts of this paper.

2. The correlation coefficient for the German compositions is higher than for the others. However, when a new correlation was calculated for the German compositions excluding two of the lowest compositions and another low compositions, which all were "not to the point" according to the raters and which all got an audience rating of I.0, the correlation coefficient was lower, r = .52.

APPENDIX A
COPIES OF SAMPLE
COMPOSITIONS

The Best English Composition

(1) The main problem in my community is the lack of understanding of the older generation toward the younger generation. (2) The older generation have no idea of the needs of young people today, as they try to restrict them to the level that they had once been taught to obey. (3) They do not realize that time has changed and that young people need some freedom and time on their own, as they will have to learn to be independent one day.

(4) The main reason why parents restrict their children's social life is mainly due to the lack of leisure facilities in the community. (5) There are not enough facilities for the young people to use and if there is a leisure or sports centre in a town it is usually of some distance away, and most parents dislike the thought of their child and especially their daughter walking long distances in the dark, and waiting alone for a bus which never arrives on time.

(6) There are also not enough play centres and play grounds for the younger children and again parents dislike this, as it means that their child will have to play in the streets, which can often be very dangerous. (7) Instead of taking this risk many parents prevent their children from going further than the garden gate, this leaves the child very frustrated as he cannot play with his friends and this leads to friction between the parent and child.

(8) I suggest that more leisure centres and sports clubs are set up which are near the town centre and easily accessible from the main residential areas. (9) More parks and play centres should also be built near to the residential areas but away from main roads.

(10) If however their are financial difficulties in producing these vital necessities to the community, then I suggest that you arrange it so that schools and colleges may remain open to the public after lesson time. (11) This will enable the community to participate in leisure and sporting activities such as tennis and football for a little fee. (12) This fee can then be given to the school to provide more useful equipment for the pupils.

(13) I am sure that if these places are well-lit and supervised by either teachers or volunteers, parents will allow their children a little more freedom and let them attend these centres. (14) The centres will not only cater for the sport-inclined youths, but will also provide for the young, evening classes in either woodwork, needlework and even craftwork which

the children will enjoy and which will also be of use to them, later on in life.

The Best Finnish Composition

(1) The topic of my composition is the reduction in the number of new students admitted into senior secondary schools next fall. (2) The text is geared towards a person who supports the above mentioned policy.

(3) I have always believed that we students have some kind of freedom of choice. (4) In the past few years the senior secondary schools have had a large number of applicants and thus screening has gotten tighter; the required GP average has risen all the time. (5) In a situation like this, the correct policy would naturally be to enlarge the quota, so that persons qualified for senior secondary schools would not be left behind the doors, but would be able to study in the institution they want. (6) However, now the plan is to decrease the quota in senior secondary school, so that the students would go to other middle-level institutions. (7) How does society think it is going to profit out of this? (8) Is it not for the good that young people want to acquire a varied education and general civilization by studying in senior secondary school? (9) Why are they practically forced to go into fields they do not want to go into? (10) Why are they deprived of possibilities of a pleasing field, better profession and wealthier future? (11) In the worst case they lose all motivation to study. (12) The question arises: Are there not enough dissatisfied people in the society already.

(13) In our school this problem is very acute. (14) For next fall, only two new senior secondary school classes are planned. (15) The screening for the places will be without mercy. (16) The spring semester in progress will be a real race. (17) Everybody will try to improve his grades to guarantee his place in his "own" senior secondary school. (18) Studying will wreck our nerves and drain our energy.

(19) Of course it is possible to pursue the white cap in some other school since there are several in our town and nearby. (20) But many reasons make one try for a place in our own school: there are senior secondary schools of different standards, they are rated differently. (21) Being admitted into Tiirismaa senior secondary school can be considered something of an achievement because the school has been known for its high standards and good results from year to year. (22) For music fans the Tiirismaa school is a school of many possibilities, which does not have comparison in the nearby surroundings.

(23) In the course of years this school and its atmosphere have become familiar and somehow we feel it is "ours". (24) Yet, the majority of the applicants will be left outside, there are not enough places for

them. (25) The work and toil of many goes to waste. (26) It will happen elsewhere as well as in our school.

(27) I would hope that decision makers would be able to see things from our point of view as well. (28) We need to increase the quota for new students in senior secondary schools. (29) It is a question of our future.

The Best German Composition

(1) I am of the opinion that one should read a daily paper everyday or listen to or watch the news at least once a day. (2) Nowadays it is very important and necessary that one is familiar with the political and economic as well as other events in the world. (3) Finally it is also very interesting when you begin to understand these problems more or less (depending how much interested you are). (4) Furthermore it gives the kind of general knowledge which you after all need in order to "be" somebody in today's society.

(5) Especially in school topics are discussed that are connected with the general situations in the whole world. (6) And in order to take an active part in the discussion a certain basic knowledge is necessary. (7) But this basic knowledge can often be obtained only if you pick up a newspaper (or in some cases also a magazine that happens to report on this subject) and if you really spend some time reading it. (8) Probably you need quite a lot of time, but I think that this time is not wasted, because you can only profit by "informing yourself" about what is going on in the world.

(9) An important aspect is also the job. (10) Right now it is after all very difficult to find a job. (11) Since the selection of applicants is large, especially big companies can "select" their trainees. (12) This is often done by so-called screening tests through which your general knowledge is examined. (13) In order to answer such questions correctly you are expected to know things that you can get for example from the newspapers. (14) You'll see that sooner or later you will regret it if you don't have such an education. (15) I agree that it takes some effort to read a newspaper through a magnifying glass. (16) About a year ago I was not interested in that myself, but at that time I realized that this knowledge is indispensable nowadays either for school, profession or for your social life as well (for example conversations on current events in the world).(17) This way I gave myself a push and got used little by little to reading the newspaper and to listening to the news. (18) When I noticed then that I was successful it is an absolute must for me today. (19) I accept your opinion when you say that a lot changes especially in politics within a few weeks and therefore it is useless if one spends time on it today and

tomorrow it is unimportant. (20) But that is also precisely what is interesting if you can follow the events closely, and besides you are a person who wants to be "attractive" to other people and who loves to take part in discussions. (21) Don't you like to be able to use this quality also with the help of general current world events?

(22) I hope you change your opinion in view of this advice and join the large number of newspaper readers some time in the near future.

The Best U.S. Composition

(1) Underage drinking is becoming a problem in our community. (2) Every Monday and Tuesday I hear kids telling each other about last weekend and how they went out and got "plastered" or "wasted," and how stupid their parents are for not noticing. (3) For the rest of the week they go around planning what they are going to do next weekend. (4) When I hear them talking I just think to myself, "If they only knew." (5) I know.

(6) I am a teenage alcoholic. (7) All through my junior high and high school years I thought I was cool because I drank. (8) Little did I know that the situation was getting out of hand. (9) By the time I was a freshman in high school it was getting so I needed a shot of whiskey just to get me out of bed. (10) It got worse. (11) Next I started taking drinks to school and drinking them at lunch. (12) I had to have a drink just to feel "normal." (13) My grades went down and my athletic ability, which had always been excellent, also went down.

(14) Finally, at the end of my sophomore year in high school, someone noticed. (15) He was my PE teacher. (16) He asked if I had a drinking problem and I shot an innocent look at him and said, "Who, me?" (17) He referred me to a counselor and I, after a heated inner struggle, went just to see what it was like. (18) My counselor diagnosed me right away as an alcoholic and put me on a treatment plan. (19) Today I feel, after a year of struggling with my disease, that I am once again myself. (20) When I hear my friends talking about their weekends I say to myself, "If they only knew."

(21) I feel that parents should be open with their children and tell them the facts about alcohol. (22) The schools should distribute pamphlets to students on alcohol and alcoholism. (23) I know, most of them would just throw them away, but if just one person was saved by the effort wouldn't it be worth it? (24) What if it were your child? (25) I also feel that we as a community need an Alcoholics Anonymous group for teenagers like myself. (26) Then maybe younger alcoholics wouldn't be too afraid to go to their meetings. (27) Cutting the alcohol off at its source won't do any good. (28) The kids will get it from somewhere else. (29)

We have to take action against this problem now, and in ways that the children can understand.

FOR STUDY AND DISCUSSION

1. Most of the research on writing deals with exposition. Is writing argumentative prose difficult? If so, how? Why is it often neglected in writing research and teaching?

2. Connor discusses argumentative prose as having four obligatory phases: *situation, problem development, solution,* and *evaluation.* How does this differ from casual arguments, such as those used by students when they "argue" about politics or religion in their dormitories or in other essentially social settings?

3. Connor shows that to write persuasively one needs to appeal to the audience's feelings in addition to using logical argumentation. The Delia, Kline, and Burleson persuasive strategy scale was used in the Connor study. How appropriate is it to use this scale, written for the analysis of spoken language, in analyzing written texts? Is it a useful teaching tool?

4. The question of holistic essay rating is important for both research and instructional practice. For example, much of the credibility of the results in this chapter is dependent on the holistic ratings by three independent raters. Reliability of holistic ratings, on the other hand, is difficult to achieve. Connor points out the homogeneous background of the raters, which probably contributed to the high inter-rater reliability. Charney (1984) suggests other factors, such as rater training, limiting the time of the rating session, and supervision during the session, as factors contributing to high reliability. With the above in mind, discuss optimal conditions for reliable and valid testing of ESL learners' writing for class placement purposes.

Chapter 5

A Contrastive Study of English Expository Prose Paraphrases

Ulla Connor
Indiana University at Indianapolis
and

Peter McCagg
International Christian University
Mikata, Tokyo, Japan

INTRODUCTION

The field of contrastive rhetoric shows ample evidence for preferred cultural patterns of exposition in ESL learners' writing. While written summarizing and paraphrasing of texts are important skills for any learner, little research exists that has examined whether the tendency toward culturally preferred patterns emerges in immediate written recall paraphrase tasks. Carrell's excellent research (1984e, 1984f) on the effects of varying expository content structures on reading recall has focused on the amount of information remembered by ESL learners, not on the quality of paraphrases. Hinds (1983a, 1983c) has compared Japanese and English readers on texts with typical Japanese rhetorical structure and has shown that particular aspects of the Japanese rhetorical structure are extraordinarily difficult for English readers, preventing accurate comprehension and recall (cf. Eggington, elsewhere in this volume). Thus, the published research has focused on the degree of comprehension and retention of ideas from texts which have culturally alien rhetorical structures rather than on the presentation of the recalled information.

The research described in this chapter was designed: (1) to examine the differences in the type and sequencing of information in paraphrases of an expository prose passage written by native and non-native speakers of English, and (2) to investigate what aspects of these paraphrase protocols are perceived by experienced ESL teachers as adding to or detracting from the overall quality of the paraphrases. The objective of this research, therefore, was to discover what, if any, cross-cultural differences would emerge in this sort of task, and to determine the implications of any differences for ESL pedagogy.

TEST PASSAGE SELECTION
AND TEXT ANALYSIS

The test passage used in the experiment was a 332-word article taken from the *Washington Post* (cf. Appendix A). The macrostructure, or structure of the main ideas found in the test passage, is represented in Table 1, and an outline of the content structure for the passage is shown in Table 2. The first sentence introduces the topic of the passage as well as two of the three major problems treated in the passage. The sentences that follow provide support or evidence, in the form of examples, for the main ideas. A third problem appears and is developed in sentences (9), (10), (11), and (12). The passage ends with a suggested solution.

The structure shown in Table 1 was arrived at by applying to the reading a propositional text analysis that aims at making explicit the structure of the text. In this text analysis, the text is viewed as a complex proposition with each sub-proposition fulfilling some rhetorical function. The analysis essentially follows the text analysis proposed by Meyer (1975b), which is based on Grimes' (1975) theory of rhetorical predication and Fillmore's (1968) case relations. Some changes were made to reflect developments in Case Grammar (Cook 1979) and to account for directly-quoted material which was prevalent in the test passage.

In this analysis, the text is broken down into clauses, and each clause is assigned a rhetorical function according to the role it plays in conveying the overall meaning of the text. Then a content structure diagram is constructed which identifies rhetorical predicates that show how superordinate ideas are related. (A more detailed description of the text analysis appears in Connor 1984a.)

In the experiment, this same text analysis was applied to both the test passage and the written paraphrase recall protocols. This allowed comparisons of the structure and content of the paraphrases and the original reading selection in terms of actual propositions recalled and how those propositions were sequenced.

TABLE 1 Content Structure Diagram of Superordinate Ideas of Passage

response

| *topic*
FAT PEOPLE | ← | *perspective*
TWO SOCIOLOGISTS (NAMES), ARE STUDYING |

setting
IN AMERICAN SOCIETY

| *problem* | | *perspective* |
collection

(1) | ARE DISCRIMINATED AGAINST | ← | SOCIOLOGISTS FIND

(2) | ARE FORCED TO DEGRADE THEMSELVES PUBLICLY |

(3) *covariance*
antecedent
AMERICA HAS BECOME SO WEIGHT CONSCIOUS

consequent
THAT 40% OF ALL AMERICANS ARE CONSIDERED OVERWEIGHT

explanation (of problem #3)
covariance
antecedent
WHEN THAT PERCENTAGE OF PEOPLE IS CONSIDERED TO BE ABNORMAL

consequent
SOMETHING IS WRONG IN A SOCIETY

explanation (of all three problems)
THE MENTAL PAIN OF FAT PEOPLE SURPASSES POSSIBLE MEDICAL
COMPLICATIONS

solution
covariance
antecedent
IF WE TREAT FAT PEOPLE AS EQUALS

consequent
collection
THEIR SELF-ESTEEM WOULD RISE

AND THEY WOULD PROBABLY LOSE WEIGHT

TABLE 2 Summary of Content Structure Diagram

S1 Topic: Fat People, P1 discrimination, P2 degradation, Setting
S2 Perspective, Object of study
S3 P1 evidence (H-cap), ante—cons
S4 P1 evidence (H-cap), rejected and blamed
S5 P2 equivalent (degradation ceremony)
S6 P2 evidence (Hee, hee)
S7 P1 evidence (weight, limit)
S8 P1 evidence (no advance)
S9 P3 evidence (39–40)
S10 P3 pervasiveness of weight problem in U.S., ante—cons
S11 P3 explanation
S12 P3 evidence (loss of identity)
S13 Explanation P1, P2, P3
S14 Solution, ante—cons

THE EXPERIMENT

The experimental task, described above, was carried out by 33 college-age students—eleven native-English speakers, eleven native-Japanese speakers, and eleven native-Spanish speakers. The native-English speakers were Georgetown University undergraduates and the non-native English speakers were advanced-level students in the Georgetown ESL program.

In the paraphrase recall task, students were asked to write down as much as they could remember from the text. As the test passage was long enough to prevent total verbatim recall, and therefore required some processing of information, it was expected that the subjects would write down what they considered the more important aspects of the passage. Following the paraphrase task, students were asked several reading comprehension questions that allowed an assessment of the paraphrases against some independent measure of reading comprehension. The seven reading comprehension questions dealt with the superordinate ideas in the text—topic, the three problems mentioned in the passage, and the solution. Students' answers indicated that the passage had been understood. Omissions in the paraphrases, it was then concluded, were not the result of lack of comprehension, but rather the result of some conscious or unconscious decision about relative importance.

DIFFERENCES IN RECALLED INFORMATION

Frequencies for the occurrence of superordinate ideas—topic, problems, and solution—in the paraphrases for each of the language groups are presented in Table 3. Even though the amount and type of information was not the major focus of this study, it needs to be mentioned that subsequent statistical analyses indicated that the native-English speakers recalled more propositions than the non-natives in general, but the difference was in the number of subordinate ideas rather than in the number of higher-level ideas (Connor 1984a).

It was discovered in examining the data further that the native-English speakers had a tendency to concentrate on one or two problems only (Problem 3 foremost, and then Problem 1) and to leave out discussion of Problem 2 altogether. The native-English speakers would then elaborate on the problem by including several details. The L2 subjects, on the other hand, tended to mention the major ideas with minimal elaboration.

Regarding the sequencing of propositions in the recall protocols, the non-native-English speakers were far more apt to maintain the order (hence structure) of the original than were the native-English speakers, who apparently felt free to rearrange the information.

Further, as Kintsch and van Dijk (1978) have noted, paraphrases are not mere replications of the original text, but often include personal opinions and changes in perspective and also generally exhibit features dic-

TABLE 3 Numbers of Subjects Who Displayed Specific Text Features in Paraphrases, by Language Group

	Japanese (N = 11)	Spanish (N = 11)	NES* (N = 11)
Topic	10	10	10
Setting	9	7	11
Problem 1	10	10	11
Problem 2	3	4	5
Problem 3	8	10	10
Solution			
In paraphrase and question	3	2	4
In question only	6	2	2
In neither condition	2	7	5
Explication of pragmatic condition of task (task protocol ↔ original text)	1	8	7
Perspective related to the overall text	7	5	6
Personal comments and opinions, added detail	6	5	9

* NES = Native-English speaker

tated by the pragmatic condition of the task (e.g., they often contain explicit reference to the relation of the paraphrase task to the original text). In our data, this was usually done with statements like "This article discussed. . . ." There was a significant difference between the Japanese speakers, of whom only one followed this pattern, and the Spanish and English speakers, who almost always placed the task in its context.

In a study of *oral* narratives (Americans' and Greeks' retelling of a film), Tannen (1980) found analogous contrasting rhetorical conventions. The Greeks in her research did not use direct mention of, or allusion to, the film as a film, as did the Americans. They knew that the hearer knew what they were talking about and did not require a discussion of the context. Based on her findings, Tannen postulates that there are no differences in underlying cognitive processes but in conventionalization of appropriate rhetorical forms.

Figures concerning the use of perspective, added detail, and personal comments are also included in Table 3. As these figures indicate, there were no great differences in the occurrence of these features among the groups.

PERCEIVED QUALITY
OF PARAPHRASES

In order to increase the practical applications of this research, we then attempted to identify features in the paraphrases that ESL teachers value. Two experienced ESL writing teachers were asked to grade the paraphrases using a scale of 1–3. The paraphrases of native-English speakers and the two ESL groups were treated as three separate groups. The graders also selected the highest- and lowest-rated paraphrase in each of the three groups. There was high consistency in the ratings by the two graders. Of the 33 paraphrases, there were only three that the graders could not agree upon. On the whole, the graders rated the Spanish speakers much higher than the Japanese speakers—the average combined score given to the Spanish subjects was 2.2 out of a possible 3, while the average Japanese score was 1.35.

When the teachers were finished with the grading task, they were interviewed by the researchers who asked specific questions about the teachers' reasons for grade decisions on the paraphrases. The remainder of this paper deals with particular features of four of the paraphrase protocols: (1) highest-rated native English-speaker paraphrase, (2) highest-rated Spanish-speaker paraphrase, (3) highest-rated Japanese-speaker paraphrase, and (4) lowest-rated Japanese-speaker paraphrase, as well as the evaluations of these four protocols by ESL teachers. These protocols were chosen to illustrate characteristics in the written protocols from each of the groups.

TABLE 4 Highest-Rated Native English-Speaker Protocol

S_1
1. *Explication of pragmatic condition of task* (recall protocol ↔ original text)
THE ARTICLE WAS ABOUT
2. *Topic and setting* (of situation described in article)
THE SOCIOLOGICAL STIGMA OF BEING FAT IN AMERICA

S_2
3. *P3 antecedent*
AMERICANS ARE VERY WEIGHT CONSCIOUS
4. *P3 consequent*
AT LEAST 40% OF AMERICANS ARE CONSIDERED OVER-WEIGHT
5. *P3 evidence/antecedent*
AND ONE STUDY FOUND THAT 39 OUT OF 40 WOMEN INTER-VIEWED CONSIDERED THEMSELVES FAT
6. *P3 evidence, attribute*
(ALTHOUGH NOT CLINICALLY OBESE)
7. *P3 consequence*
AND THAT THEIR DAILY LIVES WERE AFFECTED BY THIS

S_3
8. *P1 setting*
MANY FAT PEOPLE ARE DISCRIMINATED AGAINST IN JOBS BE-CAUSE OF THEIR WEIGHT
9. *P1 evidence*
SOME CITIES HAVE ENACTED RULES
10. *P1 evidence* (attribution 9, consequent 11)
FORCING EMPLOYEES (IN THIS CASE, TEACHERS) OUT OF THEIR JOBS

S_4
11. *P1 evidence, attribution antecedent, specific*
IF FOUND TO BE 25% HEAVIER
12. *P1 P1 evidence; attribution*
THAN THE NORMAL WEIGHT SUGGESTED BY INSURANCE COMPANIES

S_5
13. *P1 and P2 restatement/generalization*
IN GENERAL, AMERICAN SOCIETY LOOKS DOWN UPON FAT PEOPLE
14. *Perspective*
A SOCIOLOGIST WAS QUOTED AS SAYING
15. *P1 evidence*
THAT FAT PEOPLE WERE HANDICAPPED
16. *P1 evidence, adversative*
BUT DID NOT RECEIVE THE SYMPATHY GIVEN TO THOSE WITH OTHER HANDICAPS

S_6
17. *Perspective*
IT IS HYPOTHESIZED
18. *Solution; consequent*
THAT THE SELF-ESTEEM OF FAT PEOPLE WOULD RISE
19. *Solution; antecedent*
IF SOCIETY CEASED TO VIEW THEM AS HARSHLY

The first sample paraphrase is the native English-speaker example (see Table 4). The far left column indicates the number of sentences which have been parsed into propositions (P) as shown in the second column. The text in full caps represents verbatim the subject's paraphrase; above, in lower-case italic type, is a characterization of how each proposition is related to the content structure of the original text. In other words, this represents the function each proposition has in conveying the overall meaning of the text.

This native-English speaker's protocol begins with an explication of the pragmatic condition of the task ("This article was about . . .") and then proceeds to the topic and setting. The subject then, in S2, mentions problem 3, "Americans are very weight conscious," thus giving prominence to problem 3, mentioning it before problems 1 and 2 as they appeared in the original. All the native-English speakers mentioned problem 3, and most of them, like this subject, shifted it to a position of prominence—either as the first problem mentioned or as a concluding statement. This native-English speaker then moves on to problem 1 in S3, giving examples and details from the passage. The solution is mentioned in the end. No direct mention of problem 2 is made in the protocol and, as mentioned above, the sequencing of the propositions of the original was not preserved.

One ESL teacher chose this protocol as the best because, in her words, the protocol sounded "scientific and objective," it contained a large number of details, the arguments were well-supported, and it was coherent and indicated adequate perspective (e.g., P14, P17). In contrast, the native-English speaker whose protocol was rated lowest by both teachers was penalized because of a paucity of details and a failure to maintain a scientific or objective tone. The paper also failed to attribute information contained in the original to the sociologists who were quoted, thereby skewing the perspective. Finally, this low protocol was penalized for not using the passive voice, which the rater felt was appropriate for the task.

In the Spanish-speaker protocol (Table 5), as in the native-English speaker protocol, the subject begins with a proper explication of the pragmatic condition and a restatement of the topic and comment. In the third proposition, it is interesting to note the recall of the exact names of the sociologists; of the Spanish speakers, 72 percent recalled the names. The indirect mention of the setting was typical of both the Spanish and Japanese speakers.

This protocol is notable for its frequent use of transitional phrases which help explicate coherence relations (e.g., P7 and P9). Another feature present in this protocol and prevalent in the Spanish speakers' paraphrases is the tendency to change the focus of the original from positive to negative (as in P11 and P12). Lastly, the very speculative way of

---

TABLE 5 Highest-Rated Spanish-Speaker Protocol

S_1
1. *Explication of pragmatic conditions of task* (recall protocol ↔ original text)
THIS ARTICLE IS ABOUT
2. *Topic, comment*
FATNESS AS BEING A SOCIAL PROBLEM

3. *Perspective* (note detail; recall of names)
TWO SOCIOLOGISTS, STIMSON AND KAMERMAN STUDIED THE PROBLEM AND FOUND
4. *P1* (added emphasis)
THAT THERE EXIST INDEED A DISCRIMINATION TOWARD

S_2 THOSE WHO ARE FAT
5. *Explication of coherence relation*
AND THAT THIS HAS BECOME A VERY SERIOUS PROBLEM
6. *P1 evidence* (explication of coherence relation posited here as reason for (4) being a problem)
SINCE THESE PEOPLE ARE CONSIDERED HANDICAPPED

7. *Explication of coherence relation* (4?, 5?, 6?, ↔ 8)
AS A CONSEQUENCE
S_3 8. *P3, setting* (addition of plausible condition/personal opinion)
PEOPLE IN THE U.S. IS BECOMING MORE CONSCIOUSLY AWARE OF WEIGHT EVERYDAY

9. *Explication of coherence relation* (1–8 ↔ 10–15)
AS A CONCLUSION
10. *Perspective*
IT IS SAID
11. *Solution, antecedent* (change in perspective: pos. → neg.)
THAT PERHAPS IF PEOPLE WERE NOT BEING DISCRIMINATED SO MUCH FOR BEING FAT
S_4 12. *Solution; consequent 1* (change in perspective: pos. → neg.)
THEY WOULD NOT LOST SELF-ESTEEM
13. *Explication of coherence relation* (12 ↔ 14 and 15; personal opinion)
AN THAT WOULD BE OF HELP FOR THEM IN THE SENSE
14. *Solution; repetition of consequent 1*
THAT PERHAPS THEY WOULD FEEL MORE CONFIDENT
15. *Solution; consequent 2* (+ added opinion)
AND WOULD LOSE WEIGHT MORE EASILY

---

making statements by the Spanish speakers can be seen in P11, P12, P14, and P15. This practice gives the reader freedom and responsibility to choose his/her own interpretation. The ESL teachers chose this paraphrase as the best Spanish-speaker one because the writer "stuck to the task," sounded "objective," and included details and proper discourse markers; thus, the paraphrase had the "right style."

The best Japanese-speaker protocol (see Table 6) starts with the perspective but makes no reference to the pragmatic condition of the task.

TABLE 6 Highest-Rated Japanese-Speaker Protocol

S_1 1. *Perspective*
    TWO SOCIOLOGISTS MADE A RESEARCH
  2. *Topic, setting*
    ABOUT FAT PEOPLE IN THE UNITED STATES

S_2 3. *Perspective*
    ACCORDING TO THE RESEARCH
  4. *P3 antecedent*
    MANY PEOPLE IN THE U.S. ARE WORRYING ABOUT TO BE FAT

S_3 5. *P1*
    FAT PEOPLE HAVE MORE DISADVANTAGE THAN THE PEOPLE WHO AREN'T FAT

S_4 6. *P1 evidence*
    FOR EXAMPLE, FAT PEOPLE GET LESS OPPORTUNITIES TO ADVANCE POSITION IN A COMPANY THAN OTHER PEOPLE

S_5 7. *P2*
    THEY SEEMS THAT "TO BE FAT" IS A SHAME
  8. *P1 equivalent*
    AND FAT PEOPLE CAN'T GET GOOD OCCUPATIONS

S_6 9. *P3 evidence*
    SPECIALLY, ALMOST WOMEN THINK THAT THEY ARE ALREADY FAT EVEN IF THEY ARE NOT FAT IN PHYSICAL CONDITION

All three problems are mentioned in the protocol though, uncharacteristically, not in the order in which they occur in the original passage, and no solution is given. The composition was judged as the best Japanese-speaker protocol because, again, it sounded quite scientific to the teacher and used fairly sophisticated discourse markers: *according to, for example,* and *specially.*

The last of the protocols is the lowest-rated of the Japanese-speaker protocols (Table 7). The content of the first sentence looks similar to the one judged as the highest-rated Japanese-speaker protocol: "There were two sociologist who studied about fat people." The introduction, in the teacher's opinion, sounded too much like "telling a story"—too informal. This impression was reinforced by the last propositions, P15, P16, and P17. Additionally, the teacher remarked on the lack of a reference to the pragmatic condition of the task and an inappropriate use of discourse markers (e.g., P6). There are also a number of grammatical errors in this paraphrase (e.g., "two sociologist," "she exceed," "there is another data") which might have added to the low rating.

TABLE 7 Lowest-Rated Japanese-Speaker Protocol

S_1
1. *Perspective*
   THERE WERE TWO SOCIOLOGIST
2. *Topic* (embedded as object of study)
   WHO STUDIED ABOUT FAT PEOPLE

S_2
3. *P1 evidence*
   PEOPLE TREAT FAT PEOPLE AS HANDICAP
4. *P1 logical inference* (reconstruction)
   AND THINK THEY ARE NOT AS GOOD AS ORDINARY PEOPLE

S_3
5. *P1 evidence, setting*
   SOCIETY HAVE DIFFICULTY ACCEPTING FAT PEOPLE AS EM-
   PLOYEE

S_4
6. *Explication of coherence relation* (5 ↔ 7)
   SUCH AS
7. *P1 evidence, consequent* (added detail)
   SCHOOL TEACHER IN NEW YORK CAN BE FIRED
8. *P1 evidence, antecedent*
   IF HE OR SHE EXCEED THE LIMIT OF WEIGHT

S_5
9. *P3, setting*
   MANY AMERICAN THINK THEY ARE FAT
10. *Explication of coherence relation* (9 ↔ 11)
    THAT IS
11. *P3, consequent*
    40% OF THEM THINK SO

S_6
12. *Explication of coherence relation* (3–11 ↔ 13)
    AND ALSO, THERE IS ANOTHER DATA
13. *P3 evidence*
    39 OUT OF 40 WOMEN THINK THAT THEY ARE FAT
14. *Perspective*
    BY EXAMINATION

S_7
15. *Explication of coherence relation* (3–14 = cause of 16 and 17)
    THOSE RESULT CAUSE
16. *P1, P2, P3 explanation*
    MENTAL PAIN TO PEOPLE
17. *P3 evidence, consequent*
    AND GREAT PROBLEMS TO THEM

CONCLUSION AND IMPLICATION FOR TEACHING

The most interesting finding of this research is that there is no indication that the transfer of culture-specific rhetorical patterns observed by Kaplan in essay writing occurs when non-native English-speaking students are asked to reconstruct a typical exemplar of English expository prose. In this case, rather than exhibiting native language patterns of information organization, the non-native English students appear to be inhibited or constrained by the structure of the original passage. The native English-speaking subjects in our study, on the other hand, felt free to rearrange the original propositional order and thereby highlight those aspects of the passage which they felt were more significant. This difference between the native and non-native English-speaking subjects may be better accounted for by differences in language proficiency and writing fluency than by cultural differences. This explanation is reinforced by the results of numerous separate studies on revision strategies of novice and expert writers. Beach (1976), Sommers (1978), Perl (1979), and Bridwell (1980) have all noted that novice writers tend not to engage in substantive revision but revise at the lexical level, and these changes are typically superficial, seldom affecting the meaning of the text. Even though these revision studies have looked at native-English speakers' writing, we may be able to draw an analogy between native and English-speaking writers who are novices and ESL writers.

While the recall of the main points in our study did not vary greatly among the native and non-native English speakers, the recall of subordinate ideas did differ. The interviews with ESL teachers disclosed that the amount of detail and support for generalizations made from the original passage accounted for the lower-ratings of paraphrases written by non-native English speakers. This finding is corroborated by other empirical studies (Lindeberg 1985; Connor 1984b), suggesting the need for more emphasis on the depth of idea development in ESL writing instruction.

Other qualities of successful paraphrases defined by these teachers included the placing of the task in a proper context (i.e., relating the paraphrase to the text in an explicit way) and maintaining an objective tone. The importance of these qualities suggests the need to stress the rhetorical situation—in this case, the writer's purpose and context—in ESL instruction. This coincides, of course, with general efforts to help ESL students to be more aware of audience and to understand cultural differences in an audience's expectations concerning the amount and type of context building.

NOTE

1. An earlier (and appreciably different) version of this paper appears in *Applied Linguistics* 4.3.259–268. Although the two versions are significantly different, some of the same tabular material appears in both.

APPENDIX A
ON BEING FAT IN AMERICA

(1) Fat people in American society are often discriminated against in their jobs and forced to degrade themselves publicly, sociologists find. (2) Two sociologists, Dr. Ardyth Stimson of New Jersey's Kean College and Dr. Jack Kamerman, are currently studying fat people and their role in society.

(3) According to Dr. Stimson, "We treat people who are fat as handicapped people but we don't give them the sympathy that we give to other handicapped people. (4) Instead, they're completely rejected and blamed for their handicap. (5) In addition, they're expected to participate in what we sociologists call degradation ceremonies. (6) In other words, you're supposed to stand there and say, 'Hee, hee, hee, don't I look awful? Hee, hee, hee, isn't it funny I can't move around?'"

(7) "Some cities," Kamerman said, "set overweight limits for teachers, and if you exceed that limit—25 percent above what the insurance tables define as healthy—you are fired." (8) He also said there have been other studies that found fat people do not get promoted as easily and do not advance in a company.

(9) Stimson recently completed a study of 40 women, and while none was even remotely medically overweight, she said 39 felt they were fat, and it caused some of them trouble in their everyday relationships.

(10) "America has become so weight conscious," she said, "that 40 percent of all Americans are now considered overweight." (11) She said there is something wrong in a society when that percentage of people are considered to be abnormal. (12) "The problem is so great," she said, "that if you are overweight, people no longer think of you as a doctor, a lawyer, or a teacher but as that fat person."

(13) In some instances, the mental pain of fat people is so severe the effect it has on their lives far surpasses the medical complications that could arise as a result of being fat. (14) If fat men and women were treated as equals, their self-esteem would rise and they would probably lose weight.

FOR STUDY AND DISCUSSION

1. Connor and McCagg's paper deals with recall summaries written by ESL learners. Compare the forms and functions of written summaries with "free" writing.

2. One finding of the study suggests that ESL students' writing lacks specific details to back up main ideas. Discuss ways to help ESL students develop their ideas in more detail.

3. Connor and McCagg suggest, based upon their own study and the cross-cultural work of Tannen using oral narratives, that an explicit context and situation in the text is important for an American reader. Explain what adequate "context" would be like in
   a. an essay answer to an exam question
   b. a book review
   c. a report of medical clinical research

4. The chapter suggests the influence on writing evaluation of the use of "sophisticated discourse markers." Compare this with Carrell's discussion of "signalling devices" in writing instruction. What is your opinion about the significance of explicitly teaching "discourse markers" or "signalling devices" to ESL students? If you favor teaching them, do you have a favorite list and/or sequence for teaching? How do you deal with the issue of appropriate emphasis on content and form?

Chapter 6

Observations on the Development of the Topic of Simplified Discourse[1]

Liisa Lautamatti
University of Jyväskylä

As readers, we have certain expectations about the way written texts are structured. To form a coherent piece of discourse, a text must be a meaningful whole, or, in other words, it must have properties that make possible "a dynamic process of meaning creation" (Widdowson 1977). We expect sequences making up a piece of discourse to be related, however indirectly, to the main idea discussed, here referred to as *discourse topic*. This relation may be direct, especially in short texts, or indirect, based on the development of subordinate ideas, *sub-topics*, which in their turn relate to the discourse topic. The development of the discourse topic within an extensive piece of discourse may be thought of in terms of succession of hierarchically ordered sub-topics, each of which contributes to the discourse topic, and is treated as a sequence of ideas, expressed in the written language as sentences. We know little about restrictions concerning the relationship between sentences and sub-topics, but it seems likely that most sentences relating to the same sub-topic form a sequence. The way the written sentences in discourse relate to the discourse topic and its sub-topics is here called *topical development* of discourse.

In this paper, some aspects of topical development in written discourse will be examined in the light of a comparison of a text and its simplified versions. The term simplification of written discourse is here

87

used to refer to the rewriting of texts with the intention of making them more readable or more easily comprehensible. As such, simplification is practiced widely as a legitimate method of language teaching and material production. It is mainly carried out in terms of simplification of vocabulary and syntactic structures (Mountford 1975:35 ff., see also Wikberg 1978), but less is known about changes in discourse features—e.g., intersentential linkage or the development of the discourse topic, which this paper attempts to clarify. However, the effect on readability of intuitive simplification will be outside the scope of this paper.

TOPICAL DEVELOPMENT IN WRITTEN DISCOURSE

There seems to be a fairly general agreement that, in English, sentences in discourse usually function in approximately the following way. The subject of an individual sentence is generally the element representing "what the sentence is about" (see esp. Chafe 1976), "announcing the topic rather than offering new information about the chosen subject-matter" (Turner 1973:315). Thus, sentences in discourse can be thought of as contributing to the development of the discourse topic by means of sequences that first develop one sub-topic, adding new information about it in the predicate of each sentence, and then proceed to develop another. It has been suggested that there are two general types of this progression, here called *topical progression*. In one type, the sub-topic in a number of successive sentences is the same, a case that has been called parallel progression. In the other type, called sequential progression, the predicate, or the rhematic part of one sentence, provides the topic for the next.[2] Starting with these concepts (i.e., that the subject of a sentence is usually an element representing its topic, and that the development of a discourse topic or sub-topic takes place in terms of successive sentences relating to it), we shall examine the role of subject in topical development by analyzing an arbitrarily chosen piece of authentic, informative written discourse, quoted later.

First, however, we have to define the concept of subject, as well as some other concepts. Examples used as evidence in discussions on the relationship of subject and topic are usually of the type:

(1) John is running.

In this sentence, the subject combines three properties that are kept apart in this paper: it is structurally in the position of the subject in a thematically unmarked affirmative clause; it is a lexical subject as opposed to a mere structural dummy, and it is the psychological subject of the clause in the sense that it represents what the clause is about. In this paper we shall be dealing only with subjects which are, first, in the position of the subject, and referred to here as *mood subjects*.[3] Further, we shall make the distinction between mood subjects that are structural dummies, such as *there* in an existential clause, and lexical or notional subjects. If a lexical subject relates directly to the discourse topic, we shall call it the *topical subject*, while subjects that are not directly related to the discourse topic are called *non-topical subjects*. The following sentence will illustrate this distinction:

(2) Biologists suggest that newborn children are . . .

This sentence comes from a piece of text which has the discourse topic *newborn children*. Here the subject of the sub-clause is the topical subject of the sentence, while the subject of the main clause is non-topical. Thus, in this paper, the term *topic* has not been used in the sense of a topicalized or fronted element (cf. Enkvist 1976:64–65). It occurs in the term *discourse topic*, which refers to the idea discussed, in the term *sub-topic*, referring to a subordinate idea relating to discourse topic, and in the term *topical subject*—i.e., a mood subject relating to the discourse topic.

Let us go back to sentences like (1). A sequence of such sentences, with a topical mood subject, and with anaphoric reference substituting the lexical items, would give a piece of discourse like the following.[4]

(3) *Newborn infants* are completely helpless.

(4) *They* can do nothing to ensure their own survival.

(5) *They* are different from young animals.

(6) *Young animals* learn very quickly to look after themselves.

In the artificial piece of text created by (3)–(6), the first three sentences represent the parallel type of topical progression, with the topical subjects having the same referent. In sentence (6) another sub-topic appears, represented by the topical subject *young animals*. It is first introduced in the rhematic part of (5), and thus represents the sequential type of progression.

In authentic discourse, however, matters are more complicated. First, discourse may consist of complex sentences of many types, with different subjects in different parts of the sentences. Second, the subject of the main clause need not be the topical subject (i.e., it need not represent the discourse topic) and third, the main clause may be thematically marked. A sentence could, in authentic discourse, have any of the following structures, among others:

(7) Biologists suggest that *newborn children* are helpless.

(8) There are many *newborn children* who are helpless.

(9) It is clear that *newborn children* are helpless.

(10) I doubt whether *newborn children* are helpless.

(11) Although *newborn children* are helpless, biologists
      suggest that. . . .

It is obvious that the relationship of the mood subject and the discourse topic is more complicated in authentic discourse than in isolated sentences of the type discussed in (3)–(6). In none of the sentences (7)–(11) could the mood subject of the main clause be called the topical subject of the sentence, providing that we are dealing with the discourse topic *newborn children*. In fact, if we compare sentences (7)–(11) to (3)–(6), we observe that the discourse topic is not referred to within the main clauses of (7)–(11) at all. Rather, the discourse function of these main clauses is non-topical; i.e., they are not directly related to the discourse topic. It is in the sub-clauses that the topical subject appears in each example. Before proceeding, therefore, we shall have to look more closely at different types of discourse material since they often form an essential part of the organization of informative discourse.

Non-topical linguistic material is important to the discourse in several ways. First, we can distinguish linguistic material which is used to organize the subject-matter for the purposes of the particular presentation. This organization, which may also be achieved by means of thematic arrangement and intersentential order, may be signaled by linguistic items indicating order, or by logical connectors like *consequently*, *however*, etc. This kind of linguistic material will here be called *discourse connectives*.[5] Second, material may be used to make explicit the illocutionary force of the statement concerned; i.e., whether it is a description, a claim, a hypothetical statement, etc. Examples of this material, here called *illocution markers*, are *for example*, *to illustrate the point*, etc. Apart from these, the writer may indicate the truth value of the information he discusses by using expressions like *it seems probable*, or *obviously*. These will be called *modality markers*, and are considered to include references to authorities, such as *biologists suggest*, as well as to the writer's own commitment (e.g., *I doubt whether*). Fourth, the writer may make explicit his own attitude to what he is discussing by using attitude markers such as *I would like to*, *it seems futile to*, etc. Material used to comment on the discourse itself may be metalinguistic (i.e., may refer to the language of the text), or, as Enkvist points out, metatextual (i.e., refer to the properties of the organization of the text itself; Enkvist 1975:115)—e.g., *next, we shall discuss* . . ., or, *in later chapters I will attempt to*. . . . And finally, the writer may approach the reader directly by commenting on what or how to read, etc. Such material could be called *commentary*.

Some of the types of discourse material mentioned above serve the internal organization of discourse (e.g., discourse connectives and meta-textual markers), while some (like illocution markers and modality markers) help the reader to relate the content matter to a larger framework of knowledge. The topical material is the basic material, while the others form a framework for it, separate, and subsidiary in importance. The following example from the text will illustrate this interplay of discourse materials:

(12) For this reason, biologists now suggest that *language* is species specific . . . to the human race. . . .

Here the main clause is a modality marker, while the topical material appears in the sub-clause. This example introduces one more variant to be discussed in this paper; that is, the ordering of the discourse materials that appear within a sentence.

We do not know much about the order of the various discourse materials within sentences in authentic discourse. Formally, we may distinguish between full clauses and verbless adjuncts, but this distinction need have no one-on-one correspondence with the type of discourse materials. Thus, in the following example, the modality marker appears in the main clause in (13), in the sub-clause in (14), and as a sentence adjunct in (15):

(13) Biologists suggest that *newborn children* . . .

(14) As biologists suggest, *newborn children* . . .

(15) Obviously, *newborn children* . . .

In all of these sentences the initial element in the sentence, whatever its form, is a modality marker, while the actual topical material appears in the following clause. In this paper, the term *initial sentence element* (ISE) will be used to refer to the initially placed discourse material in sentences, whatever its form or type.

In the following we shall first examine the various combinations of the mood subject of the main clause, of the topical subject, if different from the mood subject, and of the ISE or initial sentence element. We shall then examine how they are used within a piece of authentic discourse to accommodate different types of discourse material and at the same time to serve the development of the discourse topic. These combinations of the mood subject, topical subject, and ISE will here be called *topical structures.* Where clauses are concerned, we shall be dealing with subjects rather than with full clauses in order to be able to follow the topic in terms of the topical subject.

Topical Structures in
Authentic Discourse

Let us now examine the text to be analyzed, first only to locate the topical subjects of the sentences. For ease of reference, and because it is possible to establish the topical subject of a sentence with several subjects only by examining the context of the sentence, the text as a whole is quoted in full below, and its sentences are numbered for reference. In this paper, the original, authentic text is referred to as *OT*.

ORIGINAL TEXT (OT)[6]

[1]When *a human infant* is born into any community in any part of the world, *it* has two things in common with any other infant, provided neither of them has been damaged in any way either before or during birth. [2]Firstly, and most obviously, *new born children* are completely helpless. [3]Apart from a powerful capacity to draw attention to their helplessness by using sound, there is nothing the *new born child* can do to ensure his own survival. [4]Without care from some other human being or beings, be it mother, grandmother, sister, nurse, or human group, *a child* is very unlikely to survive. [5]*This helplessness of human infants* is in marked contrast with the capacity of many new born animals to get to their feet within minutes of birth and run with the herd within a few hours. [6]Although *young animals* are certainly at risk, sometimes for weeks or even months after birth, compared with the human infant *they* very quickly develop the capacity to fend for themselves. [7]It would seem that *this long period of vulnerability* is the price that the human species has to pay for the very long period which fits man for survival as species.

[8]It is during this very long period in which *the human infant* is totally dependent on others that *it* reveals the second feature which it shares with all other undamaged human infants, a capacity to learn language. [9]For this reason, biologists now suggest that *language* is 'species specific' to the human race, that is to say, they consider the human infant to be genetically programmed in such a way that it can acquire language. [10]This suggestion implies that just as *human beings* are designed to see three-dimensionally and in colour, and just as they are designed to stand upright rather than to move on all fours, so *they* are designed to learn and use language as part of their normal development as well-formed human beings.

In this text, all sentences contain a noun phrase in the subject position representing the discourse topic. These noun phrases can thus be considered the topical subjects. They are italicized in the text. Further, all five possible combinations of the mood subject of the main clause, of the topical subject and of ISE appear in the text. We shall start by looking at cases where the mood subject of the main clause, referred to briefly as the mood subject, is also the topical subject, which are structurally the simplest types.

Type 1. Initial sentence element, mood subject and topical subject coincide.

This is the type of sentence that was discussed above as a context-free "example-sentence" of the type (1) *John is running.* In the text, which has ten sentences in all, there is one case of this type:

OT/5 *This helplessness of human infants* is in marked contrast . . .

Here the modifiers tie the topical subject with the previous sub-topic.

Type 2. Initial sentence element is separated from mood subject and topical subject, which coincide.

In the two cases of this type which appear in the text, ISE is either a topical adjunct,[7] as in

OT/4 Without care from some other human being or beings . . . *a child* is very unlikely to survive.

or non-topical, as in the second case:

OT/2 Firstly, and most obviously, *new born children* are completely helpless.

Here ISE consists of a discourse connective, and is followed by a modality marker.

While the above types present a fairly straightforward picture, with the topical subject coinciding with the mood subject, and thus appearing in a syntactically prominent position, most of the sentences of the text have a non-topical mood subject in the main clause, while the topical subject appears outside the main clause.

Type 3. Initial sentence element and mood subject coincide while topical subject is separate.

There are two sub-types of type 3 in the text. In the first, 3a, the mood subject of the initial main clause is a dummy, with the main clause representing topical material. One case of this kind occurs.

OT/8 It is during this very long period in which the *human infant* is totally dependent on others that *it* reveals. . . .

This sentence begins the second paragraph of the text. Its ISE summarizes an idea developed in the previous paragraph—that is, the previous sub-topic, and in this way links it with the topical subject represented by the lexical *human infant* and the anaphoric *it.*

In the other variant, 3b, the initial main clause is non-topical, while the topical subject appears in a following sub-clause. There are two cases of this kind, both with the main clause serving as a modality marker:

OT/7 It would seem that ***this period*** . . . is the price that the human species has to pay . . .[8]

OT/10 This suggestion implies that just as ***human beings*** are designed . . . so ***they*** are designed . . .

Type 4. Initial sentence element and topical subject coincide, while mood subject is separate.

The two cases of this type appearing in the text both have the topical subject in an initial sub-clause, with a cohesive anaphoric pronoun as the mood subject. The examples are the following:

OT/1 When the ***human infant*** is born . . . ***it*** has two things . . .

OT/6 Although ***young animals*** are at risk . . . ***they*** very quickly develop . . .

This structure serves to introduce or change the topical subject. The first case is the first sentence in the text, and the second case introduces a sub-topic based on the comment of the previous sentence.

Type 5. Initial sentence element, mood subject and topical subject are all separate.

The following cases occur in the text:

OT/3 Apart from a powerful capacity to draw attention to ***their*** [sic] helplessness . . . there is nothing the ***new born child*** can do. . . .

OT/9 For this reason, biologists now suggest that ***language*** is . . .

This is the most complex of the types studied and makes possible a more varied interplay of discourse materials than the others. In the first case above, ISE is topical, as is the main clause. The mood subject *there* is used to move the topical subject into the following sub-clause. The second case, discussed earlier, has ISE which consists of a discourse connective, a main clause serving as a modality marker, and a topical subject in the sub-clause.

On the basis of the very limited materials discussed here we can make the following tentative observations about the relationship of the mood subject, the topical subject, and the initial sentence element. If we analyze topical structures in written discourse keeping the topical material apart from non-topical types of material, we find that the mood subject of the main clause may consist of any type of material. In other words, the mood subject may be the topical subject or it may consist of non-topical material of discourse organization. It may also be a syntactic dummy in a topical or non-topical clause. Where the mood subject of the main clause is not the topical subject, the latter in this text appears in a sub-clause, which may precede or follow the main clause. ISE may be topical or non-topical. The non-topical ISEs in the text are modality markers or discourse connectives. At least in the text studied, then, part of the development of the discourse topic takes place in terms of sequences of subjects, though these topical subjects often appear in sub-clauses, while the main clause has a non-topical function.

Though it is likely that, with further analyses of different kinds of texts, the picture obtained here will prove too simple, the findings seem to suggest that a framework of topical development based on the notions of initial sentence element, mood subject, and topical subject, as well as on the idea of different types of linguistic material in discourse, may be applied to examination of written discourse.

We shall next proceed to apply the notion of two types of topical progression, parallel and sequential, to an analysis of the text.

Topical Progression in Authentic Discourse

Having established a kind of topical skeleton of the text in terms of the topical subjects of its individual sentences, we will now examine the way these topical subjects form different types of sequences. We shall apply the notion of parallel progression where the topical subjects of successive sentences have the same referent, and that of sequential progression where the rhematic part of one sentence gives rise to the topical subject in the following.

In Table 1, the topical subjects in the text analyzed are arranged in the order of their appearance in the sentences of the text. (The reader is advised to consult the complete text.)

In this skeleton there are sequences representing the parallel type of progression such as sentences OT/1–4, and others representing the sequential type such as sentences OT/5, 6, and 9, which are indicated by placing the sequential topical subject to the right underneath the previous one. Some of the cases, however, are less clear-cut. Sentence OT/7, for instance, has a topical subject that may be claimed to refer back to the ideas developed all through the paragraph. Sentence OT/10, on the other hand, continues the initial sub-topic, which is readopted in OT/8 and later in the comment of OT/9.

TABLE 1 Sequence of Topical Subjects in OT

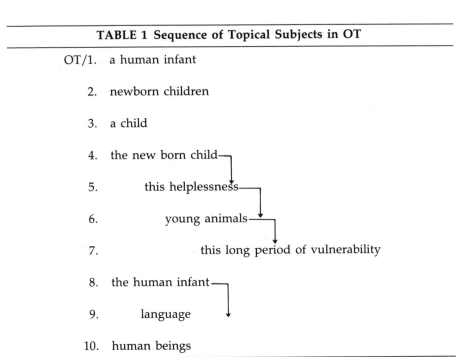

OT/1. a human infant

2. newborn children

3. a child

4. the new born child

5.   this helplessness

6.   young animals

7.   this long period of vulnerability

8. the human infant

9.   language

10. human beings

COMPARISON OF TOPICAL DEVELOPMENT IN AUTHENTIC AND SIMPLIFIED DISCOURSE

The second part of this paper consists of a description of topical development in simplified discourse, and comparison between simplified and authentic text in this respect. In order to find out whether simplification is accompanied by changes in the pattern of topical development, several experienced language teachers and applied linguists were asked to produce simplified versions of the text analyzed here. They were given no instructions as regards the kinds of changes they were expected to make, only the aim was specified: to make the text more readable for foreign language learners on the tertiary level of education.[9] It was expected that the simplifiers would then produce versions intuitively based on their knowledge of foreign learners' difficulties.

Of the versions produced, four were rewritten as discourse with resulting changes in topical development, while in the rest only occasional vocabulary items and syntactic structures had been changed. The first four will be analyzed here.

Comparison of Topical Structures

The simplified texts (see Appendix I) vary to some extent in their reproduction of the original pattern of topical structures, as seen in Table 2.

Some general trends may be observed. Compared with the percentage of types in OT, the average percentages of types in STs imply avoid-
ance of types 3a, 4, and 5. Type 2 has more or less retained its relative
frequency, as has 3b, where the main clause is a modality marker. Type
1, however, has been used proportionately much more in STs than in
OT, particularly in ST1 and ST4. All in all, the simplifiers can be said to
have favored types where the topical subject is the mood subject of the
main clause, or, where this is not the case, structures where the initial
main clause serves as a modality marker, and the topical subject follows
in a sub-clause. Sentences with a dummy subject in the main clause, with
a topical sub-clause in the initial position, or with ISE, mood subject and
topical subject separate, have been used less frequently than in OT.
Strangely enough, there is also indication that the proportion of the less
used types 3a, 4, and 5 is about the same within an individual text.

The greatly varying individual strategies used by the simplifiers are
reflected in the proportion of the types of structures, particularly in ST1
and ST3. Of these two, the first has a high percentage of Type 1 ("John
is running"). At the same time it doubles the original number of sentences. ST3, on the other hand, follows OT most faithfully both in the
number of sentences and in the proportion of the various types of struc-

**TABLE 2 Distribution of Different Types of Topical Structures
in OT and STs**

| Percentage of types | | | Number of cases | | | | | Total in |
Type	OT*	STs (av.)	OT	ST1	ST2	ST3	ST4	all STs
1	10	41	1	12	3	2	5	22
2	20	19	2	1	3	2	4	10
3a	10	0.7	1	1	1	1	1	4
3b	20	21	2	5	3	2	1	11
4	20	0.6	2	—	1	2	—	3
5	20	0.6	2	1	—	1	1	3

Type 1. ISE = topical subject = mood subject
Type 2. ISE ≠ topical subject = mood subject
Type 3. ISE = mood subject ≠ topical subject
Type 4. ISE = topical subject ≠ mood subject
Type 5. ISE ≠ topical subject ≠ mood subject

* The abbreviation OT refers to the original text, and ST1–ST4 to the four simplified
versions of this text.

tures. It uses other means of simplification, some of which will be discussed below.

It would seem then that some types of topical progression are intuitively felt to be less readable than others. The principle behind the use of the various types in simplified texts might be that of identification of the topical subject. The types in which it is separate from the mood subject and ISE, which could thus be assumed to necessitate a separate identification process by the reader, are much less frequent than those in which it occurs in the syntactically prominent position of the mood subject of the main clause. The one exception to this is type 3a, where the topical subject is separate from the mood subject; here the main clause represents non-topical material, and the topical subject appears in a subclause following the main clause. This may indicate that the use in the main clause of some kinds of non-topical material is felt to increase readability in spite of the fact that the sentence structure becomes more complex. Of course, as was noted above, these observations are based on very limited material, and may have to be modified in the light of further analyses.

New Variants of Topical Structure in Simplified Texts

The simplified texts contain some variant types of the topical structures discussed above. Thus, in addition to sub-types 3a and 3b there appear the following cases of type 3:

> ST1/3 The only thing *they* can do to persuade someone to look after them is to cry. . . .

> ST2/4 All *he* can do is cry. . . .

In these cases the main clause belongs to topical material, but an emphatic use of extrapolation moves the topical mood subject into the subclause. In the STs there are also two cases in which the main clause is metalinguistic:

> ST2/9 The use of this term means that *learning to speak a language* is . . .

> ST4/11 By this they mean that *the human infant* is. . . .

Comparison of Patterns of Topical Progression

In the discussion above, two possible types of topical progression are mentioned: the parallel type, where a sequence of sentences shares the topical subject, and the sequential type, where the topical subject of one sentence is based on some part of the comment of the previous one. In topical development, the topical subjects may be considered to develop one sub-topic at a time, while these sub-topics in turn contribute to the development of higher subtopics or of the discourse topic. We shall compare the use of the two types of progression in STs to their use in OT (See Table 1).

By applying these notions to the topical progression in OT, we get the diagram shown in Table 3.

Analyzed in this way, the passage consists of five sub-topics, of which *child* could be considered the primary sub-topic both in terms of its frequency and in terms of its initial occurrence. The notions of parallel and sequential progression, however, require some modification in the light of this analysis. Parallel progression seems either to proceed directly, as in OT/1–4, or to extend over a piece of text based on sequential progression, as in OT/4–8. Thus, in OT/8, the primary sub-topic is re-assumed without being reintroduced by sequential progression, a type we

Sentence No.	Topical depth				Sub-topic No.
	1	2	3	4	
OT/1	human infant				1
2	children				1
3	child				1
4	child				1
5		this helplessness			2
6			animals		3
7				this period of . . .	4
8	it				1
9		learning language			5
10	human beings (S)				1

TABLE 3 Topical Progression in OT

shall call *extended parallel progression*. On the other hand, in OT/10 the primary sub-topic is re-assumed after a lapse of one sentence but supported by reference in the comment of OT/9 to *human child*. This kind of parallel progression is marked (S) in the diagrams.

The diagram also shows the numbers of successive sequential types of progression, here called the *topical depth*. In this text, introduction of successive new sub-topics by sequential progression creates a topical depth of 4 in OT/4–7.

The ratio of sub-topics to the number of sentences, the proportion of the types of progression, and the depth of topical progression may be factors that contribute to the perception of a text as simple or complex. We shall compare these features in OT to the corresponding features in STs to see whether they have been affected by intuitive simplification (see Table 4).

Comparing the diagrams of STs with that of OT shows, first, that the primary sub-topic *child* has been retained in all STs, though in different lexical forms. However, the treatment of the original sub-topics varies. *Animals* appears as a sub-topic in ST1, ST2, and ST3, but not in ST4, while *helplessness* has been omitted in ST2 and replaced by *nurturing* in ST4. *Learning language* has been omitted in ST3. On the other hand, some new sub-topics appear. In ST2 there is one new sub-topic, *man's survival*, while ST1 has several: *another human being, another than mother, human brain, human eyes, human skeletons, human species, characteristics, second characteristic,* and *this characteristic*; ST4 has *second respect*.

To summarize, apart from ST1, the simplified texts have fewer sub-topics than OT (OT = 5, ST2 = 4, ST3 = 3, ST4 = 4), even though both ST2 and ST4 have increased the total number of sentences in the text from 10 to 11 and 12 respectively. ST1, however, presents another kind of picture. It has ten sub-topics, but it also doubles the total number of sentences, thus retaining the proportion of different sub-topics to number of sentences. We may conclude that the reduction of the number of sub-topics forms one strategy of simplification. It leads to a proportionate increase in sentences with the primary sub-topic as the topical subject, and a decrease in sentences with a tertiary or secondary sub-topic as the topical subject. Further, ST4 also has one case with extended sequential progression, a type that did not appear in OT. This case will be discussed below.

Increasing the number of sub-topics in ST1 also leads to an increased number of cases representing extended parallel progression—i.e., cases where the topical subject of a sentence is readopted after a number of intervening sentences. In OT, the number of these cases is two, one with extension over one sentence, and another over three sentences, both at the topical depth of 1. This may now be compared with the corresponding figure in STs (Table 5).

TABLE 4 Topical Progression in STs*
(Topical Subjects May Appear in Abbreviated Form)

ST1	No. of sub-topics
1 babies	1
2 characteristic	2
3 they	1
4 baby	1
5 another human being	3
6 another than mother	4
7 babies	1
8 animals	5
9 they	5
10 animals	5
11 child	1
12 this period	6
13 second characteristic	2
14 this characteristic	2
15 learning language	7
16 human brain	8
17 human eyes	9
18 human skeletons	10
19 ability to learn language	7
20 human species (S)	1

No. of different sub-topics: 10

TABLE 4 Continued

ST2	No. of sub-topics
1 babies	1
2 baby	1
3 baby	1
4 he	1
5 animals**	2
6 they	2
7 man's survival	3
8 babies	1
9 this capacity	4
10 babies (S)	1
11 learning to speak	4

No. of different sub-topics: 4

ST3	No. of sub-topics
1 baby	1
2 it	1
3 it	1
4 baby	1
5 helplessness	2
6 animals	3
7 humans (S)	1

TABLE 4 Continued	
ST3	**No. of sub-topics**
8 baby	1
9 humans	1
10 babies	1

No. of different sub-topics: 3

ST4	**No. of sub-topics**
1 infants	1
2 infants	1
3 they	1
4 they	1
5 they	1
6 infants———	1
7 period of nurturing	2
8 second respect———	3
9 capacity to learn language	4
10 language	4
11 human infant———	1
12 learning language	4

No. of different sub-topics: 4

* Extended progression is indicated in Tables 2 and 4 by straight vertical arrows that connect two topical subjects.

** See below for a discussion of this case, where topical progression is based on contrast.

TABLE 5 Number of Cases of Extended Progression in OT and STs

Topical depth	OT	ST1	ST2	ST3	ST4
1	1 × 1*	1 × 1	1 × 1	1 × 2	1 × 4
	1 × 3	1 × 2	1 × 3		
		1 × 3			
		1 × 8 (S)**			
2		1 × 11			
3		1 × 3			

* Read: one case extending over one sentence, etc.
** For a discussion of this case of extended sequential progression, see below.

We see from Table 5 that while OT has extended parallel progression only at the level of the primary sub-topic, ST1 has cases of a secondary and tertiary sub-topic with parallel progression. All other cases in STs occur at the level of the primary sub-topic. The number of the cases in ST2 is the same as in OT, while ST3 and ST4 have only one case of this type. The simplification strategy of ST1 has led to a more complex pattern of progression than in OT. There is a similar difference between ST1 and the other STs in the use of the different topical depths, created by successive cases of sequential progression, as shown in Table 6.

As Table 6 shows, all texts except ST1 have few cases with more than two topical levels. The reason for the more complicated pattern of topical progression in ST1 may at least partly be due to its high frequency of topical structures of Type 1—i.e., a type where the combined mood and topical subject occurs initially in the sentence. Since the sentences are short, this makes it necessary to develop subsidiary ideas in separate sentences and thus to create additional sub-topics by means of sequential progression. Table 6 also shows that parallel progression is used far more than sequential progression in all texts, and that two or more consecutive sentences with sequential progression are rare.

TABLE 6 Use of Topical Depth in OT and STs, and the Number of Topical Subjects Occurring at the Depth Concerned

Depth*	OT	ST1	ST2	ST3	ST4
1	6	6	6	8	7
2	2	8	4	1	3
3	1	3	1	1	2
4	1	3	—	—	—

* Topical depth is created by the number of successive cases of sequential progression, based on the primary sub-topic.

We could now summarize the findings concerning topical progression in simplified texts. Apart from ST1, with its highly individual strategy of simplification, the following changes occur consistently in simplified texts: slight decrease in the number of sub-topics per sentence, slight increase in the use of parallel progression, and a consequent increase in cases using topical depth of 1—i.e., cases with the primary topical subject. Cases of extended parallel progression show little change.

All the types of parallel and sequential progression observed in STs are not, however, completely representative. Some cases indicate that analysis based on this binary division is inadequate. We shall now look at these cases.

Remarks on Parallel and Sequential Types of Progression

We shall next discuss some cases that seem atypical of the basic types of progression. First, in some instances the topical development takes place more gradually than in the "pure" parallel or sequential development. The following case will illustrate this:

> OT/4–5 Without care from some other human being or beings, be it mother, grandmother, sister, nurse, or a human group, *a child* is very unlikely to survive. *This helplessness of human infants* is . . .

Here the topical subject of the last sentence may be retraced to the comment in the previous one, . . . *is very unlikely to survive.* However, it has been prepared, as it were, by the treatment of the idea in all the three sentences before it. Whether this can be considered a simple case of sequential progression is something that can perhaps best be discussed in the context of a larger sample of cases, and will not therefore be taken up here. In Tables 3 through 5, there are also cases of parallel progression of this type, which have been marked (S) to indicate that even sequential development is involved. Out of the three cases attested, the following will elucidate this:

> ST2/10 Biologists use the term "species specific" to describe how all undamaged *human babies* are genetically predisposed . . . to the learning of a language.

The topical subject of the sentence, *human babies,* may be linked with the primary sub-topic of the text, represented by the topical subject of most preceding sentences, and re-assumed here by way of extended parallel progression. But it is also linked with *the baby* in the comment of the previous sentence. Similar cases occur in ST1 and ST3. Further, in one case the gradual development of the topical subject based on parallel progression ties up with the initial sentence element of the previous sentence:

> ST4/10–11 Because all undamaged human infants learn language, and no other creatures do, biologists say that *language* is 'species specific.' By this they mean that *the human infant* is genetically programmed . . .

Again, *human infant* is re-assumed on the basis of appearing as the primary topical subject in most preceding sentences (see Table 4), but it also ties up with *all undamaged human infants* in the initial sub-clause of the previous sentence. Cases like this are here classified as instances of parallel progression, but analysis of further texts is needed to specify their character more closely.

A similar ambiguous case occurs in ST1:

> ST1/19–20 Just as these are specifically human characteristics, so, the scientists suggest, *the ability to learn language* is a specially human characteristic. *The human species* is able to survive because all normal human beings are able to learn and to use language.

The primary sub-topic in the text is *the baby* (see Table 4), but here, in the last sentence of the text, *the human species* appears. Is this to be interpreted as a case of extended parallel progression with a more inclusive concept replacing the original sub-topic, or should we see *the human species* as a case of sequential progression based on the previous sentence? It has here been considered to represent extended parallel progression with sequential ties, like the following:

> ST3/8–10 . . . when *a baby* is totally dependent . . . it shows . . . the ability to learn a language. Biologists now suggest that *normal humans* automatically learn a language. *Babies* learn language . . .

Since both cases occur at the end of the text, the use of the more general concepts representing the primary sub-topic may be caused by the conclusive character of the final sentence.

Extended parallel progression may also contain atypical features. First, while it occurs in OT only with the primary sub-topic, there are cases in some STs with a secondary and tertiary sub-topic (see Table 4). The following example contains a tertiary sub-topic extending over a sequence of three sentences:

> ST1/15–19 Biologists suggest that *learning language* . . . is an ability which is only found in the human species . . . *the human*

> *brain . . . human eyes . . . human skeleton . . . the abil-*
> *ity to learn language . . .*

There are also two cases of extended parallel and sequential progression which contain discourse organizational material (*first . . . second*) to facilitate perception of textual cohesion:

> ST1/2, 13 *The first characteristic* which all human babies share is that they are completely helpless. . . . *The second characteristic* which human babies share, develops during the long period of learning to survive.
>
> ST4/1–2, 8 *All human infants* . . . are alike in two respects. Firstly . . . *The second respect* in which all human infants are alike is . . .

In the first case, while the first topical subject is based on sequential progression, the second follows from it by parallel progression. In the second case, however, *two respects* in the first sentence is referred to by a discourse connective, *firstly,* in sentence 2, and, six sentences later, by *the second respect,* a topical subject based on sequential progression. It would seem, then, that the "topicality" value of the topical subject may vary, but further analyses are necessary.

The various ways in which a topical subject in sequential progression may be connected with the previous comment may be illustrated by the following cases:

> ST1/5–6 *The other human being* need not necessarily be the mother. *A grandmother, sister, or someone who is not related* to the child, may care for it.
>
> OT/6–7 [young animals] . . . very quickly develop the capacity to fend for themselves. It would seem that *this long period of vulnerability* . . .

In the first example above, the topical subject of the second sentence develops the comment of the previous one by listing cases of "non-mothers." In the second case, the topical subject of the last sentence arises out of a contrast with the idea in the previous comment: *learn very quickly to fend for themselves* vs. *long period of vulnerability. Vulnerability* is also cohesively linked with the notion of helplessness, which occurs several times in the preceding sentence.

In addition to the above case where sequential progression is based on the idea of contrast, there appears a similar case with parallel progression:

> ST2/3–5 A *new-born baby* is unable to survive without help. All *he* can do is to cry . . . *New-born animals,* on the other hand . . .

The topical subject, *new-born animals,* in the last sentence is introduced by contrast to the previous topical subject, *new-born baby,* as *on the other hand* makes explicit. Whether this type of progression always necessitates the use of a discourse adjunct, and whether it may be based on relationships other than contrast, will have to be discussed in a context of more extensive material.

The occurrence of these varieties of topical progression is an indication of the intricate manner in which the topic and its sub-topics are developed in discourse, and of the problems related to its analysis in terms of the binary division into sequential and parallel progression. Further investigation seems to be needed at least of the extended types of progression, of the use of nontopical material as (or with) the topical subject, and of parallel progression based not on repetition of the sub-topic but on other relationships with it, such as contrast or conceptual inclusion. Similarly, the possibility of several candidates for topical subject in one sentence, which has not been discussed in this paper, should be examined.

FOR STUDY AND DISCUSSION

The above findings can be interpreted as indicating that, in addition to the generally recognized features affecting readability such as sentence length, syntactic complexity, and type of vocabulary, some types of topical development in discourse are intuitively felt to affect readability of a text. In the light of the findings of this paper, a "simple" text would represent the following picture of topical development: it would mostly use sentences in which the topical subject is the mood subject of the main clause; or, when the main clause serves as a modality marker or has, say, a metalinguistic function, the topical subject would be the mood subject of a sub-clause immediately following the main clause. The number of sentences with a non-topical initial sentence element would be relatively small. Sentences would follow each other by means of parallel progression much more frequently than by sequential progression, with few cases of extended progression or with other features atypical of the "pure" types. Extended progression might be supported by the use of cohesive discourse adjuncts.

The simplification of a text is a process that affects a number of interrelated textual features. In the material examined here, two distinct types of simplification strategy appear, one resulting in the kind of "simple" text described above, and the other resulting in an extreme simplification of topical structures, with a proportionate increase in the type

(1) *John is running*. At the same time, the original pattern of topical progression is greatly complicated. This text shows a definite increase in extended parallel progression, not only at the level of the primary subtopic, but also on that of secondary and tertiary sub-topics. Further, it increases the number of original sub-topics and, thus, the proportion of sequential progression, which means an increased use of the different topical depths.

Further, different simplification strategies also affect features of discourse which have not been analyzed in this paper. Tentative examination of cohesion in the different texts shows that some patterns of cohesion are affected (Lautamatti 1978), as are common readability index features such as sentence length, sentence complexity, and type of vocabulary.

As was mentioned above, the evaluation of the effect on readability of the changes studied is outside the scope of this paper. However, some observations on problems relating to such evaluation are called for. First, if we wish to examine the changes brought about by simplification of topical development alone, we will have to eliminate changes that occur in vocabulary, sentence length, and sentence complexity. In the light of the present material this seems impossible because of the interrelatedness of these features. On the other hand, we might compare texts (such as ST1 and ST3) based on different simplification strategies. This, however, gives no indication of how much the effect is due to changes in individual features. It is possible that the resulting simplification is due largely to changes in vocabulary alone.

This brings us to a more basic issue: the aim of simplification in the teaching of a foreign language. Ideally, simplified texts are used in the teaching of FL reading comprehension as a ladder towards less simplified and finally authentic texts. Therefore, our aim in producing simplified reading material is not to make texts as simple and readable as possible, but rather to reduce their difficulty to a level which the students find motivating and instructive, and yet keep their informational and conceptual level intact. Rather than find ways of producing as simple discourse as possible, we can use simplification to find discourse variables that can be used in language teaching. One such variable may be topical development in discourse. For this reason, the findings discussed here might be of interest for language teachers and material producers.

Not all problems in reading comprehension are related to unfamiliar vocabulary or syntactic forms. Students may also need help in following the line of argument and in relating different parts of discourse to each other. Students who have problems on discourse level rather than word or sentence level might benefit from exercises which help them to perceive how the topic is developed in discourse and to learn to take advantage of predictability relating to topical development.

Similarly, differentiation between the types of discourse material, and familiarity with their functions, might help a foreign language learner to relate more explicitly the topical and non-topical discourse material, and in this way to use the non-topical material as the kind of supporting framework that it is meant to be, not as one more linguistic obstacle. To practice above-sentence-level predictability in FL reading comprehension, a modified cloze could be applied to various aspects of topical development. This would direct the learner's attention to discourse level and might help the teacher in locating problem areas in the handling of texts. Further, contrastive analysis of patterns of topical development in the source language and the target language could be used to predict areas where the student is likely to base his strategies for handling written discourse on misleading predictions.

NOTES

1. I would like to thank the members of the reading comprehension seminar of 1976–77 at the Department of Linguistics, University of Edinburgh, and its organizers, Alan Davies and Gillian Brown, for their help in providing me with simplified versions of the text analyzed here, and for many stimulating discussions. I am also grateful to Professor H. G. Widdowson for a brief but inspiring period of tutoring, and to Hugh Trappes-Lomax and Mahmoud Ayad for their patient and critical help in some problem areas. My stay in Edinburgh was supported by the British Council, of which this is a grateful acknowledgment. I owe a further debt of gratitude to Auli Hakulinen and Viljo Kohonen, for their help and criticism.

2. Enkvist (1974b:74) calls these *teeman toisto* ("repetition of theme") and *teemaprogressio* ("progression of theme"), but for reasons that will become obvious below, we shall be concerned with the repetition or non-repetition of what is here called the topical subject. As Enkvist points out, analysis of these two types is made difficult by the great number of cohesive references that often exist between sentences in a text. Some attempts to extend analysis into atypical cases are made on pp. 105–108. See also Holman's (1976) analysis of the two types in spoken Finnish as represented in contemporary fiction.

3. This term is used here in the same sense as in Huddleston (1971:61–62). Huddleston further distinguishes the mood subject from the prepassive subject and the concord subject. He gives the following example where the *there* is the mood subject, and *some 500 people* the concord subject, while the prepassive subject has not been expressed: *There have already been killed some 500 people.*

4. The topical subjects in the sentences analyzed are italicized. If there is

an anaphoric reference between the clauses of the sentence, both the lexical item and the pronoun are italicized.

5. Huddleston, following Halliday, calls these thematic adjuncts *discourse sentence adverbs*.

6. Doughty, Anne and Peter. 1974. *Language and Community*. London: Edward Arnold. Copyright by permission of Edward Arnold (Publishers) Ltd.

7. Huddleston uses the term *lexical* adjunct (Huddleston 1971:321).

8. Where the main clause and the subsidiary clause both have a mood subject that can be said to be topical, the mood subject of the main clause has here been considered the primary topical subject. In the text analyzed, there is one case of this type (sentence OT/7), while in some others (sentences OT/1, 6, 8, 10) there is a cohesive tie in the form of anaphoric reference between the subjects of the main clause and the sub-clause.

9. The simplifiers were given the following instruction: Simplify the following text preserving its character as a piece of discourse, to make it more readable for foreign language students on the tertiary level of education.

APPENDIX I: SIMPLIFIED TEXTS

SIMPLIFIED TEXT 1

(1) All healthy, *new-born babies,* in all countries of the world, share two characteristics.

(2) *The first characteristic* which all human babies share, is that they are completely helpless. (3) The only thing *they* can do to persuade someone to look after them is to cry, and in this way they can draw attention to themselves. (4) *A helpless baby* will only survive if another human-being looks after it. (5) *The other human-being* need not necessarily be the mother. (6) *A grandmother, sister, or someone who is not related to the child,* may care for it.

(7) *Human babies* are unusual in this characteristic, if we compare humans to other animal species. (8) *Many new-born animals* can stand on their feet very soon after being born. (9) Often *they* can run with the herd a few hours later. (10) *Young animals* may get hurt and even die during their first year, but those that survive are able to look after themselves. (11) *A young human child* takes much longer to learn to look after itself. (12) We must suppose that *this long period of learning* is necessary to allow the human race to survive as a species.

(13) *The second characteristic* which human babies share, develops during the long period of learning to survive. (14) *This characteristic* is the ability to learn language and it is shared by all babies who have normal, healthy brains. (15) Biologists suggest that *learning language,* during this time, while the young child cannot look after itself, is an ability which is only found in the human species. (16) They suggest that *the human brain* is specially designed to allow human beings to learn language. (17) We know already that *human eyes* are designed to see the world in color and to

recognize whether objects are solid or not. (18) We also know that *human skeletons* are designed to allow people to walk upright on two feet, and not use their hands as well. (19) Just as these are specially human characteristics, so, the scientists suggest, *the ability to learn language* is a specially human characteristic. (20) *The human species* is able to survive because all normal human beings are able to learn and to use language.

SIMPLIFIED TEXT 2

(1) At birth, *all babies* have two things in common with each other, wherever and whenever they are born. (2) (This is not true if *the baby* is in any way damaged.) (3) First, *a new-born baby* is unable to survive without help. (4) All *he* can do is to cry, which may attract the attention of those who can help him to survive—his mother, grandmother, sister, nurse, and so forth. (5) *New-born animals,* on the other hand, can stand on their feet very soon after birth and run with their herd a few hours later. (6) Although *animals* remain vulnerable to attack for weeks, in some cases for months, after birth, *they* become able to survive without help very much more quickly than human babies. (7) *Man's survival* as a species depends on this particularly long period of infant vulnerability. (8) Secondly, *all babies* possess a capacity to learn language. (9) *This capacity* is revealed while the baby is still dependent on others for survival. (10) Biologists use the term "species specific" to describe how *all undamaged human babies* are genetically predisposed, or programmed, to the learning of a language. (11) The use of this term means that *learning to speak a language* is part of the normal and natural development of an undamaged human being, in the same way that it is normal to see in three dimensions and in color, (and) in the same way that it is normal for a man to stand upright.

SIMPLIFIED TEXT 3

(1) When *a baby* is born (into any community anywhere) *it* has two things which it shares with all babies, providing none of them have suffered any damage. (2) First, *it* will be helpless. (3) And, apart from crying to attract attention, there is nothing *it* can do to change this helplessness. (4) Without help from other human beings *the baby* is unlikely to live.

(5) *A baby's helplessness* contrasts with the ability many young animals have—the ability to stand up a few minutes after birth and to run a few hours later. (6) Although *these young animals* are in danger for some time after their birth *they* can help themselves much better than human babies. (7) It seems that *humans* have to pay for their long period of development with a long period of helplessness.

(8) It is during this period (when the *baby* is totally dependent) that it shows the second thing *it* shares with all babies—the ability to learn a language. (9) Biologists now suggest that *normal humans* automatically learn a language. (10) *Babies* learn language because they are designed to learn one as part of their normal development, just as they are designed to see in three dimensions and in color, and to stand upright.

SIMPLIFIED TEXT 4

(1) All *human infants,* wherever they are born, are alike in two respects, so long as they are not damaged in some way before or after birth. (2) Firstly, and most obviously, *new-born infants* are completely helpless. (3) *They* are able to draw attention to themselves by crying, but, apart from this, can do nothing to ensure their own survival. (4) *They* depend entirely upon other human beings, such as mother, grandmother, sister, nurse and so on. (5) Without the care of these *they* are unlikely to survive. (6) In this respect, *human infants* are unlike many new born animals, which sometimes need to get to their feet and run with the herd within minutes of birth. (7) For humans, *the long period of nurturing* which fits man for survival as a species means that there is an equally long period of dependence and therefore vulnerability.

(8) *The second respect* in which all human infants are alike is the capacity to learn language. (9) It is during the period of vulnerability that *this capacity* is exercised. (10) Because all undamaged human infants learn language, and no other creatures do, biologists say that *language* is 'species specific.' (11) By this they mean that *the human infant* is genetically programmed so that it can acquire language. (12) *The learning of language* is as much part of the normal development of human infants as, for instance, the ability to see three-dimensionally and in color, or the characteristic of standing upright rather than going on all-fours.

FOR STUDY AND DISCUSSION

1. Williams argues:

   . . . The clearest style is one in which the grammatical structures of a sentence most redundantly support the perceived semantic structure. The more consistently the grammatical structure reinforces—or reflects—the semantic structure, the more easily a reader takes up that semantic structure. . . . It is not always possible—as demonstrated by the way in which this sentence opens—for us to write sentences in which every agent occurs in subject position and precedes what it does; in which what that agent does is expressed in a verb directly following a subject/agent. . . . But it is possible for us to come far closer to this maximally redundant pattern than most writers do. . . . Those structures that have come to be known as *rheme-theme* or *topic-comment* sequences coincide with subjects and noun/agents and the verb phrases that follow. The topic is that element in the sentence from which the rest of the sentence flows. The topic ordinarily communicates the most familiar, the previously mentioned, the implied ideas. In most languages, the topic regularly coincides with the subject. But even in English, it need not:

   In regard to style, there are many unknowns.

   The topic is *style,* but style is not the subject. The topic is regularly the first noun in the sentence, but again, it need not be:

In this paper, style has been the main subject.

Style is not the first noun, but it is still the topic. . . . The comment expresses the new ideas, ordinarily that which cannot be deduced from what is assumed or already mentioned. And the end of the comment, the end of the clause, emphasizes that new information most strongly. . . . On the basis of some preliminary evidence . . . it appears that a series of consistent topics is judged to be more clearly written than a series of sentences in which the topic is not consistently selected. And when we reinforce a consistent topic with a consistent nexus between verbs and what agents do, then the style appears to become the clearest and most efficient of all (J. Williams. 1979. Defining complexity. *College English*. 40.6.603–605).

Does Williams' notion have any bearing on the research reported by Lautamatti? Specifically, comment on the relationship between Williams' notion that ". . . a series of consistent topics is judged to be more clearly written than a series of sentences in which the topic is not consistently selected" and Lautamatti's notion of the interaction between *discourse topic* and *sub-topic*. Does Williams' notion have relationship to Carrell's idea of "top-level rhetorical organization?"

2. Do you agree that ST 1–4 really are simplified texts? Write your own simplified version of OT. Why did you do what you did in order to simplify? Compare your ST with the STs given in Lautamatti's paper. What differences do you perceive? Are there any similarities? Do these differences and/or similarities suggest anything about the concept *simplification?*

3. Select a coherent passage of between 200 and 300 words out of the middle of any randomly chosen expository text.
   a. How did you select your text? Compare your process with that outlined in Grabe.
   b. Count the number of sentences in your text that fall into the five types of topical structures identified by Lautamatti.
   c. Describe the patterns of any sentences you find in your text which do not meet the criteria of the five given patterns.
   d. Compare your counts with those given by Lautamatti for her OT and explain any discrepancies between your counts and hers.
   e. Count the number of sub-topics in your text and compare the ratio of sub-topics/sentences to the ratios reported for Lautamatti's OT. Comment on the comparison.

4. Referring to such theoreticians and methodologists as Widdowson, Munby, Rivers, Brumfit, Stevick, and Krashen, argue for or against the use of simplified (as opposed to authentic) texts in second-language instruction.

Chapter 7

Contrastive Rhetoric and Text-Type Research

William Grabe
Northern Arizona University

INTRODUCTION

Over the last ten years a large amount of research on contrastive rhetoric and L2 writing has focused on types of expository prose texts. In particular, Kaplan's (1966, 1972, 1982, 1983a, 1983b) research on contrastive rhetoric, writing instruction, and access to information/technology transfer have combined to elevate expository prose above other text-type genres in terms of practical concerns for education and literacy development. One recurring problem, however, in much of the ongoing text research on expository prose, whether in contrastive rhetoric or in reading comprehension research, is that the term *expository prose* itself is rather crude. If more, and more careful, research findings are to lead to accurate generalizations about text types, a number of basic assumptions must be validated. Among these:

1. Whether expository prose, in fact, can be defined in a somewhat objective manner;
2. If expository prose is a suitable major text genre, what sub-types are identifiable within expository prose;
3. If sub-types exist, what are their characteristics, and how do they relate to each other?

A research goal, then, would be to address these issues first in English, and second, assuming some resolution for English, to pursue similar questions for other languages. For example, does expository prose of some type exist in some other language? If it does, what are its characteristic properties? What sub-types exist? How are the sub-types different from each other? How do they relate to each other? etc. The basic issue is whether similar text-type generalizations may be made for different languages, particularly with respect to expository prose.

The above research goals provide a foundation for research in contrastive rhetoric. Much of the current research in contrastive rhetoric is centered on English compositions written by different groups of second-language students. While such an approach offers many insights (e.g., Kaplan 1966, 1982), contrastive rhetoric must include comparisons of edited texts in different languages, where the writing is somehow comparable (cf. Hinds 1980, 1983a, 1984). The research study to be discussed in this paper indicates a way to define text comparability in two or more languages. The attempt to form a better understanding of expository prose in English has clear implications for defining similar text types in other languages.

The research reported in this paper presents a methodology for defining expository prose in English as a legitimate major text genre, explores what sub-text groupings exist, how they might be characterized, and how such sub-text groupings relate to each other. The paper will first describe the methodology used to define underlying measures which discriminate different types of texts. By using multivariate statistical techniques such as factor analysis and cluster analysis, the study proposes a set of underlying textual parameters which serve to discriminate text types, as well as to group texts into definable clusters. The discussion of the results argues for a more careful division of expository text types into humanities texts, general informational texts, and two types of natural science texts, as well as for the distinction between expository text types and other genres.

METHOD

The Data Base

The study reported here hypothesized 15 possible text-type groupings, listed in Table 1. Included in these text types were texts from academic journals, freshman and sophomore introductory textbooks, and general audience popular journals. These groupings were generally based on assertions and examples in the literature relating to expository prose (e.g., Hinds 1979; Kroch and Hindle 1982). Two of the groups, fictional narratives and professional correspondences, were included as control groups since the literature refers to them as text types different from expository prose. For each group, 10 texts were collected using a variety of appropriate sampling procedures (see Grabe 1984 for more detail). These 150 texts (70,000+ words) were entered into a computer as a data base for the text analyses.

TABLE 1: Text Groups and Word Counts

Category	Words/category
1. Academic Journal Humanities (AHUM)	4833
2. Academic Journal Law (ALAW)	4591
3. Academic Journal Natural Science (ANAS)	4882
4. Academic Journal Social Science (ASOS)	4608
5. Business Reports (BURE)	4834
6. Newspaper Editorials (EDTL)	4771
7. Introductory Textbook Humanities (IHUM)	4907
8. Introductory Textbook Natural Science (INAS)	4808
9. Introductory Textbook Social Science (ISOS)	4495
10. Local News Stories (LONS)	4656
11. Fictional Narratives (NARR)	4638
12. Popular Humanities (PHUM)	4659
13. Popular Natural Science (PNAS)	4742
14. Professional Correspondences (PROC)	4760
15. Popular Social Science (PSOS)	4474
	total words = 70,658

In setting up the text-type groups, two sociolinguistic parameters—topical context and audience—were proposed to interpret variation in text types. Topical context varied along the *natural science—social science—humanities* parameter. Audience varied along the *academic—introductory university—popular* parameter. Other text types, such as newspaper editorials and local news stories, were included since earlier studies have drawn on these sorts of texts as examples of expository prose. A general arrangement of text types according to the parameters proposed is given in Table 2. The columns labeled *natural science, law, social,* and *humanities,*

TABLE 2: A Sociolinguistic Matrix of Text Types

Context Audience	NATS*	LAW	SOS	HUM	BUS	NEWS
academic	ANAS**	ALAW	ASOS	AHUM	BURE	x
introductory	INAS	x	ISOS	IHUM	x	LONS
popular	PNAS	x	PSOS	PHUM	x	EDTL
other	x	x	x	NARR	x	CORR

* NATS = Natural Science; SOS = Social Science; HUM = Humanities; BUS = Business.

** See Table 1 for a key to these abbreviations.

and the rows labeled *academic, introductory,* and *popular* represent a hypothesis on text-type variation. The other groupings are either exploratory or control groups placed in the matrix for completeness.

Variables in the Study

The texts were compared by means of syntactic and cohesion measures. The list of variables used in the study appears in Table 3. In all, 27 syntactic variables and 6 cohesion variables were included. The rationale for

---

TABLE 3: Variables counted in the Study

Syntactic Variables

1.	Prepositions (by, of, with . . .)	(PREP)
2.	Nominalizations (-tion, -ity, -ment . . .)	(NOM)
3.	1st/2nd person pronouns	(IYOU)
4.	3rd singular pronoun	(HESHE)
5.	Singular pro-verb DO	(SINGDO)
6.	Past tense	(PAST)
7.	Present tense	(PRES)
8.	Words per sentence	(WDSENT)
9.	Adjectives	(ADJ)
10.	General conjuncts (and, but, or . . .)	(GENCONJ)
11.	Precise conjuncts (namely, thus . . .)	(PRECCONJ)
12.	Subordinators (because, since . . .)	(SUBORD)
13.	Passive	(PASSIVE)
14.	Infinitives	(INFIN)
15.	WH-clauses (following verbs like tell, remember . . .)	(WHCL)
16.	THAT-clauses (following verbs like know, say . . .)	(THATCL)
17.	Relative clauses	(RELCL)
18.	Pied piping (prep. relative cl.)	(PIEPIPE)
19.	General hedges (maybe, around . . .)	(GENHDG)
20.	THAT-deletion (in complement clauses)	(THATDEL)
21.	Relative pronoun deletion	(RELDEL)
22.	Contractions (aren't . . .)	(CONTRAC)
23.	All attitude adverbs (surely, truly . . .)	(ATTALL)
24.	All clefting constructions	(CLEFTS)
25.	Split auxiliary/infinitives	(SPLITS)
26.	All questions	(QUES)
27.	All locative adverbs (e.g., of time, place)	(LOCALL)

Cohesion Variables

28.	Definite article reference	(ART)
29.	Deictic reference	(DEIC)
30.	All repetition	(REPALL)
31.	Lexical inclusion	(INCLU)
32.	Lexical comparatives	(COMPAR)
33.	Lexical synonymy/antonymy	(SYNANT)

these syntactic variables was based on claims made in the literature about significantly varying linguistic features of texts (e.g., Akinnaso 1982; Chafe 1982, 1985; Olson 1977; Rubin 1980). A review and analysis of the literature is found in Biber (1984a, in press). Twelve cohesion variables were examined for all texts following Halliday and Hasan (1976), Rottweiler (1984), and Stotsky (1983). The measures included both referential and lexical cohesion categories. The study restricted variable counts to syntactic and cohesion categories only. There is certainly much variance in text types unaccounted for by such an analysis. In the future, as discourse theory develops quantifiable coherence structures reliably, they should be added to the array of variables. In this way, variation due to larger textual organizing principles may be better understood.

Measurement Procedures

The syntactic variables were counted using a statistical program developed by Biber at the University of Southern California. The program was created to count untagged text corpora for a variety of syntactic and lexical features, many of which are included in Table 3. (A discussion of this program, as well as a description of the algorithms may be found in Biber, to appear.) Cohesion variables were analyzed by handcounts throughout the text corpus, and included only intersentential cohesion relations (following Halliday and Hasan 1976).

Analysis

The final set of variables were combined in a factor analysis to define textual parameters. The factor analysis grouped variables together which appear to be measuring the same underlying parameter. The created factors were then used to examine text-type variation.[1] After having passed a general significance test, the factors were interpreted by means of factor scales (Duncan Means) to examine whether the textual parameters did, in fact, distinguish the hypothesized text types, in what ways, and to what extent.

A different type of analysis, a cluster analysis, was also performed on the 150 texts. This procedure was used to combine texts themselves into groups, rather than combining variables into groups. The text-type labels were ignored and all 150 texts were broken up into smaller groupings based on how all the variables covaried. The purpose was to see if recognizable groups could be interpreted without hypothesizing categories beforehand.[2] The procedures used in this study are outlined in Figure 1. While a detailed account of the statistical procedures is beyond the scope of this paper, a brief review will accompany the discussion of results.

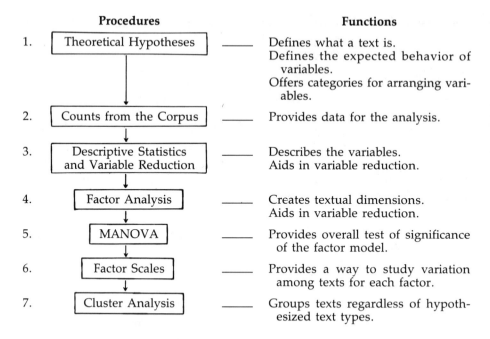

Procedures		Functions
1.	Theoretical Hypotheses	Defines what a text is. Defines the expected behavior of variables. Offers categories for arranging variables.
2.	Counts from the Corpus	Provides data for the analysis.
3.	Descriptive Statistics and Variable Reduction	Describes the variables. Aids in variable reduction.
4.	Factor Analysis	Creates textual dimensions. Aids in variable reduction.
5.	MANOVA	Provides overall test of significance of the factor model.
6.	Factor Scales	Provides a way to study variation among texts for each factor.
7.	Cluster Analysis	Groups texts regardless of hypothesized text types.

Figure 1: Steps in the Statistical Methodology

RESULTS

Factor Analysis

Factor analyses combine variables that co-occur in the texts; that is, certain variables will tend to be measuring the same underlying parameter. This co-occurrence suggests that a common underlying dimension exists which is only imperfectly measured by the surface variables (Gorsuch 1983). The purpose is to determine significant, stable factors which can then be used to examine text-type variation. Once a set of stable factors are decided upon, each factor can then be interpreted.

Factor interpretation is the attempt to name a factor, to use a label which explains why the different variables would join together to form the factor. Factor labels are only as good as the theory which suggests what each variable measures. Thus, any labeling is tentative and should not be taken as real or unchangeable (though the factor structure itself is real), but as optimal. In this study, the factors analyzed provide a useful way to discuss relations among different text types.

This study proposed a seven factor solution; that is, the statistical procedure was set to create only the first seven factors since this was considered to form the optimal solution (for discussion, see Grabe 1984;

Gorsuch 1983).[3] Apart from the numerous guidelines in Gorsuch (1983) for determining structural stability, support for this factor structure is indicated by similar stable factor structures reported in Biber (1984a, 1984b, to appear). The factor structure coefficients are given in Table 4.

TABLE 4: Factor Structure Coefficients

Variable	Fact 1	Fact 2	Fact 3	Fact 4	Fact 5	Fact 6	Fact 7
GENHDG	.0260	.3747	−.1188	−.0466	.0883	−.0810	.0547
PRECCONJ	.4963	−.0124	.0751	.0671	.0838	.3305	.0667
GENCONJ	−.0198	−.1105	−.0137	−.0183	−.5065	.0247	.1260
IYOU	.0448	.7411	.0365	−.0289	−.0173	−.0322	.1986
PRES	.7538	.4141	−.0589	.1295	.0893	.0946	−.1038
CONTRAC	−.0990	.1476	−.0868	−.1585	.0746	−.0596	.4550
HESHE	−.3308	.0250	−.3848	−.6595	.0039	−.0965	.0600
PAST	−.8212	−.1910	−.1746	−.1421	.0871	.0079	.0986
WHCL	.0528	.3953	−.1129	.0025	−.0143	.3903	−.0323
ADJ	.3236	−.0327	.1858	−.1987	−.2509	−.0894	.0363
PREP	.0004	−.1359	.6358	.1728	−.0975	−.0694	−.1324
INFIN	.0762	.5210	.2932	−.0849	.1781	−.0137	.0284
THATCL	.0320	.3554	.0371	.0355	.6194	−.0458	.3270
RELCL	.3858	.0419	.0064	−.2649	.3125	.1527	−.0886
SUBORD	.0694	.4012	−.0599	−.0011	.1924	.0707	−.2605
NOM	.2517	−.1138	.5311	.1045	.0450	.1181	−.0433
THATDEL	.0107	.1236	.0081	.0321	.5868	−.0740	.2781
RELDEL	−.2437	.1712	−.2166	.0654	.1006	−.3801	−.1387
SINGDO	.0704	.4576	−.0721	−.0869	.0779	.1387	.0487
WDSENT	.0360	.0759	.6052	−.1343	−.0402	.0965	.0639
PIEPIPE	.0934	.0712	−.0009	−.0472	.1849	.4182	−.2834
PASSIVE	−.1732	−.1449	−.0376	.5373	.0372	.3898	−.2304
ART	.0222	−.1116	−.3112	.2553	.4185	−.1393	−.1507
DEIC	.1196	.1002	−.0716	.0362	−.0052	.2355	−.2733
COMP	.3871	−.0239	−.0148	−.0045	.1054	.0451	−.3513
INCLU	−.2127	−.2580	−.1017	.2876	−.2994	−.1040	.3390
SYNANT	−.0703	−.0681	.0058	−.3654	−.0073	.1613	−.2457
ATTALL	−.0945	.0417	.0619	−.1075	−.0170	.5421	−.0031
CLEFTS	.1462	.0506	−.3208	−.0173	−.0963	.2469	.1210
SPLITS	.1620	.0050	.0394	.0604	−.1780	.4008	.0112
QUES	.0794	.1516	−.1182	.0154	.1055	.1916	.6254
REPALL	.0288	−.3500	.0440	.6348	.1870	−.1221	.0365
LOCALL	−.1949	−.0243	−.3473	−.1699	−.0299	−.3245	.0365

Prior Communality Estimates

	Factor 1	Factor 2	Factor 3	Factor 4
Eigenvalues	3.9695	3.3771	2.3946	2.1686
Proportion	.1203	.1023	.0723	.0657
Cumulative	.1203	.2226	.2949	.3606

	Factor 5	Factor 6	Factor 7
Eigenvalues	1.8800	1.7085	1.4663
Proportion	.0570	.0518	.0444
Cumulative	.4176	.4693	.5138

TABLE 4 Continued

Final Communality Estimates

GENHDG	PRECCONJ	GENCONJ	IYOU	PRES	CONTRAC	HESHE
.17473	.37731	.28615	.59420	.78758	.28035	.70603
PAST	WHCL	ADJ	PREP	INFIN	THATCL	RELCL
.77892	.32542	.25202	.48443	.40313	.62255	.34962
SUBORD	NCM	THATDEL	RELDEL	SINGDO	WDSENT	PIEPIPE
.27924	.38716	.44357	.31366	.25478	.40638	.30544
PASSIVE	ART	DEIC	COMP	INCLU	SYNANT	ATTALL
.54746	.39220	.16101	.28722	.42023	.22957	.32026
CLEFTS	SPLITS	QUESALL	REPALL	LOCALL		
.21100	.22391	.48238	.60894	.29555		

Each factor created in Table 4 is a linear combination of all the variables. Loosely, each number for each variable can be thought of as a correlation coefficient between that variable and the factor structure. Variables with high coefficients on a factor (here at or above .35) are said to load on a factor. For example, Factor 1 in Table 4 has the following variables loading positively: Present (.75), Precise Conjuncts (.50), Comparative Cohesion (.39), and Relative Clauses (.39). There is only one strong negative loading, Past ($-.82$). Thus, Factor 1 is considered to comprise these variables. The task is then to interpret the factor structure in terms of previous research on text analysis. For example, why would present tense, precise conjuncts, comparative cohesion, and relative clauses all fall together? What label can be given to make sense of this combination? Why would past tense (the complementary negative loading) be in opposition to the positive loadings? It is the researcher's task to offer the most appropriate labels. As will be seen, however, there are ways to check the strength of the interpretations given by examining factor scales.

In Figure 2, the first six factors are given interpretations; the seventh was considered uninterpretable for the present. The variables listed for each factor in Figure 2 include only those with coefficients at .35 or higher. The labeling of the factors follows in part from research in the literature, such as the discussions in Chafe (1982, 1985), Redeker (1984), Tannen (1985), etc., on the nature of written language and larger parameters said to underlie surface features. In part, the labels are drawn from, and supported by, the research of Biber (1984a, 1984b, in press, to appear) and Neu (1985). A lengthy rationale for the labeling is given in Grabe (1984).

A brief discussion of one of the factor labelings will provide an illustration of the labeling decisions. Factor 2 (in Figure 2) is labeled Orientation to Discourse. The variables that loaded positively include General Hedges, First and Second Person Pronouns, Infinitive Complements,

Factor 1	Factor 2	Factor 3	Factor 4	Factor 5	Factor 6
Immediacy of Context	Orientation of Discourse	Information Type	Presentation of Information	Informational Focus	Attitude to Content
(Immediate Context)	(Interactional)	(Abstract /Logical)	(Objective /Effaced)	(Focused)	(Careful)
Pres Precconj Relcl Compar	Genhdg Iyou Infin Thatcl Subord Singdo Pres	Nom Prep Wdsent	Passive Repall	Thatcl Thatdel Art	Whcl Piepipe Passive Attall Splits
(Distant Context)	(Informational)	(Situational)	(Expressive)	(Unfocussed)	(Loose)
Past	Repall	Heshe Locall	Heshe Synant	Genconj	Reldel

Figure 2: Factor Structure Interpretations

That-Clause Complements, Subordinators, DO as a pro-form, and Present Tense. The single negative loading is lexical repetition. Based on discussions in Tannen (1982, 1985), and Biber (to appear), it is likely that written texts include interactional features similar in nature to features found in oral language; that is, some types of writing attempt to be more interactionally oriented and less informationally oriented. Biber (1984a) found similar groupings of variables for primarily oral discourse. For this reason, I have labeled Factor 2 "Orientation to Discourse" and the two poles (positive and negative) as Interactional and Informational. This factor tends to support Tannen's notion that certain textual parameters cut across the oral/written distinction. It is also interesting to note that a number of subordinating devices are more oriented to interaction, or oral language, than is commonly noted in the research literature, where many claim subordination to be a feature of written language as opposed to oral language (e.g., Chafe 1982; Kress 1982; Kroll 1977; cf. Biber to appear).

In arriving at interpretations of the factors, as much attention should be given to the strength of the coefficient as to the combination of variables which load. For example, Present Tense and Past Tense have extremely high coefficients on Factor 1. This probably becomes more important for interpretation than finding a neat explanation for all the variables combining on that factor. Overall, the factor labels become tentative explanations for why variables loaded as they do on each factor.

Factor Scales

After having ascertained that the factors discriminated overall among the text types (by means of a MANOVA), Duncan Means were used to explore text-type variation along each factor. The Duncan Means offer a useful procedure for examining relative relationships in text-type groupings along each textual dimension (or factor), and they will therefore be referred to as factor scales.

Each factor scale is created by taking the variables which loaded on that factor, adding together the numerical counts of those variables for each text, and averaging the final number for each text type. For example, if each Professional Correspondence text had 40 occurrences of Present Tense, 5 occurrences of Relative Clauses, and 20 occurrences of Past Tense (all variables loading on Factor 1), then each of these texts would have a final sum of 25 for Factor 1. The ten texts would then be averaged, and a factor scale score for Professional Correspondences on Factor 1 would be 25. Table 5 presents factor scales for the first four factors (as they are the four most important). The r-squared figure given along each factor scale in Table 5 indicates the amount of variance in the factor explained by text-type variation.

TABLE 5: Factor Scales for Each Text Group on Each Factor

1. Immediacy of Context.
   ($F = 7.90$, $p < .0001$, $r^*r = .450$)

Mean	Text Type
59.22	Intro Natural Science (INAS)
50.87	Professional Corr (PROC)
47.37	Editorials (EDTL)
38.23	Academic Law (ALAW)
37.66	Academic Humanities (AHUM)
37.10	Popular Social Science (PSOS)
36.95	Intro Social Science (ISOS)
35.54	Intro Humanities (IHUM)
28.75	Popular Nat Science (PNAS)
20.98	Academic Soc Science (ASOS)
18.46	Academic Nat Science (ANAS)
17.82	Local News (LONS)
9.11	Annual Business Reports (BURE)
6.60	Popular Humanities (PHUM)
−11.48	Fictional Narratives (NARR)

2. Orientation of Discourse.
   ($F = 12.27$, $p > .0001$, $r^*r = .560$)

Mean	Text Type
49.21	Professional Corr (PROC)
11.46	Editorials (EDTL)
−3.05	Intro Humanities (IHUM)
−4.09	Fictional Narratives (NARR)
−4.76	Academic Humanities (AHUM)
−15.18	Popular Soc Science (PSOS)
−20.78	Intro Social Science (ISOS)
−22.76	Popular Humanities (PHUM)
−35.26	Academic Law (ALAW)
−36.62	Intro Natural Science (INAS)
−36.90	Local News (LONS)
−45.29	Popular Nat Science (PNAS)
−47.09	Academic Soc Science (ASOS)
−64.22	Annual Business Reports (BURE)
−69.87	Academic Nat Science (ANAS)

3. Informational Type.
   ($F = 12.89$, $p < .0001$, $r^*r = .572$)

Mean	Text Type
125.40	Academic Law (ALAW)
119.70	Professional Corr (PROC)
114.30	Academic Soc Science (ASOS)
112.90	Annual Business Reports (BURE)
112.60	Academic Nat Science (ANAS)

TABLE 5: Continued

---

3. Informational Type.
   ($F = 12.89$, $p < .0001$, $r^*r = .572$)

Mean	Text Type
104.00	Academic Humanities (AHUM)
102.00	Intro Soc Science (ISOS)
98.20	Intro Humanities (IHUM)
97.60	Intro Nat Science (INAS)
96.40	Popular Soc Science (PSOS)
95.70	Popular Nat Science (PNAS)
94.50	Editorials (EDTL)
92.00	Local News (LONS)
88.00	Popular Humanities (PHUM)
37.00	Fictional Narratives (NARR)

---

4. Presentation of information.
   ($F = 17.84$, $p < .0001$, $r^*r = .649$)

Mean	Text Type
107.83	Academic Nat Science (ANAS)
102.61	Intro Natural Science (INAS)
96.39	Annual Business Report (BURE)
89.22	Popular Nat Science (PNAS)
79.18	Academic Law (ALAW)
78.55	Local News (LONS)
77.84	Academic Soc Science (ASOS)
64.75	Intro Social Science (ISOS)
61.81	Popular Soc Science (PSOS)
56.53	Intro Humanities (IHUM)
43.46	Popular Humanities (PHUM)
40.15	Editorial (EDTL)
38.66	Professional Corr (PROC)
30.45	Academic Humanities (AHUM)
1.06	Fictional Narratives (NARR)

Since the factor scales arrange each text type in relation to all the other text types, they provide a way to examine the plausibility of the factor interpretations. Earlier, factor labels were suggested by the set of variables which loaded on each factor. We can now compare those labels with the arrangement of text groups on the factor scales to see if the labeling helps us to understand the ordering of text types.

The factor scales for Factor 1, the first textual dimension, offer some indication that the "Immediacy of Context" label is reasonable in light of the text-type distribution. Recall that Factor 1 involved a major distinction between Present Tense and Past Tense. Thus, texts with high scores on this factor deal more with immediate contexts, and perhaps also with generalizable information. The texts with an "Immediate Context" include Introductory texts (INAS = 59.22), Editorials (EDTL = 47.37), and Professional Correspondences (PROC = 50.87). The immediacy effect appears to represent an effort to be direct and relevant to a present time context, explaining introductory and editorial texts. Professional Correspondences, as might be expected, are among the most strongly immediate. Texts that would be considered more distant include Academic Social Science and Academic Natural Science texts. This is reasonable considering that many of these texts involve reports of completed experiments. Similarly, both Local News and Business Reports are reports of past events. This factor may be powerful in explaining distinctions between expository and other major text types—i.e., Fictional Narratives. Note that Fictional Narratives are the lowest text type for Factor 1 (as they are also for Factors 3 and 4—NARR = −11.48).

The factor scale for Factor 2, "Interactive—Informational Orientation to Discourse," seems to be supportive of the labeling. The general arrangement of groups by their means shows that Correspondences (PROC = 49.21), Editorials, Narratives, and all the Humanities are more interactive. Recall that Factor 2 included variables that could be identified with oral language features. It is, therefore, reasonable that letters, fiction, and editorials, of all the text types in this study, should have high factor means. In contrast, the Science texts (ANAS = −69.87), Business Reports, Local News, and most Academic texts are more oriented towards information than interaction. Further, the means indicate a useful distinction between the two text types for newspaper texts. (Note Factors 1 and 4 for further distinctions between these text types.) The means also indicate that this factor may be a powerful distinguisher of Professional Correspondences as this type appears with a much higher mean score than all the other text types.

The third factor, "Logical vs. Situational Context," is well supported by the factor means. The most abstract context is typically represented by the Academic Journal texts (ALAW = 125.40), Business Reports, and Professional Correspondences. The middle group consists of Introductory texts; the lower group, of Popular texts (PHUM = 88.00). This clear separation along the academic—popular parameter is a good indicator that the factor label is a reasonable one; that is, academic writing should be more abstract/logical, while popular writing should be more situational. The means of this factor also verify one dimension of the hypothesized sociolinguistic parameters discussed earlier (Table 2).

Factor 4, described as "Presentation of Information," or the writer's personality, is also well supported by the results of the factor means. Texts exhibiting effacement are the Science texts (ANAS = 107.83), as might be expected, as well as the Local News texts. This is reasonable considering that news writing is intended to convey non-commitment. In contrast, the Humanities texts, Editorials, and Fictional Narratives (NARR = 1.06) are all considered more expressive. Factor 4 also verifies the second of the sociolinguistic parameters discussed earlier—that of contextual differences from natural science to social science to humanities. Thus, Factors 3 and 4 together suggest that sociolinguistic parameters are more than heuristic organizing principles for text-type differences; rather, they represent real underlying distinctions which separate different text types.

Based upon the results of the factor scales, I have posited four important textual dimensions (the four factors) which discriminate text types. It also appears safe to suggest from these results that some earlier research on text types in literature, and basic text analyses more generally, have made generalizations based on text-type data whose categorization has been oversimplified. If the factors discussed here are real, then texts normally assumed to be equally "expository" may actually be significantly different along a number of textual dimensions.

For example, if we examine Local News and Editorials, both sub-sets of newspaper writing, we find that they cannot be readily joined as a single text type. They would appear to be similar text types if measured by variables loading on Factor 3, "Informational Type." However, if we compare the two in terms of either Factor 1 or Factor 2, we would have to conclude that they are different text types. Thus, the issue of determining text-type variation is one that requires the study of texts as multidimensional constructs. No single simple continuum can be established to study text-type differences adequately. (See especially the discussion in Biber in press.)

We may also reasonably conclude at this point that certain text types bear little resemblance to the large majority of the text types in this sample. Fictional Narratives are outliers on three of the four major dimensions. This suggests that the majority of the hypothesized text types are more closely aligned among themselves than with this anticipated non-"expository" prose type. Though less obvious, Professional Correspondences appear to follow Narratives as outlier text groups (particularly on Factor 2). We might then suggest that text-type variation is better viewed as variation along textual dimensions rather than as one-dimensional parametric variation (or dichotomous variation).

If we return to the research questions posed at the beginning of this article, some responses may now be proposed. The results of the factor scaling do suggest that there is such a larger text genre called *expository prose*. Further, it is reasonable to suggest at this point that a number of sub-groupings exist among the hypothesized text types. Academic texts,

Science texts, Humanities texts, Local News, and Editorials all appear to have consistent, explainable behavior according to the textual parameters defined by the factor analysis. Finally, it is possible to define a number of characteristic features with respect to these text types in terms of the variables contributing to different textual dimensions (the factors), as well as by the factor interpretations. A clearer conception of the relations among the text types is discernible if the factor scales for each factor are plotted in two-dimensional space.

Plotting Factor Scales

Each of the four factor scales in Table 5 can be used to plot relations between text types in two-dimensional space. For example, the factor scale for Factor 1 runs from 60 to −12; the factor scale for Factor 2, from 50 to −70, etc. Rather than presenting the text types in rank ordering, the exact distance between them can be presented, as in Figure 3 (using Factor 1 as an example).

If two factor scales are plotted together, one horizontal and the other vertical, a two-dimensional field can be created with each text type located therein. Thus, the relations among the text types are indicated in two-dimensional space for two textual parameters. Figures 4 and 5 are two-dimensional plots using the factor scales for Factors 1 and 2 (Figure 4), and Factors 3 and 4 (Figure 5). In fact, if the two figures could be combined somehow, a more accurate representation of text-type variation would emerge. That is, any given text type is related to any other text type on all four dimensions. The graphs presented here give some indication of the complexities involved in explaining text-type relations accurately. They illustrate nicely the statement that texts must be studied as multidimensional constructs.

Examining the graphs (Figures 4 and 5), one quickly notes the separation of narrative texts from all others. Figure 4 also distinguishes Professional Correspondences from all other text types. A more careful examination of Figure 4 reveals a wave-like progression from the lower-right quadrant with the first wave composed of Natural Science texts, the second wave of Social Science texts, the third wave of Humanities texts, and the last wave spreading beyond expository prose to Narratives and Professional Correspondences. A similar strong separation can be observed in Figure 5 where Natural Science, Social Science, and Humanities form distinct groups. The division between Academic, Introductory, and Popular texts is also discernible, though less strong.

The factor graphs also provide some indications about the more exploratory text types included in the study. Local News, for example, appears to be associated with Social Science writing in Figure 4, and to

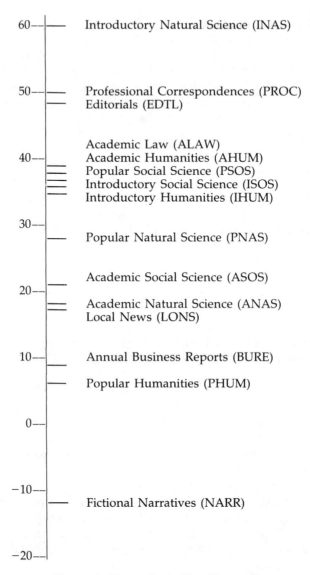

60 — Introductory Natural Science (INAS)

50 — Professional Correspondences (PROC)
Editorials (EDTL)

40 — Academic Law (ALAW)
Academic Humanities (AHUM)
Popular Social Science (PSOS)
Introductory Social Science (ISOS)
Introductory Humanities (IHUM)

30 —

Popular Natural Science (PNAS)

Academic Social Science (ASOS)
20 —
Academic Natural Science (ANAS)
Local News (LONS)

10 — Annual Business Reports (BURE)

Popular Humanities (PHUM)

0 —

−10 —
Fictional Narratives (NARR)

−20 —

Figure 3: Factor Scale Plot (Factor 1)

fall between Social Science and Natural Science in Figure 5. In Figure 5 it is also located between the levels of Introductory and Popular writing, as might be anticipated. Editorial writing, being more expressive and more interactional, appears to be more in line with Humanities writing in both graphs. A somewhat less predictable result was the close relationship between Academic Natural Science writing and Annual Business Reports

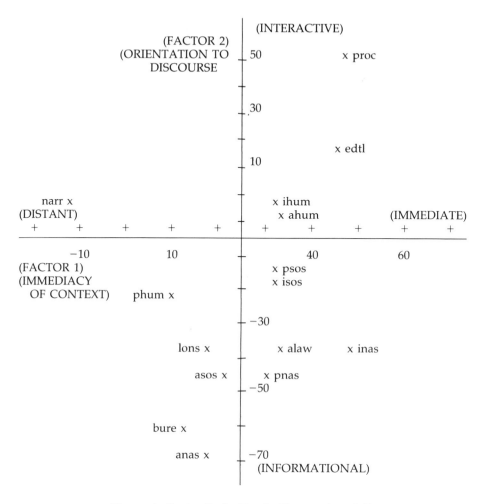

Figure 4: Factor Scale Graph (Factors 1 and 2)

indicated in both Figures. A careful consideration of the textual parameters offers some explanation for this relationship, though further research is needed here.

Cluster Analysis

To this point we have established that the hypothesized text types are a
reasonable set of categories for classifying text types and that the methods employed thus far indicate valid sub-groupings of expository prose
texts. We would like some converging evidence to support the findings

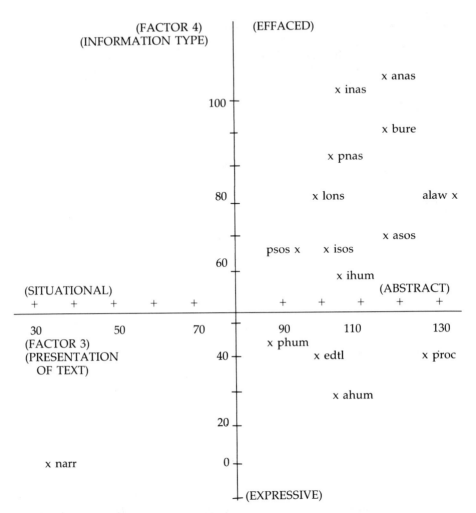

Figure 5: Factor Scale Graph (Factors 3 and 4)

above. A second way to explore the research questions raised is by means of a cluster analysis. The cluster analysis offers an independent way to examine the text types, and a way to see if the texts form groupings that suggest a major category of *expository prose*. In this analysis the labels given to the text types were ignored. Instead, the cluster analysis treated all 150 texts as potentially one group, and proceeded to form sub-groups or clusters based solely on the variables used (Table 3). When the analysis finds a set of clusters which captures a good amount of the variance in the variables, it so indicates with a Cubic Clustering Criterion (CCC) Value above 2. The best clustering was found for 8 groups (CCC = 4.66).

The result of the cluster analysis for 8 groups is given in Table 6.

Table 6 contains three sets of numbers for each text type along each cluster. The clusters are labeled 1–8 and each cluster is read horizontally. The top row of numbers is the number of texts from that genre in the particular cluster. The middle set of numbers, the row %, indicates what percentage each genre contributes to the full set of texts in a cluster. The lower set of numbers, the column %, indicates the percentage of texts from a genre which are considered part of a cluster.

A number of useful observations may be made about these results. The first is that a general *expository* prose group probably appears as Cluster 1. The only text-type groups not contributing are Fictional Narratives, Professional Correspondences, and Business Reports; all the other text-type groups have texts as part of Cluster 1. The non-occurrence in this group of Fictional Narratives, Professional Correspondences, and Business Reports strengthens the observation that Cluster 1 may represent some general *expository* grouping. This is further reinforced by Clusters 2, 5, and 6, where Fictional Narratives and Professional Correspondences form independent clusters.

Cluster 2, for example, only has eleven texts, nine of which are Fictional Narratives. Thus, this cluster may be said to represent a Narrative group of texts. Cluster 6 comprises only one text, a narrative text. This second cluster indicates that there may be more than one kind of narrative text type, though that issue is not explored here. Cluster 5 contains 20 texts, all ten Professional Correspondences are included as well as five Editorial texts. This cluster identifies correspondence writing and, perhaps, more interactional types of writing, which would account for the Editorial texts as well.

Clusters 3 and 4 provide further support for considering two separate sub-types in Academic/Science and Humanities text types. In Cluster 3, 17 out of 22 texts are Humanities texts, making a strong argument for a Humanities text type. Cluster 4 contained many Academic Law texts and a large number of Natural Science texts. This indicates some type of Academic/Science reporting style indicative of science and law writing. A second possible type of science text is indicated in Cluster 7. Cluster 7 contains three Academic Science texts and one Business Report. Cluster 8 is hard to interpret, though it may be a second type of general informational writing.

Overall, the results of the cluster analysis allow us to suggest that there is a general text type which may be labeled as *expository*, as opposed to non-expository texts such as narratives and correspondences. In addition, there appear to be a number of clearly separate sub-types within the expository umbrella (as indicated by their contributions on the general cluster), including at least two types of Science texts, a type of

TABLE 6: Cluster Analysis for Eight Groups

CLUSTER	GENRE	AHUM	ALAW	ANAS	ASOS	BURE	EDTL	IHUM	INAS	ISOS	LONS	NARR	PHUM	PNAS	PROC	PSOS
	FREQUENCY / ROW PCT / COL PCT															
1	FREQUENCY	2	2	3	3	0	5	2	6	6	5	0	2	4	0	6
	ROW PCT	4.4	4.4	6.5	6.5	0.0	10.9	4.4	13.0	13.0	10.9	0.0	4.4	8.7	0.0	13.0
	COL PCT	20.0	20.0	30.0	30.0	00.0	50.0	20.0	60.0	60.0	50.0	00.0	20.0	40.0	00.0	60.0
2	FREQUENCY	1	0	0	0	0	0	0	0	0	0	9	1	0	0	0
	ROW PCT	9.1	0.0	0.0	0.0	0.0	0.0	0.0	0.0	0.0	0.0	81.8	9.1	0.0	0.0	0.0
	COL PCT	10.0	00.0	00.0	00.0	00.0	00.0	00.0	00.0	00.0	00.0	90.0	10.0	00.0	00.0	00.0
3	FREQUENCY	7	0	0	0	1	0	4	0	2	1	0	6	0	0	1
	ROW PCT	31.8	0.0	0.0	0.0	4.6	0.0	18.2	0.0	9.1	4.6	0.0	27.3	0.0	0.0	4.6
	COL PCT	70.0	00.0	00.0	00.0	10.0	00.0	40.0	00.0	20.0	10.0	00.0	60.0	00.0	00.0	10.0
4	FREQUENCY	0	7	3	3	3	0	1	4	1	0	0	0	2	0	0
	ROW PCT	0.0	29.2	12.5	12.5	12.5	0.0	4.2	16.7	4.2	0.0	0.0	0.0	8.3	0.0	0.0
	COL PCT	00.0	70.0	30.0	30.0	30.0	00.0	10.0	40.0	10.0	00.0	00.0	00.0	20.0	00.0	00.0
5	FREQUENCY	0	1	0	0	0	5	2	0	1	0	0	0	0	10	1
	ROW PCT	0.0	5.0	0.0	0.0	0.0	25.0	10.0	0.0	5.0	0.0	0.0	0.0	0.0	50.0	5.0
	COL PCT	00.0	10.0	00.0	00.0	00.0	50.0	20.0	00.0	10.0	00.0	00.0	00.0	00.0	100.0	10.0
6	FREQUENCY	0	0	0	0	0	0	0	0	0	0	1	0	0	0	0
	ROW PCT	0.0	0.0	0.0	0.0	0.0	0.0	0.0	0.0	0.0	0.0	100.0	0.0	0.0	0.0	0.0
	COL PCT	00.0	00.0	00.0	00.0	00.0	00.0	00.0	00.0	00.0	00.0	10.0	00.0	00.0	00.0	00.0
7	FREQUENCY	0	0	3	0	1	0	0	0	0	0	0	0	0	0	0
	ROW PCT	0.0	0.0	75.0	0.0	25.0	0.0	0.0	0.0	0.0	0.0	0.0	0.0	0.0	0.0	0.0
	COL PCT	00.0	00.0	30.0	00.0	10.0	00.0	00.0	00.0	00.0	00.0	00.0	00.0	00.0	00.0	00.0
8	FREQUENCY	0	0	1	4	5	0	1	0	0	4	0	1	4	0	2
	ROW PCT	0.0	0.0	4.6	18.2	22.7	0.0	4.6	0.0	0.0	18.2	0.0	4.6	18.2	0.0	9.1
	COL PCT	00.0	00.0	10.0	40.0	50.0	00.0	10.0	00.0	00.0	40.0	00.0	10.0	40.0	00.0	20.0

Humanities text, and another type yet to be labeled. In general, these findings match the earlier findings, lending support to the research results discussed above; that is, there does seem to be a major genre type labeled *expository prose*. There do appear to be identifiable sub-types within the larger genre category of expository prose. It also seems possible to identify characteristics of each sub-type distinguished.

LIMITATIONS OF
THE STUDY

The results attained in this study were dependent on the syntactic and cohesion variables chosen. If other variables had been chosen for analysis, there may have been variation in the findings. However, recognizing the general importance attributed to most variables in this study, the measures employed represent, to a large extent, current thinking about linguistic/functional correlates of text structure. A direction for future research is to incorporate other variables. Particularly, efforts should be made to include underlying coherence relations in some quantitative form.

A second limitation of the study involves the narrow range of textual variety examined by the statistical procedures. If text types of significantly different form had been included in the study (as, for example, drama or poetry), the range of variation would undoubtedly have been greater and the discrimination of text types would have been stronger. However, because of the nature of the research question, a number of hypothesized text types were expected to show little variance. There is a danger that the textual dimensions are being drawn within a narrow textual field, allowing for some amount of correlation. But given the results of the MANOVA and the clearly distinguishable sub-text types in the study, the findings reported here appear to be valid. Also, the fact that the seven-factor solution was both stable across different rotation patterns and satisfied a number of other criteria discussed in Gorsuch (1983) supports this research.

CONCLUSION

The results of this study offer a number of relevant implications for text-type and writing research generally, and for contrastive rhetoric in particular. The research discussed here indicates that we can define expository prose as a distinct major text genre, and further, that a number of text-type distinctions exist within expository prose which we must be aware of. If these finer distinctions among text types can be repeated with a text data base in a second language, a real basis for rhetorical comparison is possible. How this could be done is a question for future research.

Another general implication to draw from this work is that many linguistic variables may be quantified and used profitably in statistical analyses. Further, such linguistic counts do seem to coalesce to represent important textual parameters in writing. Taking the logical reasoning one step further, we may be able to use such techniques to map writing development. Rather than consider surface, cohesion, and coherence features individually, measures combined to form textual parameters may yield significant insights about the acquisition of literacy skills and language transfer.

The complexity of the text types examined in this study may be extended to instructional issues as well. Both Heath (1985) and Carrell (1984c) have argued that writing expository prose requires reasoning and rhetorical arrangements which can only be gained by practice in expository writing. While writing narratives, dialogues, and letters improves certain writing abilities, these types are sufficiently different that students may still be unable to write good expository prose. The results of this study support the notion that expository prose is a distinct text genre, with its own particular textual dimensions, requiring its own instruction. Such an implication ties in well with practical aspects of contrastive rhetoric research.

An additional set of implications from this research is that certain surface features are more prevalent for different text types. For example, as has been noted elsewhere, nominalizations and passives are more prevalent in Natural Science writing. It turns out that extensive repetition is also an important device. Interestingly, in this study, nominalizations were not a distinguishing characteristic of Science writing, but of Academic Journal writing generally. Thus, more careful text-type distinctions clarify some of the more general statements in the literature. The relevance of this sort of research for instruction in ESL is not well-established, but it should have implications for research in contrastive rhetoric, particularly for indirect research approaches; that is, second language essays may be examined and differentiated following these insights.

Finally, for contrastive rhetoric research in two languages, this approach provides a way to determine whether text types exist, how they can be defined, and how they can be related to other text types. If contrastive rhetoric is to examine text materials in a number of languages, at some point in the future, the research will first have to establish which texts in different languages are, in fact, similar. Such research would indicate textual dimensions that differ from English textual parameters, and perhaps also from each other. If this approach is combined with studies of students' uses of writing in various countries, more careful research in contrastive rhetoric will be possible, and a more realistic assessment of indirect English L2 studies will emerge.

NOTES

1. The factors were tested for significance by means of Multiple Analysis of Variance (MANOVA). The factors were significant at $F = 6.61$ (Wilk's criterion), $F < .0001$.

2. The general methodology and the procedures for display used here are outlined in Biber (in press; to appear).

3. The factor analysis used was an iterated principle factor analysis (a common factors analysis) with a varimax rotation, and with the number of factors set at seven. The analysis was run on the SAS (1982) package installed at the University Computing Center, University of Southern California.

FOR STUDY AND DISCUSSION

1. Grabe uses sophisticated statistical analyses (e.g., factor analysis, ANOVA, MANOVA, Duncan Means, etc.). Is such statistical analysis essential for contemporary discourse study? Is it helpful? What will be necessary to make this type of research readily available to teachers?

2. In analyzing the corpus texts Grabe used three types of variables; indeed he suggests that a text is a multifaceted structure. Classically, linguistics has been interested in the description of syntactic structure. How would you classify Grabe's research? Is it linguistics? Is it sociolinguistics? Is it pragmatics? Why?

3. Grabe suggests that there is indeed an "expository prose," but further suggests that the class is not monolithic but is composed of a number of significantly different sub-types. What are the implications of this claim for traditional rhetorical studies? What does it mean in terms of English-for-Special-Purposes teaching?

4. In the light of Grabe's claim, comment on the contribution to discourse studies made by Connor, Connor and McCagg, Carrell, Eggington, Hinds, and Ostler.

Part III
Inter-Language Studies

Chapter 8

Reader Versus Writer Responsibility: A New Typology[1]

John Hinds
Pennsylvania State University

This paper investigates the notion of reader responsibility, in contrast to writer responsibility. Its focal point is that there are different expectations with regard to the degree of involvement a reader will have, and that this degree of involvement will depend on the language of the reader. In this sense, this paper is concerned with language typology.

The concern with language typology, in its modern sense, dates from Greenberg's (1963) classic article in which he postulated a typology that involves certain basic factors of word order. Greenberg (1963:77) proposed that there are three common word order types, illustrated in Table 1.

The significance of Greenberg's typology is that it allowed him to postulate a number of "implicational universals." That is, by knowing that a language is SOV, for instance, it follows that that language will

TABLE 1 Basic Word Orders		
SVO	*SOV*	*VSO*
English	Japanese	Tagalog
Fulani	Korean	Welsh
Thai	Burmese	Zapotec

141

have postpositions rather than prepositions, that there will be no invariant rule for fronting question words, and so on.

Another typology has been suggested in Li and Thompson (1976). They suggest that languages display different characteristics depending on whether grammatical subject or grammatical topic is more prominent. They identify four basic types of languages, shown in Table 2.

In subject-prominent languages, the structure of sentences favors a description in which the grammatical relation *subject-predicate* assumes primary importance. In topic-prominent languages, the grammatical role *topic-comment* is most important. For languages like Japanese and Korean, both constructions are reputed to be equally important, while for languages like Tagalog, subject and topic are said to have merged and to be indistinguishable in all sentence types.

Other typologies have been suggested as well. Thompson (1978), for instance, has discussed a typology in which languages differ in the way they utilize word order. Languages like English typically use word order to indicate grammatical relationships, while languages like Spanish, in which the movement of constituents is fairly free of grammatical restrictions, use word order to indicate pragmatic relationships, such as theme-rheme distinctions.

Monane and Rogers (1977), in a much more restricted study, have suggested that Japanese and English differ with respect to whether sentences are typically "situation-focus" or "person-focus." That is, for Japanese speakers, it appears to be enough simply to state that a situation has occurred. For English speakers, not only the situation but also the persons involved in the situation are typically stated. Monane and Rogers (1977:135) offer convincing examples, several of which are presented in Table 3.

TABLE 2

Subject-prominent Languages	Topic-prominent Languages
Indo-European	Chinese
Niger-Congo	Lahu (Lolo-Burmese)
Finno-Ugric	Lisu (Lolo-Burmese)

Subject-prominent and Topic-prominent Languages	Neither Subject-prominent nor Topic-prominent Languages
Japanese	Tagalog
Korean	Ilocano

TABLE 3

Situation-focus	Person-focus
sakebigoe ga shita zo. (lit.) A shouting voice occurred.	I just heard someone shout.
yama ga mieru (lit.) The mountain can be seen.	I can see the mountain.

In this paper, I suggest a typology that is based on speaker and/or writer responsibility as opposed to listener and/or reader responsibility. What this means is that in some languages, such as English, the person primarily responsible for effective communication is the speaker, while in other languages, such as Japanese, the person primarily responsible for effective communication is the listener. The lexical hedge "primarily" in the previous two clauses is important since the phenomena under discussion constitute tendencies rather than exceptionless "rules." This means, of course, that there may be circumstances in which English listeners are responsible for effective communication, in which Japanese speakers are responsible for effective communication, or in which that responsibility is shared by the listener and speaker. What is described here is the neutral situation.[2] The implications of this typology are discussed below with respect to specific grammatical manifestations of this distinction.

I take as a starting point the position that English speakers, by and large, charge the writer, or speaker, with the responsibility to make clear and well-organized statements. If there is a breakdown in communication, for instance, it is because the speaker/writer has not been clear enough, not because the listener/reader has not exerted enough effort in an attempt to understand.

This view has strong historical precedent. Havelock (1963, 1976), cited by Hildyard and Olson, has pointed out that:

> . . . with the emphasis on literacy both in classical Greece and in post-reformation England there was a great concern to make sentences say exactly, neither more nor less than what they meant. Poetry and proverbial sayings which mean both more and less than what they say, were rejected as a means of expressing truth both by Plato and 2000 years later by members of the Royal Society of London . . . (1982:20).

Chafe, in discussing differences between speakers and writers, has reiterated this position.

> . . . the speaker is aware of an obligation to communicate what he

or she has in mind in a way that reflects the richness of his or her thoughts . . .; the writer [is] . . . concerned with producing something that will be consistent and defensible when read by different people at different times in different places, something that will stand the test of time (1982:45).

The desire to write or speak clearly in English permeates our culture. This point of view has even been made into an aphorism for public speaking: "Tell 'em what you're going to tell 'em, tell 'em, then tell 'em what you told 'em." It is the responsibility of the speaker to communicate a message.

In Japan, perhaps in Korea, and certainly in Ancient China, there is a different way of looking at the communication process. In Japan, it is the responsibility of the listener (or reader) to understand what it is that the speaker or author had intended to say. This difference may be illustrated quite effectively by an anecdote presented in Naotsuka *et al.* (1981:16). An American woman was taking a taxi to the Ginza Tokyu Hotel. The taxi driver mistakenly took her to the Ginza Daiichi Hotel. She said, "I'm sorry, I should have spoken more clearly." This, I take to be an indication of her speaker-responsible upbringing. The taxi driver demonstrated his listener-responsible background when he replied, "No, no, I should have listened more carefully."

This difference in the way of looking at the act of communication permeates the thoughts of anyone who operates as a functioning Japanese-American bicultural. Yoshikawa gives considerable insight into this situation. He states that the Japanese actually have a mistrust of verbal language.

> What is often verbally expressed and what is actually intended are two different things. What is verbally expressed is probably important enough to maintain friendship, and it is generally called *tatemae* which means simply "in principle" but what is not verbalized counts most—*honne* which means "true mind." Although it is not expressed verbally, you are supposed to know it by *kan*—"intuition" (1978:228–229).

Yoshikawa attributes this ability on the part of the listener to intuit a speaker's meaning to the fact that Japan is a homogeneous country. Whether this explanation is correct is not the issue, although it is the case that most Japanese believe it is true. Yoshikawa further states that the basic principle of communication in Japan, the fact that what is verbally expressed and what is actually intended are two different things, is something that Japanese people are supposed to be aware of.

Suzuki (1975:31, ff.) addresses this same theme. He compares the

French attitude toward clarity in language, exemplified by the expression *ce qui n'est pas clair n'est pas francais* (that which is not clear is not French), with the Japanese attitude. Suzuki claims that Japanese authors do not like to give clarifications or full explanations of their views. They like to give dark hints and to leave them behind nuances. Moreover, Suzuki claims that it is exactly this type of prose which gets the highest praise from readers. He states that Japanese readers "anticipate with pleasure the opportunities that such writing offers them to savor this kind of 'mystification' of language."

This attitude toward reader responsibility is not limited to Japan, but is shared at least by Classical Chinese. Li and Thompson (1982:81, ff.) discuss a Classical Chinese text in which many statements are what they call "telegraphic." Concerning this passage, they state:

> The next clause . . . then states: "The logic is profound and abstruse" without clarifying what logic or whose logic is being referred to. Thus, in order to extract the correct message . . ., the reader has to rely heavily on inference based on his/her knowledge of the world and the information provided by the earlier clauses of the paragraph (1982:83).

Of another sentence in this same passage, they state that the author "left it to the reader to extrapolate that the town was his home-town." This is especially of interest since in the present-day Mandarin translation of this passage, the translator

> made it clear that the town was Zichuan. In order to provide this piece of information to the reader, however, the translator had to research the life of the author and add a footnote to point out that Zichuan was the home-town of the author. . . .

Thus, there appears to be a major shift in typological style between Classical and Modern Chinese. Classical Chinese appears to be more like Japanese in that it is a reader-responsible language, while Modern Chinese is more like English in that it is a writer-responsible language.

I turn now to a discussion of the implications of this typology on current-day Japanese writing. My point of departure is that there are greater consequences for a reader-responsible language than merely tolerance for ambiguity and imprecision of statement, although this also occurs. It goes beyond attitudes toward writing, such that English-speaking writers go through draft after draft to come up with a final product, while Japanese authors frequently compose exactly one draft which becomes the finished product.

There are specific differences between English and Japanese in the way that authors present expository materials, and these differences help to demonstrate this typology. Kaplan (1966) originally suggested that there are differences in rhetorical styles from language to language. He cites a number of rhetoricians to demonstrate that good English writing is characterized by unity and coherence. Hughes and Duhamel (1962), cited by Kaplan, provide definitions for these terms:

> Unity is the quality attributed to writing which has all its necessary and sufficient parts. Coherence is the quality attributed to the presentation of material in a sequence which is intelligible to its reader (Kaplan 1966:4).

In a series of recent papers (Hinds 1980, 1983, 1984b), I have attempted to discuss differences in Japanese and English writing with respect to coherence. The area in which speaker and reader responsibility operates, however, is with respect to unity. That is, for English readers, unity is important because readers expect, and require, landmarks along the way. Transition statements are very important. It is the writer's task to provide appropriate transition statements so that the reader can piece together the thread of the writer's logic which binds the composition together.

In Japanese, on the other hand, the landmarks may be absent or attenuated since it is the reader's responsibility to determine the relationship between any one part of an essay and the essay as a whole. This is not to say that there are no transition statements in Japanese. There are. It is only to say that these transition devices may be more subtle and require a more active role for the reader.

In Japanese grammar, there is a continuing effort to determine the functions of two postpositional particles, *wa* and *ga*, since these two particles may frequently be interchanged. In typical analyses, *ga* is considered to be a subject marker, while *wa* is considered to be a topic marker. Kuno (1972) specifically addresses the distribution of these two particles and concludes that *ga* indicates that the subject of a sentence represents new unpredictable information, while *wa* indicates that this same noun phrase represents old, predictable information. Thus, in answer to the question "Who went to Nara?" (1), with *ga*, is appropriate since Akiko is new, or unpredictable information.

(1) *Akiko ga Nara e ikimashita.*
                   to went

    Akiko went to Nara.

On the other hand, in answer to a question like "What did Akiko do last week?" (2) is appropriate because we have been talking about Akiko; that is, Akiko constitutes old, predictable information.

(2) **Akiko _wa_ Nara e ikimashita.**

Akiko went to Nara.

While Kuno's characterization of the distribution of these particles is generally correct [but see Maynard 1981, Hinds 1984b], there is a systematic violation of this general tendency in certain types of Japanese expository writing. This may best be seen through an examination of an expository essay. The essay to be examined was taken from the **Asahi Shimbun's** daily column **Tensei Jingo** "Vox Populi, Vox Dei." The English translation of this column appears one day later in the English language version of **Asahi Shimbun.** New paragraphs are indicated by a number in parentheses preceding the sentence.

(1) **shokudoo de waribashi o tsukau.**
We use "waribashi" (half-split throw away chopsticks) to eat.

tsukaisute de aru.
After use, they are thrown away.

suterareta hashi wa ittai doo naru no daroo.
What happens to them after they are thrown away?

mottainai na, to omou no wa senchuuha no ijimashisha daroo ka.
Is it merely the stinginess of those who lived through the war to feel that it is a waste?

(2) **aru shokudoo no hanashi de wa, mikka de ichimanbon no waribashi o tsukaisuteru to iu.**
According to the owner of one restaurant, his restaurant uses and throws away 10,000 pairs of chopsticks every three days.

nihon-zentai de wa, ki no waribashi wa ichinen ni yaku 100-oku-zen mo tsukawareru soo da.
In Japan as a whole, about 10,000 million pairs of wooden chopsticks are used each year.

sore dake no ryoo mokuzai ga ichido tsukawareta dake de, suterareru. kangaete mireba zeitaku na hanashi de aru.
That much wood is used just once and thrown away.

kami no genryoo ni suru tame kaishuu shi, saisei sareru to iu hanashi wa kikanai.
We have never heard about wooden chopsticks being collected and reused as raw material to make paper.

kaishuuhiyoo ga kakarisugite saisan ga awanai, to iu koto daroo ka.
Is it because it would not be a paying proposition since collecting the chopsticks would cost too much money?

(3) ***tabemono o kuchi ni hakobu no ni hashi o tsukau iwayuru hashi-bunkaken wa chuugoku, choosenhantoo, betonamu, soshite nihon, to natte iru.***

The so-called "chopsticks culture" sphere includes China, the Korean Peninsula, Vietnam, and Japan.

sono naka de mo nihon-igai no kuni wa hashi to saji no hiyoo de aru.

But all these other countries use spoons as well as chopsticks.

hashi o kihon to suru nihon-ryoori wa kiwamete tokui na sonzai na no da.

Japanese cooking which is based on chopsticks, is a very special thing.

(4) ***mukashi wa waribashi to ieba yoshino-san no sugi-bashi datta.***

Before the war, "waribashi" were Japanese cedar chopsticks from Yoshino.

yoshino no akasugi no hashi o te ni toru to, mizumizushii sugi no kaori ga suru.

When you pick up a pair of chopsticks made of red Japanese cedar from Yoshino, you can smell the fresh odor of the cedar.

karukute, yawarakami ga aru.

They are light and smooth to the touch.

masame ga sutto tootte ite sugata ga ii.

They are straightgrained and look good to the eye.

ichizen no sugibashi ni wa nihonjin no biishiki ga komerarete iru yoo ni omou.

We feel that the aesthetic feelings of the Japanese are concentrated in a pair of Japanese cedar chopsticks.

(5) ***rikyuu wa, kyaku o motenasu hi no asa, akasugi no hashizai o toridashi, ninsuu ni oojite hashi o kezuri, kezuritate no sugi no kaori o kyoo shita to iu densetsu ga aru.***

On the mornings of those days on which he was expecting visitors, the tea ceremony master Rikyu got out some red Japanese cedar wood and whittled just enough pairs of chopsticks for the expected number of visitors. He then presented the guests with the odor of freshly-cut Japanese cedar.

sore ga rikyuu-bashi no umare da.

This is the origin of the "Rikyu-bashi" (Rikyu chopsticks).

nihonjin wa hashi no atarashisa, kiyoraka na o mometa.

The Japanese demanded freshness and purity in their chopsticks.

(6) *jibun no hashi ga tanin ni tsukawareru koto, hito no hashi o tsukau koto o kirau no wa, keppekikan dake de wa nai.*

It is not just out of fastidiousness that the Japanese do not like others to use their chopsticks and also do not like to use the chopsticks of others.

mukashi no hito wa hashi ni wa sore o tsukau hito no reiryoku ga yadoru to shinjita. dakara jibun no reiryoku ga tadotta hashi o tanin ni tsukawaseru koto o kiratta no da, to iu setsu mo aru. (Honda Soichiro: *Hashi no Hon.*)

In ancient times, people believed that the spirit of the person resided in the chopsticks that he used and it is said that this is why people hated to have their chopsticks used by others. (*Hashi no Hon*—Book on Chopsticks—by Soichiro Honda.)

(7) *saikin wa hokkaidoo-san no, ezomatsu, kaba, shina nado de tsukurareta waribashi no zensei jidai de aru.*

It is now the heyday of "waribashi" made from the silver firs, birches and Japanese lindens of Hokkaido.

korera no waribashi ga tairyoo ni seisan sarehajimeta no wa koo-doseichooki ni haitte kara da.

These "waribashi" made from Hokkaido wood began to be produced in large quantities after the age of high economic growth started.

ima, demawatte iru waribashi no hanbun wa hokkaidoo-san da to omotte ii.

Half the "waribashi" used now are produced in Hokkaido.

(8) *waribashi no tsukaisute sono mono o futei suru tsumori wa nai.*

We have no intention of condemning the use-and-throw-away system in connection with "waribashi."

shikashi nenkan 100-okuzen-bun no ki ga sono mama kieshimau no wa ika ni mo mottainai.

But it is very wasteful when trees amounting to 10,000 millions pairs of wooden chopsticks disappear each year.

With the exception of the first paragraph, the initial noun phrase in each paragraph is marked by *wa*. There are, of course, other noun phrases marked by *wa*, but they will not be considered. The question to be asked is why each of these noun phrases can be marked by *wa*. To answer this question, it is necessary to understand the rhetorical pattern that organizes this essay.

The essay is organized according to a pattern known as *ki-shoo-ten-ketsu* [see Hinds 1983, 1984b]. This rhetorical style is described by Takemata (1976).

A. *ki* 結 First, begin one's argument.

B. *shoo* 起 Next, develop that.

C. *ten* 承 At the point where this development is finished, turn the idea to a subtheme where there is a connection, but not a directly connected association [to the major theme].

D. *ketsu* 転 Last, bring all of this together and reach a conclusion.

The version of the rhetorical pattern which is used in this essay has a proliferation of *ten*. This means that there are a number of tangentially related subtopics brought up with few overt transition markers. The function of each paragraph in this essay is listed in Table 4.

I will focus my remarks on paragraph 5. The overall topic of the essay is *waribashi*, or throwaway chopsticks. This topic is introduced and expanded in paragraphs 1 and 2. In paragraph 3, a different perspective on chopsticks is given; that is, that there are other "chopsticks cultures," but that Japan is unique in using only chopsticks and no other utensils. The theme of paragraph 4 is the material that goes into desirable chopsticks.

Paragraph 5 begins with the phrase *rikyuu wa*, which can perhaps be translated literally as "As for Rikyu." Rikyu is certainly not old, predictable information. The appearance of this noun phrase is unpredictable, yet it is marked by *wa*.

The function of *wa* in this case is a signal to the reader that the noun phrase so marked has some kind of connection with the overall theme of the essay. It informs the reader that there is in fact some connection, and that the reader should make an effort to place this noun phrase in its proper perspective in the essay as a whole. It tells the reader, in effect, that this noun phrase should be treated as if it were old, predictable information, even though it is not. In this respect, the function of *wa* when it marks the first noun phrase of a *ten* is very similar to English transition statements such as, "The following may seem to be unrelated to the major point, but the connection between Rikyu and chopsticks will become clear in due time."

	TABLE 4		
(1)	*ki*	(5)	*ten*
(2)	*shoo*	(6)	*ten*
(3)	*ten*	(7)	*ten*
(4)	*ten*	(8)	*ketsu*

Japanese readers, then, are required to build transitions themselves in the course of reading an essay organized along these lines. The responsibility for creating the bridge lies with the reader in Japanese, while it lies with the writer in English.

This may be seen more clearly by examining statements made by Clark and Haviland (1974) and Haviland and Clark (1974) with respect to the way information is comprehended. They claim that the primary function of language is to impart new information. Thus, the speaker's purpose is to provide new information while the listener's task is to extract this new information and to integrate it with old information already in memory. Haviland and Clark state:

> The listener's strategy, therefore, is to identify the syntactically marked Given and New information, treat the Given information as an address to information already in memory, and then integrate the New information into memory at that point (1974:513).

For Haviland and Clark, communicative success depends on how well the speaker has coded given and new information:

> The listener's success with the Given-New Strategy depends critically on whether the Given information, as so marked by the speaker, actually does match information already in memory. To borrow a term normally associated with pronominalization, the Given information must have an Antecedent in memory. If there is no Antecedent, the listener must construct one by elaborating information he already has, or he must construct one from scratch (1974:513).

Thus, for the Japanese reader, *wa* indicates that information is given, or old. This indicates that there should be an antecedent in memory. There is none, of course, in the example taken from *Tensei Jingo*. The Japanese reader, though, understands that it is the reader's responsibility to treat this noun phrase as if it were old information in order to integrate the new information in the paragraph into the appropriate place in memory.

While the facts involved in this description are straightforward, and the application to language typology relatively clear, the implications for ESL classrooms are less obvious. Numerous researchers have debated the role of transfer versus developmental processes in second language acquisition, and the findings reported here assume relevance only on the condition that transfer of native rhetorical patterns exists (cf. Kaplan 1966; Hinds 1983, 1984a). If this position is in fact correct, there are implications for classroom application. In addition to teaching students in ESL writing classes that there are differences in rhetorical styles between English and their native language, it may be necessary to take a further step and teach a new way to conceptualize the writing process. It may be necessary to instruct students from certain countries, such as Japan, that the writing process in English involves a different set of assumptions from the ones they are accustomed to working with. It is not enough for them to write with the view that there is a sympathetic reader who believes a reader's task is to ferret out whatever meaning the author has intended. Such non-native English writers will have to learn that effective written communication in English is the sole provenience of the writer.[3]

NOTES

1. I would like to thank Ulla Connor and Wako Hinds for specific comments that helped to strengthen this paper. Responsibility remains with the writer for errors of fact or judgment.

2. This is not an uncommon disclaimer in typological studies. Even Greenberg's word order taxonomy admits to variant possibilities under circumscribed situations. English, for example, an SVO language, allows OSV structures in such constructions as "Beans I like." Monane and Rogers also admit that Japanese, a situation-focus language, allows a variant person-focus construction. Thus, along with the situation-focus *kuruma ga aru*, "a car exists (= I have a car)," the person-focus construction *kuruma o motte-iru*, "I have a car," also exists.

3. As simplistic as this may sound, it will be instructive for some writers from Japan to be informed that even native speakers of English frequently go through several drafts of a paper before being satisfied that information is presented in the most effective way.

FOR STUDY AND DISCUSSION

1. What "folk evidence" can you find to support Hinds' notion that the need to speak and write clearly permeates English?

2. What is the difference between "intuiting" meaning from a text and drawing inferences from a text?

3. Hinds notes "the writer's task to provide appropriate transition statements so that the reader can piece together the thread of the writer's logic" in English. What kind of "appropriate transitions" does Hinds mean? Can you provide a taxonomy of such structures?

4. Hinds suggests that *coherence* in texts is due to unity and appropriate transitions between expressed ideas. What is your own definition of coherence? How is it different from cohesion?

5. Choose a newspaper article written in English and analyze it for its unity as Hinds has done, noting the degree of inferencing readers need to make. Compare with Hinds' Japanese passage.

Chapter 9

Written Academic Discourse in Korean: Implications for Effective Communication

William G. Eggington
Darwin Institute of Technology

This paper has two main purposes: the first, to conduct a general overview of Korean academic written discourse; and the second, to investigate an interesting feature of modern Korean discourse style.

WRITTEN DISCOURSE FEATURES

Although greatly influenced by China throughout their cultural heritage, the Korean people have been able to develop a distinctively Korean culture, philosophical approach, and artistic method—factors which, following Kaplan's (1972) assertion of the relationship between culture and discourse patterns, have contributed to equally distinctive rhetorical styles. In the following section, certain salient features of written Korean discourse will be briefly examined.

Korean discourse structure is described by Kaplan as being

> . . . marked by what may be called an approach by indirection. In this kind of writing the development of the paragraph may be said to be "turning and turning in a widening gyre." The circles or gyres turn around the subject and show it from a variety of tangential views,

but the subject is never looked at directly. Things are developed in terms of what they are not, rather than in terms of what they are (1972:46).

Example 1, which together with the ensuing samples has been translated from Korean, supports Kaplan's notion. From the initial sentence, the topic of the discourse unit, one is led away from, and then back to the subject, which is renewed in the first sentence of the second paragraph.

Example 1:

Foreigners who reside in Korea as well as those who study the Korean language in foreign countries are, despite their deep interest, ignorant of the basis on which the Korean alphabet, Hangul, was formulated. The Korean alphabet, composed of combinations of lines and curves, at first seems more difficult than Japanese kana for those who use the Roman alphabet, and as the combination of vowels and consonants multiplies, it appears more difficult to memorize all the combinations. This seemingly complicated combination of vowels and consonants can, on the contrary, be mastered with no more effort than is needed to learn the Roman alphabet or Japanese kana, for one must merely memorize two dozen vowels and consonants, the principal letters of the Korean alphabet.

The principal concern of foreign as well as Korean scholars has been on what foundation the Korean alphabet was formulated (Kang and Kim 1979:5).

Example 2 defines the topic in terms of what it is not rather than what it is.

Example 2:

The sounds of these five words are of the same kind as *k, t, p, s, ch,* however they are named hard sounds because the sounds are harder than *k, t, p, s, ch.* Some people think that these sounds are the same as *g, d, b, z, j,* because *st, sp, ps, sch* which are used with *g, d, b* as sounds today are combination words. And some people say, "The words which mark hard sounds are *sk, st, sp.*" They say, "*g, d, b* are not Korean. These were made to mark Chinese." So they wanted to take *g, d, b* out of Korean (Lee 1973:60).

Note also the use of the "some people say" formula, which appears very common in Korean discourse when one is taking a somewhat controversial stand, either to protect one's own position by enlisting anonymous support, or to appear not too direct when criticizing another's position. In a debate conducted in a national journal over the inclusion of Chinese characters in the public school curriculum, a professor of Liberal Arts and Sciences at Seoul National University used this formula, or one of its variations, seven times in a four-page article. Variations of the formula included "some claim that . . .," "some scholars have . . .," "there are men who . . .," "a professor whom I know . . .," "it is grievous to find some men holding the position that . . .," and "it is also said that . . ." (Huh 1972). This may also be indicative of an oral influence on written discourse (Ong 1979).

An example of extended discourse comes from an article (Pae 1982) taken from the English edition (a direct translation of the Korean edition) of the *Korean Times*, one of the major newspapers in Korea. The author, Pae Yang-seo, is a Hanyang University professor. In the interests of space a paragraph-by-paragraph synopsis is given here.

Example 3:

Paragraph #1.

The Ministry of Home Affairs is planning to lengthen the period of training for public officials from 3 days to 6 days per year in order to solidify the spirituality of the public officials. The training is to be conducted at the Spiritual Cultural Institute which is rendered in English as the Institute for Korean Studies.

Paragraph #2.

A new meaning of "national" is attached to the word "spiritual." Perhaps this comes from the term "spiritual culture."

Paragraph #3.

A member of the Korean Alphabet Society complained that the architectural design of the Institute for Korean Studies resembles a Buddhist Temple and thus is not Korean. This is not so because Buddhism, though imported from India, is a Korean religion. Likewise Christianity is a Korean religion.

Paragraph #4.

Any attempt to label what is national and what is foreign fails.

Paragraph #5.

Perhaps too much emphasis on nationalism may do more harm than good.

Paragraph #6.

Instead of inspiring nationalism we should be appealing to universal reason and proper moral conduct. The civil spirit must take precedence over the national spirit.

Paragraph #7.

I am reminded of this when, changing trains at the subway, I witness the rush to occupy seats on route to the sports center where the Olympic Games are to be held. How do we enhance the nation's prestige through a sports event? As a teacher I am partly responsible for this situation.

Paragraph #8.

Spiritual poverty is best observed in a metropolitan area like Seoul. Why is our public transport system so multi-layered with standing buses at the bottom, then regular buses charging three times more than standing buses, and finally taxis which move constantly to catch more passengers?

Paragraph #9.

Once you catch a taxi you have to listen to the loud radio controlled by the driver.

Paragraph #10.

"Dear administrators, please do not talk about spiritual things unless you are interested in implementing concrete ethical conduct."

Thus, commencing with a search for a definition of "spiritual" by alluding to a government retraining program and the name of, and architectural style of, the building the program is to be held in, the main point, that civil spirit should take precedence over national spirit, is reached in paragraph #6. From a western English interpretation, loosely related examples of spiritual poverty are then given, including a description of the subway rush hour, a mention of the Olympic Games, a description of the transit system in the city, and finally a complaint about loud radios in taxis. The brief conclusion is an appeal not to think about spirituality until a level of ethical conduct is reached. The organization of the article appears to follow the indirect patterns shown in the previous paragraph examples. The main idea of the article is briefly stated halfway through the article and alluded to in the conclusion. There is no direct development of this theme, but rather from an English perspective, what is developed is a view of what the main idea is not.

Hinds (1982) has shown that one of the preferred rhetorical patterns of Japanese (*ki-shoo-ten-ketsu*) has its origin in classical Chinese poetry, where the first section (*ki*) begins the argument, the second section (*shoo*) develops the argument, the third section (*ten*), immediately after finishing the argument, abruptly changes the direction of the argument towards an indirectly connected sub-theme, and the fourth section (*ketsu*) reaches a conclusion. A Korean preferred rhetorical structure, *ki-sung-chon-kyul*, appears to follow the same pattern—a pattern which may be seen in Example 3 where paragraph #1 begins the argument; paragraphs #2, #3, #4, #5 loosely develop that argument, paragraph #6 states the main point of the argument; paragraphs #7, #8, #9 state concepts indirectly connected with the argument; and paragraph #10 concludes the main theme.

In contrast to American students who receive substantial instruction in structural rhetoric, Korean students are not exposed to formal instruction on writing styles. Models, such as the above mentioned *ki-sung-chon-kyul*, are given in discussions of literature, and students are asked to emulate them in their writing. In discussion between this researcher and a number of Korean students, mention was made by the Koreans that, if one wishes to write academic prose, one writes in the *ki-sung-chon-kyul* style, leaving out the *chon* (change) stage, thus creating a "beginning, development, end" pattern. Although this may bear some resemblance to the preferred English rhetorical pattern of "introduction, body, conclusion," the Korean interpretation of "beginning," "development," and "end" appears to be different from the American equivalents, as can be seen in Examples 1, 2, and 3. One can presume that Koreans would have little difficulty in gaining a clear understanding of the above texts and would not view them as being "out of focus" as native English speakers would. It appears that the discourse styles shown above constitute the preferred rhetorical pattern of Korean academic writing.

However, another rhetorical style is evident when one surveys Korean academic journals of the type written in Korean and English and especially when one concentrates on articles written by those authors who publish in both Korean and English and have earned academic degrees in English-speaking universities. The following example, translated from Korean, taken from a Korean-English journal published in Korea, written by a scholar who also contributes to the journal in English, and who has degrees from an American university, shows a linear, general-to-specific rhetorical pattern which, despite being slightly non-idiomatic, appears to be coherent and cohesive.

Example 4:

However the following problem is not solved by the [above] methodology. This problem is the fact that the effect of the "Saemaeul Movement" as well as any other effects, are part of natural changes of life. That is to say that this is a problem of history, and historical change. This means that the elevation of the standard of living on the farming and fishing communities is effected by the rapid progress of various economic fields, the construction of facilities and the improvement of international trade (Kim 1979:135).

It would appear that some Korean scholars who seem to be more proficient in English exhibit certain aspects of a linear structure in their Korean writing as seen in Example 4, while Korean scholars who are not proficient in English and who have not studied at English-speaking universities, exhibit the particular non-linear rhetorical patterns illustrated in Examples 1, 2, and 3.

A rather clear contrast between the more traditional rhetorical pattern and the apparently English-influenced pattern can be seen by examining any number of volumes on Korean-related studies containing contributions from Korean scholars. For the sake of the reader who may not be proficient in Korean, a brief examination of a journal containing articles written by Korean scholars which have either been written in English or translated into English is given below. The volume under examination (Sohn 1975) contains nine articles, eight written by Korean scholars and one by an American scholar. Six of the eight Korean scholars hold positions in American universities. Seven of the eight articles written by Korean scholars are structured in the organizational style typically found in most English academic journals, with an introduction containing a statement of the purpose of the paper and a thesis statement, a review of the literature, an examination of the subject, and a conclusion followed by a bibliography. Examination of these bibliographies shows a significant number of citations referencing English sources. One article, the eighth, however, has seven bibliographic citations all referencing Chinese or Korean sources; there are no references to English sources in the article. An examination of the article shows no statement of purpose; for the reader unfamiliar with Korean rhetorical patterns, there appears to be no thesis development, but rather a list of points revolving loosely around an unstated central theme. The brief conclusion of the article is as follows:

> In this paper I have raised a small problem in the structure of middle Korean, and I have tried to explain my own view on the structure of plosives of Middle Korean, particularly on the problems of doen-shori (alpapranas) (Gim 1975:100).

This is the first time the reader is informed of the purpose of the paper. Obviously Gim is employing a different rhetorical pattern than the other seven Korean contributors to the journal. The fact that Gim references only Korean sources and that he is teaching in a Korean university may lead one to suspect that the rhetorical style he employs is one which has not been much influenced by English patterns; whereas the many English references cited by the other seven authors, as well as the fact that six of the seven are employed at American universities, would suggest that these scholars have been influenced by English rhetorical patterns.

It is interesting to note a finding by Clyne, who states, in his discussion of English/German rhetorical patterns, that:

There appear to be some disciplines (e.g., mathematics, engineering) in which German scientists have adopted a basically linear discourse structure. This may be conditioned by the discipline or by leadership in the discipline of English speakers. In other fields of science (e.g., chemistry), the non-linear structure is quite common in German (1981:64).

Perhaps the academic rhetorical patterns of many languages of the world are adjusting to fit a linear style. Gonzalez notes, in a description of the languages of the Philippines, that a priest will commence his sermon in the local language, but "switches to English if the topic is academic and theological in nature, a function of the probability that the preacher did his studies primarily in English during his seminary days" (Gonzalez 1981:55).

If such a code switch is possible in oral discourse, it seems plausible that Korean scholars, for example, who have studied in the United States and who have been immersed in English for an extended period of time, have also been immersed in the written discourse features of English. Indeed most of the scholars' knowledge was gained, developed, discussed, argued, expounded, and defended in the rhetorical patterns of written English. Upon returning to Korea, these scholars may have been required to transfer knowledge gained in English into Korean. Obviously there would have been some difficulty, for Korean does not have the direct lexical equivalents of English. Another more subtle problem emerges, however. As previously indicated, English has rhetorical patterns different from Korean that may cause the writer either: (1) to adjust concepts developed in the preferred rhetorical style of English to fit the rhetorical patterns of Korean; (2) to translate the language from English to Korean, but retain the rhetorical patterns of English; (3) to develop some compromise between the rhetorical patterns of Korean and English. All three choices would seem to present impediments to effective communication. The previous discussion would indicate that many Korean scholars are (consciously or unconsciously) adopting the second of the choices; that is, writing in Korean while retaining the rhetorical structures of English. Thus, Koreans unfamiliar with English and its rhetorical patterns will find information presented in the English-preferred rhetorical patterns difficult to comprehend, even though that information is presented in written Korean.

The concept that differences in rhetorical patterns between writer and reader hinder optimal communication can be verified by reference to, for example, Clyne, who in a discussion of the English linear versus the German non-linear structure reports:

> The English translation of Norbert Dittmar's book, *Soziolinguistik*, a landmark in the development of sociolinguistics in West Germany, was described by Bills (1979) as "chaotic" and criticized for its "lack of focus and cohesiveness," "haphazardness of presentation," and "desultory organization." None of the four reviews of the original written by scholars from Central European universities (Rein 1974; Geye 1974; Leodolter 1974; Purcha 1974) make any criticism of this kind (Clyne 1981:64).

Obviously the translators of *Soziolinguistik* translated the language but not the discourse structure, and since one must presume that important information can be lost when one is reading "chaotic" material, the English speaking, non-German speaking, student must be missing vital information when reading the English version of *Soziolinguistik* because of the difference in rhetorical styles between these two languages. Thus, in many fields of German-English scholarship some breakdowns in communication must be caused by scholars trying to put English rhetorical patterns into German and German rhetorical patterns into English. If difficulties of this type exist between such linguistically related languages as German and English, one must presume that there will be significant difficulties between such linguistically more distant languages as English and Korean.

Krulee, Fairweather, and Berquist (1979) have supported the concept that optimal information transfer occurs when the organizational structure of a unit of written discourse agrees with the reader's preconceived notions of what that structure should be. These authors have shown that subjects are better able to comprehend and recall information when the discourse structure and the subject's personal organizational structure are compatible. Hinds (1983c) has also demonstrated a similar finding cross-culturally. Japanese students and English-speaking American students were asked to read and then recall, immediately and then after a week, information contained in an essay written in one of the desired rhetorical patterns of Japanese. The essays were in the respective subject's native language. Results indicated that there is "a difference in the ability of Japanese and English readers to retain information in memory, depending on the organizational schema in which the information is presented" (1983c:22). The Japanese readers were able to retain information better than the English readers because the Japanese readers were operating within a familiar rhetorical framework.

Such research is of importance when consideration is given to the huge amounts of information currently being transferrred, not only cross-linguistically, but cross-culturally as well. Hinds (1983c) verifies the position first taken by Kaplan (1966) that culturally influenced rhetorical patterns play an important role in effective communication through the written medium. It may be that, in the case of Korea, the English-influenced linear style some scholars prefer represents an impediment to effective communication between those scholars and other Korean scholars, as well as the general Korean public, who prefer the more traditional discourse patterns and who have had only limited exposure to the linear structures. In other words, do Koreans regard the linear structure of the type shown in Example 4 as being as unclear as English speakers would regard the non-linear structure shown in Examples 1, 2, and 3?

A preliminary investigation of this question was undertaken by collecting a corpus of eight samples of academic Korean writing. Four of the samples followed the preferred non-linear style of Korean while the remaining four followed the linear patterns of English. The eight samples dealt with public administration, political science, and linguistics, and were carefully selected to be comparable in content complexity. Fourteen Korean students who had all been in the United States for less than six months, and who had beginning ability in English, were asked to rank the samples from easiest to read to most difficult to read. If discourse structure had an effect on the ranking, it was predicted that the samples following the preferred Korean discourse pattern (sample numbers 1, 3, 4, and 6) would be judged easier to read than the sample which followed the English-influenced linear rhetorical pattern (sample numbers 2, 5, 7, and 8). The results indicated that samples 1, 3, 4, and 6 were ranked as being easier to read 71% of all the choices available, and samples, 2, 5, 7, and 8 were ranked as being more difficult to read 69% of all the available choices.

Thus, although it was recognized that the research technique was rather crude, the results stimulated further research in this area. Another study was conducted using the research design developed by Hinds (1983c). The hypothesis of this study is that Korean speakers will be better able to reproduce information presented in the more traditional non-linear rhetorical framework than information presented in the linear rhetorical pattern frequently used by Korean scholars who have been influenced by the preferred rhetorical pattern of academic English.

METHOD

Subjects

Thirty-seven Korean adults newly arrived in the United States were asked to participate voluntarily in the study. Twenty-eight of the participants were college students in Korea and were planning to attend an American college once they had an acceptable English competency, while the remaining nine participants were more mature adults who planned to enter the workforce at the completion of an intensive English course. Ten of the subjects had been used in the pilot study.

Materials

Two paragraphs from separate articles in the October 1980 edition of the *Korean Journal of Public Administration* were selected. One of the paragraphs (Example 5) reflects the non-linear preferred rhetorical style of Korean written academic discourse. A simplified discourse analysis of the English translation of the paragraph is given below. The bracketed numbers are not part of the text and are included to identify sentences to assist in the discussion of the text.

Example 5:

[1] We intend to describe the general decision making process in Korean Government administrative offices in this report. [2] The term administrative organization means the housing, department, place and office structure of the office. [3] The purpose of this report is to research the decision making process. [4] However the theory of office decisions is developed by involving formal and informal aspects. [5] Therefore this distinction is for convenient management. [6] Because the nature of office management is very complicated, my thinking, to help in understanding it, is to divide it into business, place, formal and informal parts (Cho 1980:248).

This paragraph begins with a statement of purpose in the first sentence. The second sentence is subordinated to the first by giving a definition regarding the administrative organization of an office. The third sentence runs parallel to the discussion of the purpose of the text begun in the first sentence and does not seem to have any linear relationship with the second sentence. The fourth sentence seems to be more related to the second sentence than to the third sentence by its reference to office procedures and the separation of that theme into formal and informal aspects. The fifth sentence is subordinated to the fourth sentence by giving an explanation of why the distinctions are made. The sixth and final sentence continues the divisions begun in the fourth sentence and seems to be an expansion of the fourth sentence and not related to the fifth sentence. The paragraph development appears to follow a two strand ordering, which may be graphically depicted as:

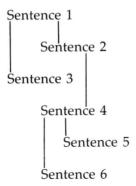

The other paragraph (Example 6) was written in a more linear style. The English translation of the text is given below. Once again the bracketed numbers identify sentences and are not part of the original text.

Example 6:

[1] In order to use the collective goods approach, it is necessary to characterize the cultural values of the social environment so that ramifications can be subdivided which enable individual preferences to be developed. [2] In general, "cultural values" may be regarded as a stock of institutionalized survival strategies written by present attitudinal and behavioral rules. [3] Cultural values can be conceptualized in this way because all societies make forms of values and rules through the mutual reaction between the individual and the group. [4] If these values and rules are instituted, they have a tendency to continue under a neutral, or even a little hostile environment (Hoon 1980:15).

The first sentence explains the rationale of the following discussion. The second sentence is subordinated to the first by explaining in more specific detail the term "cultural values." The third sentence shows why "cultural values" can be explained in this particular way and appears to be coordinate to the second sentence. The fourth sentence is subordinated to the third by its expansion of the "values and rules" concept introduced in the third sentence. The organization of this paragraph follows a hierarchical subordinate-coordinate structure common in English academic writing (McDaniel 1980), and may be graphically represented as:

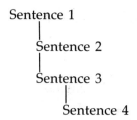

As previous research (Eggington 1983) has indicated, many Koreans have difficulty comprehending Chinese characters that are often inserted into Korean academic texts for no apparent communicative function. Since the ability to comprehend Chinese characters was not the purpose of this study, this distraction was removed and the subjects were given the paragraphs written only in Hangul (the indigenous Korean script). Thus, except for the replacement of the Chinese characters with Hangul, the paragraphs are natural in the sense that the words and the discourse elements remain exactly as they are in the original journal articles.

Procedure

The subjects were divided into two groups, one receiving the Korean version of Example 5, and the other receiving the Korean version of Example 6. The subjects were asked to read and study the paragraphs for two minutes and were told that they would be required to recall as much information from the paragraphs as they could. After two minutes the paragraphs were taken away; the subjects were given a blank piece of paper and were requested to write all that they remembered from the paragraph within eight minutes. At the conclusion of this task, the subjects were asked to return the following week for another test. Upon their return, the subjects were asked once again to reproduce as much as they could remember of the paragraph they had been exposed to the week before.

Scoring

A clausal analysis of the original paragraphs was conducted. It was found that, in Korean, Example 5 contained nine clauses, and Example 6 contained eleven clauses. The subjects' responses were also analyzed in the same fashion by three independent raters who were unfamiliar with the purposes of the research. Responses were scored on a five-point scale so that, if the information contained in a subject's clause agreed exactly with the original, then a score of 1 was assigned to the recalled clause; partial agreement resulted in a score of 2, 3, or 4 depending on the closeness of the information in the subject's clause to the original, while total disagreement, or no mention of the clause, resulted in a score of 5. Thus the higher the score, the less information was recalled. No penalty was given for any new information not found in the original, and the particular ordering of the recalled clauses had no effect on the scoring system.

Statistical Analysis

A standard two-tailed parametric T-test was used to test the reproduction differences between the traditional Korean text and the linear text in both immediate and delay conditions.

Results

Table 1 shows the mean of each group, the standard deviation from the mean, and the results of the T-tests. The null hypothesis of this study is that the means of the recalled scores of the traditional non-linear text will be statistically equal to their linear counterparts; i.e.,

$$X[nli] = X[li]$$

and

$$X[nld] = X[ld]$$

where

X = sample mean of the recalled averages
nli = the non-linear text in the immediate recall condition
li = the linear text in the immediate recall condition
nld = the non-linear text in the delayed recall condition
ld = the linear text in the delayed recall condition

The T-test analysis revealed that in the immediate recall condition, the differences in the means of the groups were not sufficient to reject the null hypothesis. Thus, in the immediate condition the subjects were

		TABLE 1		
	nli	*li*	*nld*	*ld*
Mean	3.49	3.73	3.73	4.47
St. Dev.	0.50	0.52	0.48	0.31

Two-tailed T-test for immediate condition (i.e., *nli* and *li*) 1.22 (NS)
Two-tailed T-test for delayed condition (i.e., *nld* and *ld*) 4.80 (prob < .001)
df = 25 for both tests.

able to recall approximately the same amount of information from both the traditional text and the linear text. However, in the delayed condition there were significant differences ($p < .001$). Thus, in the delayed condition the null hypothesis is rejected, and the assumption can be made that Koreans do have more difficulty recalling information after a period of time when that information is presented in a linear rhetorical style.

DISCUSSION

If reading is to be considered a "psycholinguistic guessing game," as Goodman (1970:93) has posited, then readers and writers have certain built-in expectations about the ordering of ideas in any stretch of discourse. In an optimal condition, the reader shares the same expectations of what is to follow what as does the writer. Breakdowns in communication between writer and reader occur when these expectations are violated (Martin 1980; Clyne 1980). Studies by Kintsch and Greene (1978), Meyer (1975b), and Thorndyke (1979) have shown the relationship between long-term memory recall and the particular organization through which information was presented. Over a delayed condition, information is retained far better when it is presented in a manner compatible with the reader's expectations. It would appear that this present study verifies these findings. Of more importance than the verifications, however, is the fact that the texts used in the study were written by Koreans for Korean consumption, and that the information contained within the texts has potential importance to the development of the Korean nation.

If, as this study indicates, a significant portion of Korean academic prose is written in a linear style, and if, as this study also indicates, significant segments of the Korean population, including college students, are unable to retain the information presented in this linear style as well as they can retain information presented in a more traditional non-linear style, then written academic communication in Korea must be suffering. Clearly, the size of the data base in this study is too small to permit any generalization, yet some preliminary recommendations will be attempted.

IMPLICATIONS
AND RECOMMENDATIONS

If the government of the Republic of South Korea wishes to continue its objective of modernizing the Korean society, then it must recognize that a key factor in this development is the creation of a highly efficient and openly available system of information storage and retrieval. Such a system does not come about through natural processes. The present system has the potential of creating an elite group of Korean academics who have had sufficient exposure to English education to enable them to acquire English as well as the preferred rhetorical patterns of English and thus be able to tap into the vast amount of current information available in English.

Another group of Korean scholars, numbering more than the preceding group, have not had the opportunity to acquire English, let alone the preferred rhetorical patterns of English, and thus must rely on their more fortunate colleagues to share that information with them. However, as the preceding study has shown, one group in this process of communication is using one written rhetorical pattern while the other group is using a different written rhetorical pattern—a situation which inhibits information recall and the optimal transfer of vital knowledge, as well as the optimal development of the nation.

It seems that a number of options are available to Korean educational authorities, should they desire to improve the present situation. At the present time there does not appear to be an academic written rhetorical component in the Korean educational system, but rather an informal system in which students in elementary and secondary schools are exposed to the rhetorics of classical literature and told that they should emulate these styles in their writing. Tertiary education places little importance on written style. What is needed, then, is the introduction of instruction in writing into the system. It would smack of linguistic imperialism if one were to advocate the preferred linear rhetorical pattern of academic English as the only rhetorical style to be taught in this curriculum. A better approach would be to teach both the traditional Korean styles and the English-influenced academic style. But it seems clear that the problem of differing rhetorical styles in Korean deserves serious attention.

FOR STUDY AND DISCUSSION

1. Compare Eggington's findings with those of Hinds. Are they compatible?

2. Take the English translation of the Japanese text offered by Hinds and the English translation of the Korean text offered by Eggington and count in each the five types of topical structures identified by Lautamatti. Compare your results with those provided by Lautamatti. Explain any variations.

3. Both Hinds and Eggington talk about an implied "contract" between reader and writer and the notion that readers expect information to be provided in certain order. If their contentions are valid, is cross-cultural communication possible? Why or why not?

4. Carrell talks about understanding of top-level rhetorical structure as being necessary to comprehension and recollection of texts read and ordering of texts written. Eggington makes certain policy recommendations deriving from the comparison of rhetorical styles in Korean and English. Is there any connection between the two discussions? What is that connection? Does Carrell's discussion help to clarify Eggington's point?

5. Eggington suggests that, in developing countries (e.g., Korea), access to scientific and technical literature (essential for modernization) may be enhanced by introducing into the indigenous (national) language a "linear" rhetorical mode like that in English science and technology texts. Would it be more efficient simply to teach English? If it were more efficient to introduce English language teaching, what would be the implications for ESL as a field? Where would the teachers be drawn from? Which English might be taught? What sorts of materials might be used? At which grade level might instruction best begin?

Chapter 10

English in Parallels: A Comparison of English and Arabic Prose

Shirley E. Ostler
University of Southern California

INTRODUCTION

The thesis of this paper is that various cultures organize the development of ideas differently when writing expository prose and that these differences persist when speakers of these cultures learn to write in a new language. The structure of twenty-one expository essays, written in English by Saudi Arabian students, is compared with writing by native-English speakers. The quantitative measures used are the T-unit and the Discourse Bloc; both clearly show the distinctive differences in written form between cultures. The implication is that ESL teachers need first to appreciate the differences in rhetoric in different cultures and then learn to teach these distinctions, as an aid to improving both the reading and writing skills of their students.

This paper seeks to answer, at least in part, the question of why, when Arabic-speaking students seem to have mastered most of the English grammatical forms and idioms, they still produce "foreign sounding" essays, and why it is that experienced ESL writing teachers can identify Arabic-speaking students' English essays as having been written by Arabic-speakers, even when these essays are free of grammatical errors. Following is an essay written by an Arabic-speaking student under test conditions:

1[1]   We face two serious problems on my country. The first problem is that we import many things from other countries and we cannot depend on ourselves in producing the things we need. We import different kinds of food, electric materials, cars and chothes [*sic*].

The second problem is that we depend on one source of income and that is the oil. Our national economy depends on it. We have a lot of revenues each year from oil export that come to us from selling this material. It is not good for our country to depend only on one source and it has to vary its resources. We can't insure that the oil will be enough forever.

We can solve the first problem by building many factories and we have to develop our soil to be useful to agriculture. We have to form educated people to serve and to develop their country. We can solve the second problem by seeking for other resources that we have in my country not to depend on one source like oil. Finally we will become a developed country and we can insure our future and our life.

This student writes English fairly well. He makes only five grammatical and seven lexical errors, and one spelling mistake. Further, the essay is well organized, beginning with a clearly defined topic sentence, the predicate of which is well supported. All of the syntactic devices which an ESL teacher teaches to students this writer seems to use with relative ease and yet, even if all of the errors are corrected, this sample would still sound foreign.

The primary hypothesis of this paper is that the cause of this "foreignness" derives from the rhetorical pattern used in this and other essays written in English by Arabic-speakers. This rhetorical form reflects that employed in Classical Arabic, a form which differs in several ways from that used by modern English writers.

It is difficult to discuss the differences in rhetorical form across cultures; relatively little linguistic research has been done on written discourse in English beyond the level of the sentence. Keenan and Bennett (1977), Loban (1976), and Hunt (1965) all use written discourse for part or all of their data base, but their concerns are syntactic.

However, there have been a few exceptions. Winterowd (1967, 1970) argues that there are regular relationships in written discourse which create coherence, and that if a paragraph is a recognizable convention, then there must be a "discoverable grammar of form" for units larger than the sentence. Christensen (1963, 1967) began work on the functional integrity of the paragraph, and Pitkin (1969) elucidated and expanded Christensen's concepts. Looking for an index to reflect the relationships among ideas as well as the relationships among blocs of ideas in context, Pitkin developed the Discourse Bloc.

The above studies addressed themselves to written English discourse. Kaplan (1972) argues not only that there is a regularity to discourse patterns in English, but that this pattern is contrastive across cultures, that the writing of individuals will reflect the rhetorical patterns esteemed in their native cultures, and that, when individuals write in other than their native languages, they tend to use their native patterns in that discourse. This paper is designed to probe the validity of Kaplan's contention, at least in terms of the comparison of two rhetorics, those of English speakers and of Arabic-speaking Saudi Arabian writers.

Specifically, the hypothesis of this paper is that the rhetoric of Classical Arabic is closely tied to the system of that language, that this rhetoric differs in several ways from that used by native English writers, and that the differences between the rhetoric used by English writers and that used by Arabic-speaking students writing in English can be shown quantitatively. Two corpora are analyzed—an English corpus of ten paragraphs, each selected at random from ten English publications, and an Arabic corpus of twenty-two short essays written in English by Saudi Arabian students. Two quantitative measures are used—the Pitkin (1969) Discourse Bloc as modified by Kaplan (1972) and Kellog Hunt's (1965) T-unit. However, before describing the method of data collection and analysis, it is important to describe the rhetorics of the two languages under discussion.

THE EVOLUTION
OF RHETORIC IN THE
ENGLISH LANGUAGE

English, like all other natural languages, was once an oral language; that is, the majority of its speakers were not literate. However, as it became a literate language, its rhetorical patterns evolved from those in which copia was achieved through the use of formulaic expressions to those esteeming originality and creative thought, its syntax from one of repetitive parallels and rhythmic balance to a preference for deletion and subordination. The oral style probably reached its pinnacle in the work of the late-sixteenth-century writer John Lyly. His style, known for its balance, antithesis, parallelism, alliteration, assonance, and rhyme, its emphasis of sound over sense, had its beginnings with the rhetorical development in ancient Greece; but before Lyly's death the influence of Ramus and the rising influence of the middle class in England had already signaled the end of such elaboration as a productive style in English (Houppert 1975; Scollon and Scollon 1981).

This is not to say that the oral traditions disappeared in the sixteenth century. The King James translation of the Bible is rich in examples of metrically balanced parallel constructions; the Psalms in the Old Testament and the Beatitudes in the New Testament are only two of many examples. Ong (1972) notes that copia, so highly prized by the humanist, was achieved through the use of "commonplaces," formulaic phrases which could be combined to produce elaborately developed discourse. Milton published his own collection of commonplaces. The most readily accessible example of the use of commonplaces for the modern scholar would be the Preface to the King James Bible.

These oral characteristics slowly disappeared as literacy became more general among English speakers. Ong (1972) considers the eighteenth century "a significant watershed dividing a residually oral culture from the typological culture," but he notes that the use of oral structures still continued in many settings. Charles Dickens' success in giving platform readings of his novels is directly attributable to his skill as an "oral writer," and McGuffey's *Eclectic Readers* (regularly published and revised between 1836 and 1920) introduced their readers to "sound-conscious" literature intended to train students to become adroit public speakers (Ong 1979). Thus, it was not until perhaps the early part of this century that the modern style of subordination and deletion became preferred over repetition. In modern English, alliteration has given way to end rhyme, the repetition of parallel constructions has been replaced by deletion and subordination, commonplaces are now considered clichés. Indeed, a modern English rhetoric (Birk and Birk 1972) warns students that the repetition of sound, sentence length, or sentence structure are undesirable because they "will be irritating to the reader or lull him into disinterest."

THE RHETORIC OF ARABIC

In contrast to the evolution of English from an oral to a literate language, Classical Arabic is still closely tied to oral traditions. Prior to the rise of Islam, Arabic had developed a rich oral tradition of elaborate poetry and rhymed prose. During the lifetime of Mohammed (A.D. 570–632), reading and writing were generally available for commercial uses only. Mohammed himself was probably illiterate and dictated many of the *suras* of the *Qu'ran* to *huffaz* (memorizers). The first Caliph began collecting these *suras*, and the second Caliph put them into book form about A.D. 651. So, although there are a few inscriptions in Arabic on a tombstone dated A.D. 328 and two similar ones from the fifth or sixth century, the *Qu'ran* is the earliest surviving document of written Arabic. The transcription of the oral literature began in the eighth and ninth centuries. Some of these transcribed works, among which is "The Seven Odes," are still popular today (Bateson 1967; Chejne 1969; Beeston 1970).

Thus, even though the language of the *Qu'ran* is written, its structure is oral. Indeed, the word *qu'ran* means reading or recitation. As was once done (and in some instances still is) with the traditional Christian scriptural literature, so in the mosques and marketplaces of the Islamic world, Moslems sit today, rhythmically swaying as they chant its verses.

The influence of Islam spread rapidly across Africa and Asia Minor into India, but with its success came the problems of language change. In the eighth century, scholars of the *Qu'ran*, concerned that Classical Arabic would be reshaped by these new languages into structures so different that the sacred language used by the Prophet Mohammed would be lost, devised an elaborate science of Arabic grammar and lexicography, and linked instruction in language to the study of the *Qu'ran* in the schools. The results are that, eleven centuries later, virtually this same grammar is taught in Arabic schools. Although a diglossic condition (Ferguson 1959) has developed among native Arabic-speakers, Classical Arabic has been preserved (Beeston 1970).

Ferguson (1968) describes how fond the Arabs are of their language. He notes that when classical poetry or formal or semiformal oratory is being recited, both the speaker and the listeners become deeply involved emotionally with the rhythms and phonetic symbolism. Even illiterate peasants prefer the highly literate, Classical Arabic, which they perhaps only partially understand, to the vernacular in which they are fluent. As was true in the England of John Lyly, the beauty of form is valued more highly than content (Houppert 1975).

Not only is written Arabic bound philosophically to the *Qu'ran*, but the very structure of the language, the frequent and diverse use of parallel constructions, seem to be those of the *Qu'ran*. Syntactically, the language seems to strive for a balance, a rhythmical coordination, between related components. This symmetry can be shown in the determination of sentential word order, the use of the adjective, and the formation of the relative clause.

One way that sentential balance is achieved is through the determination of word order (Wright 1862; Beeston 1970). Native Arabic-speaking grammarians say that there are two parts to a sentence, a subject and a predicate. The relationship between them is said to have "the relation of attribution, the act of leaning (one thing against another)" (Wright 1862). The language, for example, requires a maximal break in the sentence between the theme and predicate in thematic structures and between the verb and the agent in verbal structures. This break must occur about halfway through the total length of the sentence, as determined by the number of lexical items, and sentence order is arranged so that the predicate can remain at midpoint (Beeston 1970). From the introductory essay comes an example of such a verbal construction:

1   Our national economy (3) depends on it. (3)

and from another essay a thematic sentence:

> 7   The family plans and enjoyments is (6)
>   to be shared for all of them. (7)

(The parentheses indicate the number of lexical items in each part of the
sentence, and XXX indicate indecipherable items.) Though word order
cannot be altered with as much facility in English as it can be in Arabic,
the Arabic-speaking students who wrote the essays used as the corpus
in this study still manage to construct sentences that have equal balance
between subject and predicate.

Rhythmical balance is also achieved in the adjectival modification of
a noun. In Arabic there is no word class as such for adjectives. Historically, nouns and their modifiers were a coordination between two nouns,
similar to the appositive *James, the king* (Beeston 1970). In the Arabic corpus are found sentences that illustrate this coordination:

> 5   We have to put a new system for our education.
> 18 . . . the owner of it each of them.

There is always a danger of bias when a researcher rewrites data, but
these sentences might sound more like English if they were written so
the adjective preceded the noun:

> 5'   We need a new educational system.
> 18' . . . each of the owners.

Arabic also retains this appositive relationship between the relative
clause and the matrix it modifies (Socin 1927; Beeston 1970; Benveniste
1971). When the subordinated noun is undetermined, there is no relative
pronoun marker, making it similar to the appositive-like nature of the
adjective. When the subordinated noun is determined, the relative marker
is actually a demonstrative, thus a determiner by function. In both the
adjective and relative clause formation, then, the parallel balance of ap-
position is maintained, rather than the subordination more commonly
used in English. From the student essay quoted above come these two
relative clause constructions.

> 1   We have a lot of revenues each year from oil export (11)
>   that come to us from selling this material. (8)
>
> 1   We can solve the second problem by seeking for other resources
>   (11)
>   that we have in my country not to depend on one source like oil.
>   (14)

The matrices and relative clauses in both sentences are of nearly the same length in terms of the number of lexical items, thus retaining in English the balance of form so important in Arabic.

There is a similar balance between the elements that are coordinated. When coordination particles equivalent to the English *and* and *or* are used in Arabic, the two speech items they link must have exact parity of syntactic status (Beeston 1970).

> 13 My father about 85 years old age. (7)
> and he like all his family to learn and study, (10)
> So one of my older brother is proffessor in univ—Dean (11)
> and the other one is official in the government. (9)
> and I hope to get it on soon XXXX. (9)

Here the efforts to transfer stylistic preferences are evident. As mentioned in the earlier description of the principle of balance in word order, there is a general balance in the number of lexical items in each clause. All but the second clause end in prepositional phrases. Assuming an underlying *be* verb in the first clause, three of the five strings are predicate nominative constructions, and the two that are not are the final clause with *that* subject head.

In addition to the syntactic characteristics that differentiate Arabic from English, there are also stylistic ones. The Arabians' ancient oratorical prose, though no longer fashionable in its pure form, has left ineffaceable marks on the habits of thought and on contemporary writing, even when the writer is not attempting to be oratorical. Known as "saj," this prose, like most ancient Semitic literature, relies for its effect on a rhythmical balance between two and occasionally three clauses, which are marked by a careful parallelism of sense either as contrast or as similarity (Bateson 1967; Beeston 1970, 1977).

The most noticeable effect of "saj" on contemporary writing is the very common practice of writing elaborately structured paragraphs, similar to the English usage of the sixteenth century and earlier. This elaboration occurs even when the writer has no intention of writing "high-flown" prose. It is rare to find in Arabic a cumulative series of short sentences of the modern English style. Indeed, it is rare in written Arabic to find within a paragraph a new main sentence which is not linked to its preceding sentence by a coordinator. The following is an example of these sentence paragraphs:

> 2 So as in many countries of the (third) world, young people like to go from the villages to the cities, because the life in country side or in the villages are not attractive enough, the infrastructure is not very good and the jobs are rare.

Commonplaces or formulas are another stylistic characteristic of the

Arabic essay. Ong (1972) presents ample evidence that these proverbial sayings were "stock in trade" of ancient oral cultures. In the Arabic corpus are found such formulas as this proverb-like statement which one student used to close his essay:

> 14   I think its' very simple to solve it the country's problems for *there is nothing difficult while everybody use his mind honestly* [italics added].

Since very little work is available in Arabic text linguistics, the above remarks will have to suffice. Even so, the evidence seems rather clear. The language of the *Qu'ran* is the literary language which serves as a model for modern Arabic writers; this and "saj" have shaped their ideas of what is the preferred writing style. As English and the other languages of the Anglo-European tradition have moved into the era of the printed word, the preferred rhetorical form in those languages has changed from one of repetition and metrical balance to one of variety in sentence structure and of the use of subordination and deletion. The writers in each period have reflected the culturally approved forms of their time. The same is true of Arabic writers. Their culture trains them to write in the preferred mode—one based on the *Qu'ran* and on "saj." Their language forms support that mode. Their writing, even when they are writing in English and under test conditions, still reflects the preference of their Arabic culture.

DESCRIPTION
OF CORPORA

This study is based on the analysis of two corpora. The first consists of twenty-two short essays written in English, as part of an English placement test, by Saudi Arabian students entering the University of Southern California. This corpus represents the entire Saudi population taking the exam for that particular time period, except for two papers in which there were no fully developed sentences. The Saudi Arabian population was selected for two reasons: there were a reasonable number with which to work, and it was hoped that by using data from a single native population, the variable of spoken dialect differences would be reduced. Since these essays were part of a formal evaluation, it can be reasonably assumed that the participants exercised their very best linguistic skills to produce papers which would receive the highest possible ratings.

The English corpus consists of ten paragraphs from books found in a Los Angeles public library, selected at random from each of the ten divisions of the Dewey classification system; the middle paragraph on page 166 was used, unless there was no text on the page (i.e., the space being occupied by a chart, table, diagram, etc.) or unless the paragraphing prevented identification of an appropriate segment. In this case, specified other alternatives were employed. This random method was used to obtain a cross section of writing characteristic of the various disciplines. It is assumed that both corpora are random samples representing their respective populations.

In analyzing the Arabic corpus, the entire paper is used rather than the paragraph division used in the English corpus. There are several reasons for this. First, of course, there is a logical relationship between the topic sentence of the paragraph and the controlling purpose of a longer work. Each has a topic or basic idea and a predication or comment on that subject, so that there is justification for counting them both as controlling concepts. Word count of the two corpora is another criterion. The average for the English paragraphs is 119 words; that for the Saudi papers is 173. Although there is a 31% difference in word count, had the decision been to use Arabic-speakers' paragraphs, another difficult problem would have arisen. The Arabic-speaking writers appear to have a quite different concept of what constitutes a paragraph from that of the English writers; it would not have been possible to find comparable paragraphs. Finally, perhaps because the Saudi writers were given a topic on which to write, or perhaps because this is part of their rhetorical tradition, only one of the twenty-two papers is not organized around a controlling purpose or, as it is called in this analysis, a topic sentence. Hence, for the purposes of this paper, the English paragraphs and the Saudi papers are counted as rhetorically equivalent.

One more difference between the two corpora needs to be discussed. The English corpus is drawn from professional writing; the Arabic corpus has been elicited from students writing in a second language. But it is proposed here that there is, in this seeming difference, a strong similarity. Both sets of writers are writing in the best rhetorical style of the culture they represent and within which they learned to write. The English writers must achieve literary standards approved by their editors and widely acceptable to their reading audience. The Arabic students know that these essays are part of the evaluation which will determine whether they must take English classes and how many. In striving for the highest possible score, they will attend to grammatical, syntactical, and lexical concerns, because they have been taught these by their English teachers (but see Raimes 1985). They will probably not concern themselves with rhetorical arrangements. Berman (1980) notes that rhetorical arrangement is the feature most difficult to change, because it is the one of which language learners are not even aware. These skills are rarely taught in language classes. Instead, learners will write to please the only audience with whom they have had any experience, the members of their native-language communities.

QUANTITATIVE INDICES

Two indices are used to analyze the corpora: Kellog Hunt's T-unit and Pitkin's Discourse Bloc, as modified by Kaplan. The T-unit is a grammatical index defined by Hunt (1965). In his study of school children's writings, he found some difficulty in accounting for the strings written by immature students who, much like the Arabic students, had a tendency to connect long strings of words with *and*, or merely join them without a coordinator or punctuation. At other times the children punctuated as a sentence a string which was missing either a subject or a finite verb, hence making it incomplete. To accommodate this type of writing, Hunt devised the "terminal unit" (T-unit)—the shortest possible sentential unit which is still grammatical.

The Discourse Bloc is less familiar to many than is the T-unit. Pitkin (1969) first proposed the term to describe a "context," "an extended unit of discourse" larger than a sentence. The boundary of a Discourse Bloc may or may not be coterminus with a paragraph, depending upon the structure of the context. Indeed, in this study all of the Arabic papers are complete themes; all of the English samples are paragraphs. Both are counted as Discourse Blocs.

At a minimum a Discourse Bloc is that unit which recognizes that several ideas are related to each other at two levels, syntactic and semantic. Syntactically they are related through superordination, coordination, and subordination. Semantically they are related through anaphoric, cataphoric, and endophoric reference (Halliday and Hasan 1976). Within a Discourse Bloc are related units called Discourse Units. Such units are related semantically and syntactically to the Discourse Bloc and may or may not be equivalent to sentences.

Figure 1 shows the student essay quoted above in Discourse Bloc form. At first the Discourse Bloc looks like a traditional outline, but it should be noted that it is not prescriptive in nature; rather, it is based entirely on the syntactic and semantic interrelationships of the passage being analyzed, and will vary considerably according to the style of the writer. The central idea is placed at the Discourse Bloc level. The supporting ideas are Discourse Units. Each Discourse Unit must support and explicate the Discourse Bloc and stand independently in its relationship to that Bloc. The A and B sub-headings have the same relationship to their individual units as the Discourse Unit does to its Discourse Bloc. Inasmuch as the T-unit is a sentential measure and the Discourse Bloc is

---

Figure 1: Sample Student Essay in Discourse Bloc Form

DB.* We face two serious problems in my country

DU I.* The first problem is that
A. 1. we import many things from other countries and
2. we cannot depend on ourselves
in producing the things we need.
B. We import different kinds of food, electric materials, cars and chothes [*sic*].

DU II. The second problem is that
A. 1. we depend on one source of income and
2. that is the oil.
B. Our national economy depends on it.
C. 1. We have a lot of revenues each year from oil export
2. that come to us from selling this material.
D. 1. It is not good for our country
to depend on one source and
2. it has to vary its resources.

DU III. We can solve the first problem
by building many factories and
A. we have to develop our soil
to be useful for agriculture.
B. We have to form educated people
to serve
and to develop their country.

DU IV. We can solve the second problem
A. by seeking for other resources
that we have in my country
B. not to depend on one source like oil.

DU V. A. Finally we will become a developed country and
B. we can insure our future and our life.

---

* DB = Discourse Bloc; DU = Discourse Unit

an extra-sentential measure, the results of the T-unit will be discussed first.

Results of T-Unit Analysis

All of the words in each essay were counted, and then the corpora were segmented according to the number of T-units, defined by Hunt (1965) as "the shortest grammatically allowable sentences into which the theme could be divided." The number of these T-units was counted as well as the total number of dependent clauses per T-unit. From these was calculated the total number of words per T-unit and the total number of dependent adverbial and adjectival clauses per T-unit. Table 1 displays the summary of these findings. There are three main divisions: the findings for *All Clauses, Main Clauses,* and *Coordinate Clauses.* Each of these divisions is classified into categories, following the Hunt model: the total number of words used, the number of T-units, the number of words per T-unit, the number of dependent clauses, and the number of such clauses per T-unit. Figures for the Arabic and English corpora are shown in their respective columns for the total number and the mean in each division and category.

The figures in the division labeled *All Clauses* show that the mean number of words per essay for Arabic-speakers was 173 and that for English-speakers was 118, a 32% difference. Thus it would seem logical that, if the two corpora were from the same population, the other categories would show similar differences. Instead, the mean number of T-units was twice as high in the essays written by Arabic speakers, 18% greater than the predicted difference. The mean length of T-units was 70% greater in the English corpus, and the mean number of dependent clauses was 69% less than were the respective means in the corpus of essays written by Arabic-speakers. Thus, it becomes clear that there are some notable differences in the length and type of T-units between the two corpora.

Earlier, this paper discussed the fact that the Arabic language uses large numbers of coordinated structures. To ascertain whether these same coordinate patterns would occur when the Arabic-speaking students were writing in English, coordinate clauses were tabulated. The corpus figures shown under *All Clauses* were divided into *Main Clauses,* those which were not preceded by a coordinating conjunction (*and, or, but*), and *Coordinate Clauses,* those which were so preceded. Here the differences were statistically significant. Of the 3805 words used in the essays written by Arabic-speakers, 26% were used in coordinate clauses; of the 1179 words used in the English corpus, only 7% occurred in such clauses. Twenty-eight percent of the T-units written by Arabic-speaking writers were coordinate clauses; only 11% of the English T-units were. A pooled T-test was used to compute the significance of the differences in the occurrence of coordinate clauses between the two corpora. The T-score on the total number of words in coordinate clauses was 4.16, and on the total number of T-units in coordinate clauses 5.36 (both $p < .001$).

An even more definitive contrast between the two corpora can be found in the development of main and coordinate clauses. In the category of *Main Clauses,* under *Total Number of Dependent Clauses per T-Unit,* the means of the two corpora show only a 32% difference. But in *Coordinate Clauses* under the same classification, not a single occurrence of an

TABLE 1 Classification of T-Units

	Total Number of Words in Corpora		Total Number of T-Units		Total Number of Words Per T-Unit		Total Number of Dependent Clauses		Total Number of Dependent Clauses per T-Unit	
	Arabic	English	Arabic	English	Arabic	English	Arabic	English	Arabic	English
All Clauses										
Total	3805	1179	304	66			77	24		
Mean	173	118	13	7	12.6	18	3.5	2.4	3.9	2.75
Main Clauses										
Total	2805	1099	220	59			60	24		
Mean	128	110	10	6	12.8	18.6	3	2.4	3.7	2.5
Coordinate Clauses										
Total	1000	80	84	7			17	00		
Mean	45	8	4	.7	12	11	.8	00	4.9	00
t Score	4.16*	5.37*								

* These findings are the results of a pooled T-test @ 30 df., $p < .001$ level.

English coordinate clause being modified by a dependent clause shows up. The Arabic-speaking corpus shows 17 clauses (20%) with such modification.

Thus the data analyzed by T-units supports the hypothesis that the tendency of the Arabic-speaking writer to strive for balance between clauses continues when the Arabic-speaking student is writing in English. Further, if the corpus is representative of the general writing of the English-speaking population, the T-unit analysis then indicates that there is indeed a reluctance among writers of English to use clausal modification in coordinate clauses.

Results of Discourse Bloc Analysis

For the Discourse Bloc analysis each essay in both corpora was treated as described in "Quantitative Indices" (above). The total number of each of these classifications was tabulated; the means of these figures are shown in the histogram in Table 2.

The Arabic-speaking essays summarized in the top histograph and the English-speaking essays in the bottom one show an almost consistent use of a topic sentence, with the reasonable likelihood it will be subdivided in some way. There is also a strong chance each Discourse Bloc will have at least two Discourse Units with a minimum of A and B subdivisions: these subdivisions have a better than 30% chance of having a minimum of one further subdivision. Therefore a typical, though by no means minimal, pattern would be:

> Discourse Bloc D. B.
>
> Discourse Unit I A
>   B
>
> Discourse Unit II A
>   B

However, the similarity ends here. Almost one-fourth of the Arabic-speakers' papers begin with a superordinate (SO), generally a universal statement only globally related to the topic of the paper. For example, on the topic "My Family" one essay begins:

> 6 All the families in my country have a special
>   tradition different from the other families in the world. . . .

Further, although this structure does not show in the Discourse Bloc histograms, almost one-fourth of the Arabic-speakers' papers end with some type of formulaic or proverbial statement.

TABLE 2 Histograms of Discourse Blocs

Arabic Corpus

```
100%
              XX
              XX    XX
              XX    XXXX   XX
              XX    XXXX   XXXX   XX
              XX    XXXX   XXXX   XXXX   XX
              XX    XXXX   XXXX   XXXX   XX
              XXXX  XXXXXXX XXXXXX XXXX  XXXX
  XX  XX      XXXXXXX XXXXXXXXX XXXXXXXX XXXXXXXX XXXX  XXXX   XX
 10% XX  XXXXXXX XXXXXXXXX XXXXXXXX XXXXXXXX XXXXXXXX XXXXXXXX XXXXXXX XX
  SO  DB A B C  I A B C D E  II A B C D  III A B C  IV A B C  V A B  VI
```

English Corpus

```
100%
  XX
  XX    XX
  XX    XXXX
  XX    XXXX   XX
  XX    XXXXXX XXXXXX
  XXXX  XXXXXX XXXXXX
  XXXX  XXXXXX XXXXXX
  XXXX  XXXXXXXX XXXXXX
  XXXX  XXXXXXXX XXXXXX
 10% XXXXXX XXXXXXXXX XXXXXX
  DB A B  I A B C D  II A B
```

Shown here are the mean occurrences of the Superordinates (SO), Discourse Blocs (DB), Discourse Units (I, II, etc.), and the main subdivisions (A, B, etc.). Further subdivisions occurred with great regularity, but not in significant percentages.

183

5   all that to bring water, and to bring life.

Neither of these forms occurs in the English papers.

The most dramatic difference between the two corpora, however, is clearly seen in the histograms. There are simply fewer subdivisions in the English writing than there are in the Arabic-speakers' papers. No English paper contains more than two Discourse Units; 77% of the Arabic papers have three, almost half have four, and four of the twenty-two have five Discourse Units. Although the mean length of the Arabic-speakers' papers is 32% greater than that of the English paragraphs, that difference alone cannot account for the great difference in the number of Discourse Units per Discourse Bloc. The explanation can be found in the mean length of main clauses. The English main clauses are 2.5 times longer than the English coordinate clauses. English writers express themselves in complex strings of adjectival, prepositional, and verbal phrases which, lacking finite verbal constructions, do not appear in the tabulations of a clausal analysis. When coordinate clauses do occur in English, they seem to be used merely as another form of this phrasal modification. The Arabic-speakers' papers express equally complex ideas, but they do so in compound constructions which, because they contain finite verbs, *do* appear in a clausal analysis. Because the Discourse Bloc measure depends upon fully developed ideas (i.e., clauses instead of phrases), the very nature of Arabic-speakers' writing is revealed in the Discourse Bloc histograms.

IMPLICATIONS

The hypothesis of this paper is that the rhetorical style of Classical Arabic is closely tied to the linguistic system of that language. Because of this, the prose style of Arabic-speaking students writing in English has been shown to be quantitatively different from that of English-speaking writers. These differences have been shown in a comparison of T-unit development and in a comparison of Discourse Bloc histograms. The results pose further questions. Can these results be found in comparing other language groups with English? If so, is the cause merely free variation, or is there an underlying reason? While these are speculative questions, they point directions for future research and, like other papers in this volume, suggest areas that must be explored if we are to have a clear sense of how text is organized in various languages and how writing may be taught to native and non-native speakers.

NOTE

1. The number preceding each text example is a code permitting identification of the text in the research corpus, which is not reproduced here in the interests of brevity.

FOR STUDY AND DISCUSSION

1. Ostler compares student compositions with professional writing. On the surface, the two sets seem not to be comparable. Is the use of professional writing for comparison a problem? Why? If it is a problem, how can it be addressed?

2. Compare the mechanisms used to collect a corpus for analysis in Ostler, Grabe, Connor, and Carrell. What does such a comparison tell you about the problems of assembling a text corpus? What solutions to these problems can you suggest?

3. Ostler argues that the structure of some varieties of written Arabic resemble the structures that occur commonly in Koranic literature. Is there a comparable similarity between some varieties of written English and Biblical literature? If so, why should this phenomenon occur? What does the existence of the phenomenon suggest for the study of written text?

4. Do Ostler's findings compare at all with Eggington's or Hinds'? If so, what ideas do the three studies together suggest? What directions for research? If not, is there any validity to the notion that written structures are culture/language specific, or is that notion really only a reflection of superficial syntactic differences among languages?

Bibliography

Akinnaso, F. N. 1982. On the differences between spoken and written language. *Language and speech.* 25.1.97–125.

Alptekin, C. and M. Alptekin. 1983. The role of content schemata in ESL composition. *TESOL reporter.* 16.4.63–66.

Aston, G. 1977. Comprehending value: Aspects of the structure of argumentative discourse. *Studi italiani di linguistica teorica ed applicata.* 6.465–509.

Banker, J. 1980. How can we improve our translations stylistically? *Notes on translation.* 78.31–36.

Bartlett, B. J. 1978. Use of top-level structure as an organizational strategy in prose recall. Arizona State University. Ph.D. diss.

Bateson, M. C. 1967. *The Arabic language handbook.* Washington, DC: Center for Applied Linguistics.

Beach, R. 1976. Self-evaluation strategies of extensive revisers and non-revisers. *College composition and communication.* 27.160–164.

Beaman, K. 1984. Coordination and subordination revisited: Syntactic complexity in spoken and written narrative discourse. In D. Tannen (ed.) *Coherence in spoken and written discourse.* Norwood, NJ: Ablex. 45–80.

Beaugrande, R. de. 1980. *Text, discourse, and process: Toward a multi-disciplinary science of texts.* Norwood, NJ: Ablex. [Advances in Discourse Processes, Vol. IV.]

———. 1982a. Psychology and composition: Past, present, and future. In M. Nystrand (ed.) *What writers know: The language, process, and structure of written discourse.* New York: Academic Press. 211–267.

———. 1982b. *The science of composition: A program for research in theory and method.* Norwood, NJ: Ablex.

———. 1984. Linguistics as discourse. *Word.* 35.1.15–58.

——— and W. Dressler. 1981. *Introduction to text linguistics.* London: Longman.

Beekman, J. and J. Callow. 1974. *Translating the word of God.* Grand Rapids, MI: Zondervan Publishing House.

———, et al. 1981. *The semantic structure of written communication.* 5th ed. Dallas: Summer Institute of Linguistics.

Beeston, A. F. L. 1970. *The Arabic language today.* London: Hutchinson University Library.

————. 1977. *Samples of Arabic prose in its historical development.* London: Oxford University Press.

Bendor-Samuel, P. 1976. Titus: Analysis of the larger semantic units. *Notes on translation.* 61.2–8.

Benveniste, E. 1971. *Problems in general linguistics.* Miami: University of Miami Press. [Tr. Mary Weeks.]

Berman, R. 1980. Postposing, lexical repetition and the like: A study in contrastive stylistics. *Journal of applied linguistics.* 2.3–25.

Bever, T. G. and D. J. Townsend. 1979. Perceptual mechanisms and formal properties of main and subordinate clauses. In W. E. Cooper and E. C. T. Walker (eds.) *Sentence processing: Psycholinguistic studies presented to Merrill Garrett.* Hillsdale, NJ: Erlbaum. 159–226.

Biber, D. 1984a. A model of textual relations within the written and spoken modes. University of Southern California. Ph.D. diss.

————. 1984b. A textual comparison of British and American writing. Paper presented at NWAVE XIII, Philadelphia, November.

————. In Press. Spoken and written textual dimensions in English: Resolving the contradictory findings. *Language.*

————. To Appear. *Textual relations in speech and writing.* New York: Cambridge University Press.

Birk, N. and G. Birk. 1972. *Understanding and using English.* New York: Bobbs Merrill.

Blight, R. 1977. A literary-semantic analysis of Paul's first discourse to Timothy. Mimeo.

Blood, D. and D. Blood. 1979. Overview of Acts. *Notes on translation.* 74.2–36.

Bower, G. H. 1976. Experiments on story understanding and recall. *Quarterly journal of experimental psychology.* 28.511–534.

Bransford, J. D. and N. S. McCarrell. 1974. A sketch of a cognitive approach to comprehension: Some thoughts about understanding what it means to comprehend. In W. Weimer and D. Palermo (eds.) *Cognition and the symbolic processes.* Hillsdale, NJ: Erlbaum.

Bridwell, L. S. 1980. Revising strategies in twelfth grade students' transactional writing. *Research in the teaching of English.* 14.197–222.

Brown, G. and G. Yule. 1983. *Discourse analysis.* Cambridge: Cambridge University Press.

Carramazza, A. and M. McCloskey, 1981. Theory and problems in psycholinguistics. In R. B. Kaplan, *et al.* (eds.) *Annual review of applied linguistics, I.* Rowley, MA: Newbury House. 71–90.

Carrell, P. L. 1982. Cohesion is not coherence. *TESOL quarterly.* 16.4.479–488.

————. 1983a. Reply to Ghadessy. *TESOL quarterly.* 17.4.687–691.

————. 1983b. Some issues in studying the role of schemata, or background knowledge, in second language comprehension. *Reading in a foreign language.* 1.2.81–92.

———. 1984a. The effects of rhetorical organization on ESL readers. *TESOL quarterly.* 18.3.441–469.

———. 1984b. Evidence of a formal schema in second language comprehension. *Language learning.* 34.2.87–112.

———. 1984c. Facilitating reading comprehension by teaching text structure: What the research shows. Paper presented at the Eighteenth Annual TESOL Convention, Houston, March.

———. 1984d. Reading comprehension and the rhetorical organization of text. Paper presented at the Seventh World Conference of the International Association of Applied Linguistics, Brussels, August.

———. 1984e. Reply to Rankin. *TESOL quarterly.* 18.1.161–168.

———. 1984f. Review of *Introduction to text linguistics,* Robert de Beaugrande and W. Dressler. *Language learning.* 34.1.111–117.

Chafe, W. L. 1976. Givenness, contrastiveness, definiteness, subjects and topics. In C. N. Li (ed.) *Subject and topic.* New York: Academic Press.

———. 1980. *The pear stories.* Norwood, NJ: Ablex.

———. 1982. Integration and involvement in speaking, writing and oral literature. In D. Tannen (ed.) *Exploring orality and literacy.* Norwood, NJ: Ablex. 35–54.

———. 1985. Linguistic differences produced by differences between speaking and writing. In D. Olsen, N. Torrance, and A. Hilyard (eds.) *Literacy, language and learning.* New York: Cambridge University Press. 105–123.

——— and J. Danielowicz. In Press. Properties of spoken and written language. In R. Horowitz and S. J. Samuels (eds.) *Comprehending oral and written language.* New York: Academic Press.

Chang, S. J. 1983. Linguistics and written discourse in particular languages: Contrastive studies: English and Korean. In R. B. Kaplan, *et al.* (eds.) *Annual review of applied linguistics, III.* Rowley, MA: Newbury House. 85–98.

Charney, D. 1984. The validity of using holistic scoring to evaluate writing: A critical overview. *Research in the teaching of English.* 18.1.65–81.

Chejne, A. G. 1969. *The Arabic language, its role in history.* Minneapolis: University of Minnesota Press.

Cho, S. C. 1980. Inter-agency decision process in the Korean government. *Korean journal of public administration.* 1.140–151.

Chomsky, N. 1957. *Syntactic structures.* The Hague: Mouton.

Christensen, F. 1963. A generative rhetoric of the paragraph. *College composition and communication.* 14.155–161.

———. 1967. *Notes toward a new rhetoric.* New York: Harper and Row.

Clark, H. H. 1978. Inferring what is meant. In W. J. M. Levelt and G. B. Flores d'Arcais (eds.) *Studies in the perception of language.* Chichester: Wiley. 295–322.

――― and S. Haviland. 1974. Psychological processes as linguistic explanation. In D. Cohen (ed.) *Explaining linguistic phenomena*. Washington, DC: V. H. Winston. 1–40.

Clyne, M. 1980. Writing, testing, and culture. *The secondary teacher*. 11:13–16.

―――. 1981. Culture and discourse structure. *Journal of pragmatics*. 5.61–66.

Comrie, B. 1981 (1983). *Language universals and linguistic typology*. Chicago: University of Chicago Press. [Reprint Oxford: Blackwell.]

Connor, U. 1984a. Recall of text: Differences between first and second language readers. *TESOL quarterly*. 18.2.239–255.

―――. 1984b. A study of cohesion and coherence in English as a second language students' writing. *Papers in linguistics: International journal of human communication*. 17.3.301–316.

――― and M. Farmer. 1985. The teaching of topical structure analysis as a revision strategy: An exploratory study. Paper presented at the American Educational Research Association Conference, Chicago, April.

――― and P. McCagg. 1983. Crosscultural differences and perceived quality in written paraphrases of English expository prose. *Applied linguistics*. 4.3.259–268.

――― and S. Takala. 1984. Argumentative patterns in student compositions: An exploratory study. Paper presented at the Eighteenth Annual TESOL Convention, Houston, March.

Cook, W. 1979. *Case grammar: Development of the matrix model*. Washington, DC: Georgetown University Press.

Cooper, M. 1983. An investigation of the structure of academic written text with particular reference to sentence connection. University of Birmingham. Ph.D. diss.

Corbett, E. P. J. 1973. *The little English handbook: Choices and conventions*. New York: Wiley.

Crothers, E. J. 1978. Inference and coherence. *Discourse processes*. 1.51–71.

―――. 1979. *Paragraph structure inference*. Norwood, NJ: Ablex.

Cressy, D. 1980. *Literacy and the social order: Reading and writing in Tudor and Stuart England*. Cambridge: Cambridge University Press.

Daiker, D. A., A. Kerek, and M. Morenberg. 1979. *The writer's options: College sentence combining*. New York: Harper and Row.

Daneš, F. 1974. Functional sentence perspective and the organization of the text. In F. Daneš (ed.) *Papers on functional sentence perspective*. Prague: Academia. 106–128.

―――. (ed.) 1974. *Papers on functional sentence perspective*. Prague: Academia.

Dehghanpisheh, E. 1973. Contrastive analysis of Persian and English paragraphs. *Proceedings of the second annual seminar of the association of professors of English in Iran*. Tehran: Association of Professors of English in Iran.

Delia, J. G., S. L. Kline, and B. R. Burleson. 1979. The development of persuasive communication strategies in kindergarteners through twelfth-graders. *Communication monographs*. 46.241–256.

Dressler, W. 1972. *Einführung in die textlinguistik*. Tübingen: Niemeyer.

———. (ed.) 1978. *Current trends in text linguistics*. Berlin: de Gruyter.

Dryden, J. 1883. *The works of John Dryden*. Ed. George Saintsbury. Vol. V. Edinburgh: William Paterson.

Edmondson, W. 1981. *Spoken discourse: A model for analysis*. London: Longman.

Eggington, W. G. 1983. Impediments to effective communication in Korean academic writing. Unpublished paper. University of Southern California.

Enkvist, N. E. 1973. *Linguistic stylistics*. The Hague: Mouton.

———. 1974a. Theme dynamics and style: An experiment. *Studia Anglica Posnaniensia*. 5.127–136.

———. 1974b. *Tekstilingvistiikan peruskäsitteitä*. Helsinki: Gaudeamus.

———. 1976. Notes on valency, semantic scope and thematic perspective as parameters of adverbial placement in English. In N. E. Enkvist and V. Kohonen (eds.) *Reports on text linguistics: Approaches to word order*. Åbo, Finland: Meddelanden från Stiftelsens för Åbo Akademi Forskningsinstitut, nr. 8.

———. 1979. Marked focus: Functions and constraints. In S. Greenbaum, G. Leech, and J. Svartvik (eds.) *Studies in English linguistics for Randolph Quirk*. London: Longman. 134–152.

———. 1981. Experiential iconicism in text strategy. *Text*. 1.77–111.

———. 1984. Contrastive linguistics and text linguistics. In J. Fisiak (ed.) *Contrastive linguistics: Prospects and problems*. The Hague: Mouton.

———. In Press a. A parametric view of word order. In E. Sözer (ed.) *Text connexity, text coherence: Papiere zur textlinguistik*. Hamburg: Buske.

———. In Press b. Textualization as conflict and conspiracy. In H. Karlgren and F. Kiefer (eds.) *Linking in text*. North Holland: Reidel.

——— and V. Kohonen (eds.) 1976. *Reports on text linguistics: Approaches to word order*. Åbo, Finland: Meddelanden från Stiftelsens för Åbo Akademi Forskningsinstitut, nr. 8.

——— and H. Nordström. 1978. On textual aspects of intonation in Finland-Swedish newscasts. *Studia linguistica*. 32.63–79.

——— and M. von Wright. 1978. Problems in the study of textual factors in topicalization. In E. Anderson (ed.) *Working papers on computer-processing of syntactic data*. Åbo, Finland: Meddelanden från Stiftelsens för Åbo Akademi Forskningsinstitut, nr. 37.

Ferguson, C. 1959. Diglossia. *Word*. 15.325–340.

———. 1968. Myths about Arabic. In J. Fishman (ed.) *Readings in the sociology of language*. The Hague: Mouton. 375–381.

Fillmore, C. 1968. The case for case. In E. Bach and R. T. Harms (eds.) *Linguistic theory*. New York: Holt, Rinehart and Winston. 1–88.

Findler, N. V. (ed.) 1979. *Associative networks*. New York: Academic Press.

Flores d'Arcais, G. B. and R. J. Jarvella (eds.) 1983. *The process of language understanding.* Chichester: Wiley.

Flower, L. and J. R. Hayes. 1981. A cognitive process theory of writing. *College composition and communication.* 32.365–387.

Forster, K. I. 1978. Accessing the internal lexicon. In E. W. Walker (ed.) *Explorations in the biology of language.* Montgomery, VT: Bradford Books. 139–174.

Frawley, W. 1982. Universal grammar and composition: Relativization, complementation, and quantification. In W. Frawley (ed.) *Linguistics and literacy.* New York: Plenum Press. 65–90.

Frederiksen, C. H. 1972. Effects of task-induced cognitive operations on comprehension and memory processes. In R. Freedle and J. B. Carroll (eds.) *Language comprehension and the acquisition of knowledge.* Washington, DC: Winston. 211–246.

———. 1975. Representing logical and semantic structure of knowledge acquired from discourse. *Cognitive psychology.* 4.371–458.

Fries, C. C. 1952. *The structure of English.* New York: Harcourt.

Fuller, S. L. 1984. Schema theory and the comparative analysis of discourse patterns. University of Southern California. Ph.D. diss.

Garrod, S. and A. Sanford. 1983. Topic dependent effects in language processing. In G. B. Flores d'Arcais and R. J. Jarvella (eds.) *The process of language understanding.* Chichester: Wiley. 271–296.

Gim, S. G. 1975. The phonological structure of middle Korean plosives. In H. M. Sohn (ed.) *The Korean language: Its structure and social projection.* Honolulu: The Center for Korean Studies. 91–102.

Glass, A. L. and K. J. Holyoak. 1974/75. Alternative conceptions of semantic memory. *Cognition.* 3.313–339.

Gonzalez, A., FSC. 1982. Language policy and language-in-education policy in the Philippines. In R. B. Kaplan, *et al.* (eds.) *Annual review of applied linguistics, II.* Rowley, MA: Newbury House. 48–59.

Goodman, K. S. 1970. Reading: A psycholinguistic guessing game. In H. Singer and R. B. Ruddell (eds.) *Theoretical models and processes in reading.* Newark, DE: International Reading Association. 497–508.

Gorsuch, R. 1983. *Factor analysis.* 2nd Ed. Hillsdale, NJ: Erlbaum.

Grabe, W. 1984. Towards defining expository prose within a theory of text construction. University of Southern California. Ph.D. diss.

———. 1985. Towards defining expository prose: Implications for research and instruction. Paper presented at the Nineteenth Annual TESOL Convention. New York, April.

Greenberg, J. H. 1963. Some universals of grammar with particular reference to the order of meaningful elements. In J. H. Greenberg (ed.) *Universals of language.* Cambridge, MA: MIT Press. 73–113.

Grimes, J. E. 1975. *The thread of discourse.* The Hague: Mouton.

Halliday, M. A. K. and R. Hasan. 1976. *Cohesion in English.* London: Longman. [English Language Series, No. 9.]

Harris, Z. 1970. *Papers in structural and transformational linguistics.* Dordrecht: D. Reidel.

Hasan, R. 1978. On the notion of a text. In J. S. Petöfi (ed.) *Text vs. sentence.* Hamburg: H. Buske.

Haviland, S. and H. H. Clark. 1974. What's new? Acquiring new information as a process in comprehension. *Journal of verbal learning and verbal behavior.* 13.512–521.

Hawkins, J. A. 1983. *Word order universals.* New York: Academic Press.

Headland, T. N. 1981. Information rate, information overload, and communication problems in the Casiguran Damagat New Testament. *Notes on translation.* 83.18–27.

Heath, S. B. 1985. Literacy or literate skills? Considerations for ESL/EFL learners. In P. Larson, E. Judd, and D. Messerschmitt (eds.) *ON TESOL 84.* Washington, DC: TESOL. 15–28.

Hildyard, A. and D. R. Olson. 1982. On the comprehension and memory of oral vs. written discourse. In D. Tannen (ed.) *Spoken and written language.* Norwood, NJ: Ablex. 17–34.

Hinds, J. 1979. Organizational patterns in discourse. In T. Givón (ed.) *Syntax and semantics 12: Discourse and syntax.* New York: Academic Press. 135–157.

———. 1980. Japanese expository prose. *Papers in linguistics.* 13.117–158.

———. 1982a. Contrastive rhetoric: Japanese and English. Paper given at the Sixteenth Annual TESOL Convention, Honolulu, March.

———. 1982b. *Ellipsis in Japanese.* Edmonton: Linguistic Research, Inc.

———. 1983a. Contrastive rhetoric: Japanese and English. *Text.* 3.2.183–195.

———. 1983b. Linguistics and written discourse in particular languages: Contrastive studies: English and Japanese. In R. B. Kaplan, *et al.* (eds.) *Annual review of applied linguistics, III.* Rowley, MA: Newbury House. 78–84.

———. 1983c. Retention of information using a Japanese style of presentation. Paper presented at the Seventeenth Annual TESOL Convention, Toronto, March.

———. 1984a. Retention of information using a Japanese style of organization. *Studies in linguistics.* 8.45–69.

———. 1984b. Thematization as a staging device in Japanese expository prose. Paper presented at the Association for Asian Studies, Washington, DC, March.

———. 1984c. Topical maintenance in Japanese narratives and Japanese conversational interaction. *Discourse processes.* 7.4.465–482.

Hoey, M. P. 1979. *Signalling in discourse.* Birmingham: English Language Research, University of Birmingham. [Discourse Analysis Monographs, No. 6.]

———. 1983. *On the surface of discourse.* London: George Allen and Unwin.

Holman, E. 1976. Some thoughts on variable word-order. In N. E. Enkvist and V. Kohonen (eds.) *Reports on text linguistics: Approaches to word order.* Åbo, Finland: Meddelanden från Stiftelsens för Åbo Akademi Forskningsinstitut, nr. 8.

Hoon, Y. and D. S. Bark. 1980. An evaluation of the saemaul movement. *Korean journal of public administration.* 1.1–25.

Houghton, D. 1980. The writing problems of Iranian students. *ELT documents. 109: Study modes and academic development of overseas students.* London: The British Council. 79–90.

───── and M. P. Hoey. 1983. Linguistics and written discourse: Contrastive rhetorics. In R. B. Kaplan, *et al.* (eds.) *Annual review of applied linguistics, III.* Rowley, MA: Newbury House. 2–22.

Houppert, J. W. 1975. *John Lyly.* Boston: Twayne Publishers.

Huddleston, R. D. 1971. *The sentence in written English.* Cambridge: Cambridge University Press. [Cambridge Studies in Linguistics, 3.]

Hughes, R. and P. A. Duhamel. 1962. *Rhetoric: Principles and usage.* Englewood Cliffs, NJ: Prentice-Hall.

Huh, W. 1972. Exclusive use of Hangul and Hanmun education. *Korea journal.* 4.45–48.

Hunt, K. 1965. *Grammatical structures written at three grade levels.* Urbana, IL: National Council of Teachers of English. [Research Report No. 3.]

Jarvella, R. J. and J. Engelkamp. 1983. Pragmatic influences in producing and perceiving language: A critical and historical perspective. In G. B. Flores d'Arcais and R. J. Jarvella (eds.) *The process of language understanding.* Chichester: Wiley.

Kang, Y. H. and M. H. Kim. 1979. *Hankuko.* Seoul: Ihwa University Press.

Kaplan, R. B. 1966. Cultural thought patterns in intercultural education. *Language learning.* 16.1–20. (Reprinted in R. G. Bander. 1981. *American English rhetoric.* [Instructor's Manual] New York: Holt, Reinhart and Winston; also in H. B. Allen and R. N. Campbell (eds.) 1972. *Teaching English as a second language.* New York: McGraw-Hill; also in K. Croft (ed.) 1972. *Readings on English as a second language for teachers and teacher trainees.* Cambridge, MA: Winthrop. 2nd ed. 1980.)

─────. 1972. *The anatomy of rhetoric: Prolegomena to a functional theory of rhetoric.* Philadelphia: Center for Curriculum Development. (Distributed by Heinle & Heinle.)

─────. 1982. Information science and ESP. Paper presented at the Sixteenth Annual TESOL Convention, Honolulu, May.

─────. 1983a. Contrastive Rhetorics: Some implications for the writing process. In A. Freedman, I. Pringle, and J. Yalden (eds.) *Learning to write: First language/ second language.* New York: Longman. 139–161.

─────. 1983b. The cultures of science and technology. [Editorial.] *Science.* 224.4644.

─────. 1983c. An introduction to the study of written texts: The "Discourse compact." In R. B. Kaplan, *et al.* (eds.) *Annual review of applied linguistics, III.* Rowley, MA: Newbury House. 138–151.

─────. 1983d. Reading and writing, technology and planning: To do what and with what and to whom? In J. E. Alatis, H. H. Stern, and P. Strevens (eds.) *Applied linguistics and the preparation of second language teachers: Toward a rationale.* Washington, DC: Georgetown University Press. [Georgetown University Round Table on Languages and Linguistics.] 242–254.

───── and P. A. Shaw. 1983. *Exploring academic discourse.* Rowley, MA: Newbury House.

Keenan, E. O. and T. Bennett. 1977. (eds.) *Discourse across time and space.* Los Angeles: Department of Linguistics, University of Southern California. [Southern California Occasional Papers in Linguistics, No. 5.]

Kim, C. W. 1977. Divergence in language policies in Korea. In C. W. Kim (ed.) *Papers in Korean linguistics.* Columbia, SC: Hornbeam Press. 245–258.

Kim, H. D. 1979. Q.L.I. of Korean rural populace: An individual approach to social indicators. *Korean journal of public administration.* 3.134–170.

Kinneavy, J. L. 1971. *A theory of discourse.* Englewood Cliffs, NJ: Prentice-Hall.

Kintsch, W. 1974. *The representation of meaning in memory.* Hillsdale, NJ: Erlbaum.

———. 1977. On comprehending stories. In M. A. Just and P. A. Carpenter (eds.) *Cognitive processes in comprehension.* Hillsdale, NJ: Erlbaum. 33–62.

——— and E. Greene. 1978. The role of culture-specific schemata in the comprehension and recall of stories. *Discourse processes.* 1.1–13.

——— and T. A. van Dijk. 1978. Toward a model of text comprehension and production. *Psychological review.* 85.363–394.

Klenina, A. V. 1975. Kommunikativnaja svjaz' samostojatel'nyx predlozenij v naucnom tekste. *Russkij Jazyk za Rubezom.* 6.74–77.

Kress, G. 1982. *Learning to write.* Boston: Routledge and Kegan Paul.

Kroch, A. and D. Hindle. 1982. *A quantitative study of the syntax of speech and writing.* NIE Report #G78-0169.

Kroll, B. 1977. Combining ideas in written and spoken English: A look at subordination and coordination. In E. O. Keenan and T. L. Bennett (eds.) *Discourse across time and space.* Los Angeles: Department of Linguistics, University of Southern California. [Southern California Occasional Papers in Linguistics, No. 5.]

Krulee, G. K., P. G. Fairweather, and S. R. Berquist. 1979. Organizing factors in the comprehension and recall of connected discourse. *Journal of psycholinguistic research.* 8.141–163.

Kummer, W. 1972. Aspects of a theory of argumentation. In E. Gülich and W. Raible (eds.) *Text sorten.* Frankfurt am Main: Athenäum. 25–49.

Kuno, S. 1972. Functional sentence perspective—A case study from Japanese and English. *Linguistic inquiry.* 3.269–320.

Labov, W. 1972. *Language in the inner city.* Oxford: Blackwell.

Lautamatti, L. 1978. Observations on the development of the topic in simplified discourse. In V. Kohonen and N. E. Enkvist (eds.) *Text linguistics, cognitive learning and language teaching.* Turku, Finland: Publications de l'Association Finlandaise de Linguistique Appliquee. [AFinLA, 22]

Lautamatti, L. 1980. Subject and Theme in English Discourse. K. Sajavaara and J. Lehtonen (eds.) *Papers in discourse and contrastive discourse analysis.* Reports from the Department of English. University of Jyväskyla. Jyväskyla, Finland.

Lee, P. K. 1973. *Hyuntae hankukoeo sangsong ununron.* Seoul: Seoul National University Press.

Levinson, S. C. 1983. *Pragmatics.* Cambridge: Cambridge University Press.

Lewis, W. 1972 (1937). *The revenge for love*. Harmondsworth: Penguin.

Li, C. N. 1976. *Subject and topic*. New York: Academic Press.

——. (ed.) 1975. *Word order and word order change*. Austin, TX: University of Texas Press.

—— and S. A. Thompson. 1976. Subject and topic: A new typology of language. In C. N. Li (ed.) *Subject and topic*. New York: Academic Press. 457–489.

——. 1982. The gulf between spoken and written language: A case study in Chinese. In D. Tannen (ed.) *Spoken and written language*. Norwood, NJ: Ablex. 77–88.

Lindeberg, A. 1985. Cohesion, coherence patterns, and ESL essay evaluation. In N. E. Enkvist (ed.) *Coherence and composition: A symposium*. Åbo: Meddelanden från Stiftelsens för Åbo Akademi Forskningsinstitut, nr. 101. 67–92.

Loban, W. 1976. *Language development: Kindergarten through grade 12*. Urbana, IL: National Council of Teachers of English [Research Report No. 18.]

Longacre, R. 1968. *Discourse, paragraph and sentence structure in selected Philippine languages*. Santa Ana, CA: Summer Institute of Linguistics.

——. 1972. *Hierarchy and universality of discourse constituents in New Guinea languages*. Washington, DC: Georgetown University Press.

——. 1976. *An anatomy of speech notions*. Lisse: The Peter de Ridder Press.

——. 1982. *Grammar of discourse: A revision of an anatomy of speech notions*. New York: Plenum Press.

Lowe, I. 1969. An algebraic theory of English pronominal reference (Part I). *Semiotica*. 1.4.397–421.

——. 1974a. An algebraic theory of English pronominal reference (Part II): Plurals from singulars. *Semiotica*. 10.1.43–73.

——. 1974b. An algebraic theory of English pronominal reference (Part III): Applications to three participant conversations. *Semiotica*. 10.3.233–253.

Mandler, J. M. and N. S. Johnson. 1977. Remembrance of things parsed: Story structure and recall. *Cognitive psychology*. 9.111–151.

Martin, A. V. 1980. Proficiency of university level advanced ESL students and native speakers of English in processing hierarchical information in context. University of Southern California. Ph.D. diss.

Maynard, S. 1981. The given/new distinction and the analysis of the Japanese particles *-wa* and *-ga*. *Papers in linguistics*. 14.109–130.

McCloskey, M. and S. Glucksberg. 1979. Natural categories: Well defined or fuzzy sets? *Memory and cognition*. 6.462–472.

McDaniel, B. A. 1980. Contrastive rhetoric: Diagnosing problems in coherence. *The English quarterly*. 13.3.65–75.

McGee, L. M. 1982. Awareness of text structure: Effects on children's recall of expository text. *Reading research quarterly*. 17.4.581–590.

Meyer, B. J. F. 1975a. Identification of the structure of prose and its implications for the study of reading and memory. *Journal of reading behavior*. 7.7–47.

———. 1975b. *The organization of prose and its effects on memory.* Amsterdam: North-Holland Publishing Company.

———. 1977. The structure of prose: Effects on learning and memory and implications for educational practice. In R. C. Anderson, R. J. Spiro, and W. E. Montague (eds.) *Schooling and the acquisition of knowledge.* Hillsdale, NJ: Erlbaum. 179–200.

———. 1982. Reading research and the composition teacher: The importance of plans. *College composition and communication.* 33.37–49.

——— and R. O. Freedle. 1984. The effects of different discourse types on recall. *American educational research journal.* 21.1.121–143.

——— and G. E. Rice. 1982. The interaction of reader strategies and the organization of text. *Text.* 2.155–192.

———, D. M. Brandt, and G. J. Bluth. 1980. Use to top-level structure in text: Key for reading comprehension of ninth grade students. *Reading research quarterly.* 16.72–103.

Miller, R. A. 1967. *The Japanese language.* Chicago: University of Chicago Press.

Monane, T. and L. Rogers. 1977. Cognitive features of Japanese language and culture and their implications for language teaching. In J. Hinds (ed.) *Proceedings of the second annual meeting of the University of Hawaii–Hawaii Association of Teachers of Japanese.* Honolulu: University of Hawaii. 129–137.

Morgan, J. L. and M. B. Sellner. 1980. Discourse and linguistic theory. In R. J. Spiro, B. C. Bruce, and W. F. Brewer (eds.) *Theoretical issues in reading comprehension.* Hillsdale, NJ: Erlbaum. 165–200.

Morton, J. 1979. Word recognition. In J. Morton and J. Marshall (eds.) *Psycholinguistics 2: Structures and processes.* Cambridge, MA: MIT Press. 107–156.

Mosenthal, J. H. and R. J. Tierney. 1983. Cohesion: Problems with talking about text: A brief commentary. *Technical report no. 298.* Champaign, IL: Center for the Study of Reading, University of Illinois.

Mountford, A. J. 1975. *Discourse analysis and the simplification of reading materials for English for special purposes.* Edinburgh University. M. Litt.

Naotsuka, R., et al. 1981. *Mutual understanding of different cultures.* Tokyo: Taishukan.

Neu, J. 1985. A multivariate linguistic analysis of business negotiations. University of Southern California. Ph.D. diss.

Newsham, G. 1982. The paragraph in English and French. Unpublished paper. Concordia University. Montreal.

Ohmann, R. 1964. Generative grammars and the concept of literary style. *Word.* 20.424–439.

Olson, D. 1977. From utterance to text: The bias of language in speech and writing. *Harvard educational review.* 47.3.257–281.

O'Keefe, B. and J. G. Delia. 1979. Construct comprehensiveness and cognitive complexity as predicators of the number and strategic adaptation of arguments and appeals in a persuasive message. *Communication monographs.* 46.231–240.

Ong, W. J., S. J. 1972. *The presence of the word: Some prolegomena for cultural and religious history.* New Haven: Yale University Press.

———. 1979. Literacy and orality in our times. *Profession 79.* New York: Modern Language Association. 1–7.

Ostler, S. E. 1981. English in parallels: A study of Arabic style. Unpublished paper. University of Southern California.

Pae, Y. S. 1982. Thoughts of our times: What is spiritual? *The Korean times.* Seoul: The Korean Times Press.

Perl, S. 1979. The composing process of unskilled college writers. *Research in the teaching of English.* 13.317–336.

Pike, K. L. 1967. *Language in relation to a unified theory of the structure of human behavior.* The Hague: Mouton.

——— and E. G. Pike. 1977. *Grammatical analysis.* Dallas: Summer Institute of Linguistics. [S.I.L. Publications in Linguistics, No. 53.]

Pitkin, W. L. 1969. Discourse Blocs. *College composition and communication.* 20.2.138–148.

Purves, A. and S. Takala. (eds.) 1982. *An international perspective on the evaluation of written communication.* New York: Pergamon Press.

Pytlik, B. P. 1982. Decision style, purpose of discourse, and direction of communication: The impact on writing styles of selected accountants in a big eight accounting firm. University of Southern California. Ph.D. diss.

Raimes, A. 1977. *Focus on composition.* Oxford: Oxford University Press.

———. 1985. What unskilled ESL students do as they write: A classroom study of composing. *TESOL quarterly.* 19.2.229–258.

Redeker, G. 1984. On differences between spoken and written language. *Discourse processes.* 7.1.43–55.

Rosch, E. 1978. Principles of categorization. In E. Rosch and B. B. Lloyd (eds.) *Cognition and categorization.* Hillsdale, NJ: Erlbaum.

Rose, P. I. (ed.) 1978. *Views from abroad.* Washington, DC: Voice of America. [Forum Series of the Voice of America.]

Rottweiler, G. P. 1984. Systemic cohesion in published general academic English: Analysis and register description. Rutgers University, Ph.D. diss.

Rubin, A. 1980. A theoretic taxonomy of the differences between oral and written language. In R. J. Spiro, B. C. Bruce, and W. F. Brewer (eds.) *Theoretical issues in reading comprehension.* Hillsdale, NJ: Erlbaum. 411–438.

Rumelhart, D. E. 1975. Notes on a schema for stories. In D. G. Bobrow and A. M. Collins (eds.) *Representation and understanding: Studies in cognitive science.* New York: Academic Press. 211–236.

———. 1977. Understanding and summarizing brief stories. In D. La Berge and S. J. Samuels (eds.) *Basic processes in reading.* Hillsdale, NJ: Erlbaum. 265–303.

————. 1980. Schemata: The building blocks of cognition. In R. J. Spiro, B. C. Bruce, and W. F. Brewer (eds.) *Theoretical issues in reading comprehension.* Hillsdale, NJ: Erlbaum. 33–58.

Sacks, H., E. A. Schegloff, and G. Jefferson. 1974. A simplest semantics for the organization of turn-taking for conversation. *Language.* 50.696–735.

Sanford, A. J. and S. C. Garrod. 1981. *Understanding written language: Explorations in comprehension beyond the sentence.* Chichester: Wiley.

Schank, R. C. and R. P. Abelson. 1977. *Scripts, plans, goals and understanding.* Hillsdale, NJ: Erlbaum.

Scollon, R. and S. B. K. Scollon. 1981. *Narrative, literacy and face in interethnic communication.* Norwood, NJ: Ablex. [Advances in Discourse Processes, 7.]

Selinker, L., R. M. Todd-Trimble, and L. Trimble. 1976. Presuppositional rhetorical information in EST discourse. *TESOL quarterly.* 10.3.281–290.

Sheetz-Brunetti, J. and T. Johnson. 1983. Using simple diagrams to teach composition skills. *TECFORS.* 6.2.1–7.

Socin, A. 1927. *Arabic grammar.* Berlin: Reuther and Reichard. [Tr. A. R. S. Kennedy.]

Sohn, H. M. (ed.) 1975. *The Korean language: Its structure and social projection.* Honolulu: The Center for Korean Studies.

Sommers, N. 1978. Revision in the composing process: A case study of experimental writers and student writers. Boston University. Ph.D. diss.

Stein, N. L. and C. G. Glenn. 1979. An analysis of story comprehension in elementary school children. In R. O. Freedle (ed.) *New Directions in discourse processing.* Norwood, NJ: Ablex. 53–120.

Stotsky, S. 1983. Types of lexical cohesion in expository prose: Implications for developing the vocabulary of academic discourse. *College composition and communication.* 34.4.430–446.

Suzuki, T. 1975. *Tozasareta Gengo: Nihongo no sekai [A bound language: The world of Japanese].* Tokyo: Shinshiosha.

Tadros, A. 1981. Linguistic prediction in economics. University of Birmingham. Ph.D. diss.

Takemata, K. 1976. *Genkoo shippitsu nyuumon [An introduction to writing manuscripts].* Tokyo: Natsumesha.

Tannen, D. 1980. A comparative analysis of oral narrative strategies: Athenian Greek and American English. In W. L. Chafe (ed.) *The pear stories: Cognitive, cultural, linguistic aspects of narrative production.* Norwood, NJ: Ablex. 51–88.

————. 1981. *Analyzing discourse: Text and talk.* Washington, DC: Georgetown University Press. [Georgetown University Round Table on Language and Linguistics.]

————. 1982. Oral and literate strategies in spoken and written narratives. *Language.* 58.1.1–21.

————. 1985. Relative focus on involvement in oral and written discourse. In D.

Olson, N. Torrance, and A. Hilyard (eds.) *Literacy, language and learning.* New York: Cambridge University Press. 124–147.

Taylor, B. 1979. Children's and adults' recall of general concepts and details after reading. In M. Kamil and A. Moe (eds.) *Reading research: Studies and applications.* Clemson, SC: National Reading Conference. 123–128.

———. 1980. Children's memory for expository text after reading. *Reading research quarterly.* 15.399–411.

Thompson, S. A. 1978. Modern English from a typological point of view: Some implications of the function of word order. *Linguistische berichte.* 54.19–35.

Thorndyke, P. 1979. Knowledge acquisition from newspaper stories. *Discourse processes.* 2.95–112.

Tirkkonen-Condit, S. 1984. Towards a description of argumentative text structure. In H. Ringbom and M. Rissanen (eds.) *Proceedings from the second Nordic conference for English studies.* Åbo: Meddelanden från Stiftelsens för Åbo Akademi Forskningsinstitut nr. 92.

Toulmin, S. E. 1958. The uses of argument. Cambridge: Cambridge University Press.

———, R. Rieke, and A. Janik. 1979. *An introduction to reasoning.* New York: Macmillan.

Tsao, F.-F. 1983. Linguistics and written discourse in particular languages: English and Mandarin. In R. B. Kaplan, *et al.* (eds.) *Annual review of applied linguistics, III.* Rowley, MA: Newbury House. 99–117.

Turner, G. W. 1973. *Stylistics.* Harmondsworth: Penguin.

van Dijk, T. A. 1972. *Some aspects of text grammars: A study of theoretical linguistics and poetics.* The Hague: Mouton.

———. 1977. *Text and context: Explorations in the semantics and pragmatics of discourse.* London: Longman.

———. 1980. *Macrostructures: An interdisciplinary study of global structures in discourse, interaction, and cognition.* Hillsdale, NJ: Erlbaum.

———. (ed.) 1985. *Handbook of discourse analysis.* Vols. 1 and 2. London: Academic Press.

——— and W. Kintsch. 1978. Cognitive psychology and discourse: Recalling and summarizing stories. In W. Dressler (ed.) *Current trends in textlinguistics.* Berlin: de Gruyter. 61–80.

———. 1983. *Strategies of discourse comprehension.* New York: Academic Press.

Werlich, E. 1976. *A text grammar of English.* Heidelberg: Quelle and Meyer.

Widdowson, H. G. 1977. Approaches to discourse. Department of Linguistics, University of Edinburgh. Mimeo.

Wikberg, K. 1978. On Applications of Text Linguistics to the Analysis and Writing of Foreign Language Teaching Materials. V. Kohonen and N. E. Enkvist (eds.) *Text linguistics, cognitive learning and language teaching.* Turku, Finland: Publications de l'Association Finlandaise de Linguistique Appliquée.

Wilson, A. 1958. *The middle age of Mrs. Eliot.* London: Secker and Warburg.

Winter, E. O. 1977. A clause-relational approach to English texts: A study of some predictive lexical items in written discourse. *Instructional science.* 6.1–91. [Special issue.]

———. 1979. Replacement as a fundamental function of the sentence in context. *Forum linguisticum.* 4.2.95–133.

Winterowd, R. 1967. Style, a matter of manner. *The quarterly journal of speech.* 56.160–167.

———. 1970. The grammar of coherence. *College English.* 32.8.828–835.

———. 1975. *Contemporary rhetoric: A conceptual background with readings.* New York: Harcourt Brace Jovanovich.

Witte, S. P. 1983. Topical structure and invention: An exploratory study. *College composition and communication.* 34.3.313–341.

Wright, W. 1862. *A grammar of the Arabic language.* London: Williams and Norgale.

Yoshikawa, M. 1978. Some Japanese and American cultural characteristics. In M. H. Prosser (ed.) *The cultural dialogue: An introduction to intercultural communication.* Boston: Houghton Mifflin. 220–230.

About the Authors

CARRELL, Patricia L. Ph.D. Professor of Linguistics and Psychology and Dean of the Graduate School, Southern Illinois University at Carbondale. Her teaching and research interests include first- and second-language acquisition, text/discourse analysis, and comprehension and pragmatics. She has published extensively in the area of schema theory, text structure, and coherence, and has explored the applications of these lines of research in ESL reading and writing. Her work appears in *Language Learning, MLJ, Reading in a Foreign Language,* and *TESOL Quarterly.*

CONNOR, Ulla Ph.D. Assistant Professor of English, Indiana University in Indianapolis. She is a native of Finland but has spent the past thirteen years in the ESL field in the U.S. She has taught ESL at the University of Wisconsin-Madison and in the Madison Public Schools, has directed ESL programs at Purdue University and at the Indiana University in Indianapolis, and has been involved in ESL teacher-training at Georgetown University. Her research on second-language reading and writing has been published in such journals as *Applied Linguistics, Language Learning, TESOL Quarterly,* and *Text.* She is currently principal investigator in an Exxon Foundation grant to develop a comprehensive linguistic description and evaluation of student writing across cultures.

EGGINGTON, William G., Ph.D., Lecturer, Darwin Institute of Technology, Australia. He has completed his dissertation at the University of Southern California on the attitudes of various populations to language and to the communities of speakers of various languages. He has a broad range of interests, including contrastive study of discourse, particularly in Korean, ESL teaching and teacher preparation, and language policy and language planning. He has published articles pertaining to his interests in such journals as *CATESOL Occasional Papers* and *TESOL Quarterly.*

ENKVIST, Nils Erik, Ph.D., Professor of Stylistics and Textlinguistics and Director of the Research Institute at Åbo Akademi in Turku, Finland. He holds honorary doctoral degrees from the University of Poznan, Purdue University, and the University of Stockholm. His interests lie in the area of the theory and application of textlinguistics, and his publications in these areas extend to more than 300 books and articles in the most important journals in the field both in the United States and in Europe.

GRABE, William Ph.D. Assistant Professor of English at Northern Arizona University. He is primarily interested in the analysis of written discourse; his dissertation was concerned with an attempt to identify in linguistic terms the structure of expository prose as distinct from other text genres. He is also interested in sociolinguistics and in ESL and has taught ESL in Morocco and in the People's Republic of China. He has published in such important journals as *TESOL Quarterly*.

HINDS, John Ph.D. Associate Professor of Speech Communication at Pennsylvania State University. He is interested in contrastive text structure and has written widely particularly on contrastive elements in the text structures of English and Japanese. He has a broader interest in Japanese and has also published research on linguistic features of Japanese; additionally, his interests extend into issues of language universals and language typology. He has published widely, including such journals as *Language Learning* and *TESOL Quarterly*.

KAPLAN, Robert B. Ph.D. Professor of Applied Linguistics at the University of Southern California. He has long been interested in contrastive rhetoric and in the pedagogical implications of text linguistics, particularly in ESL. He currently serves as the Editor-in-Chief of the *Annual Review of Applied Linguistics* and has, in addition, published widely in major journals in the United States, Asia, and Europe. He has also been interested in international educational exchanges and has served as President of the National Association for Foreign Student Affairs.

LAUTAMATTI, Liisa Ph.D. Associate Professor of English at the University of Jyväskylä, Finland. She teaches courses on spoken and written discourse analysis of English and trains EFL teachers. She has published extensively, and her publications range from the analysis of cohesion in student essays to interactional analysis of TV interviews with presidential candidates in Finland to stylistic analyses of English literature. Her work on the identification and development of topic in English discourse was pioneering and provides inspiration to applied linguists around the world.

McCAGG, Peter Ph.D. Assistant Professor of Linguistics at International Christian University, Tokyo. He received his doctorate from the Department of Linguistics at Georgetown University where he wrote his dissertation on inferencing skills of Japanese EFL learners reading in English. His research interests include ESL reading, pragmatics, speech-act theory, and the evaluation of ESL language proficiency. He has published in *Applied Linguistics* and elsewhere and has presented numerous research papers at international conferences.

OSTLER, Shirley Teaching Assistant, Freshman Writing Program, University of Southern California. She has broad experience in the teaching of writing to both native and non-native speakers of English, having taught at the California Polytechnical University (Pomona) and at the University of Southern California in the undergraduate writing programs as well as in the American Language Institute at USC. Her primary interest is in writing research. She has presented a number of research papers at national and international conferences. She is presently completing her doctoral research at the University of Southern California.